Israel's New Strategic Dilemmas: Survival or Revival?

By Raphael Israeli

Strategic Book Publishing and Rights Co.

Strategic Book Publishing and Rights Co.
12620 FM 1960, Suite A4-507
Houston, TX 77065
www.sbpra.com

ISBN: 978-1-61897-180-7

Design: Dedicated Book Services, Inc. (www.netdbs.com)

Table of Contents

Apologia

The revived state of Israel, whose seeds were sown in the 1880s in the desolate land of Palestine, was hanging on a thin thread when declared in 1948, and only escaped by the skin of its teeth from the devastating War of Independence (1948-9). But up to the 1967 War, struggling Israel was at the peak of its popularity in the West, for its pioneering spirit, its state of siege by the Arabs who had tried to annihilate it on its birth but dismally failed, its democracy in the midst of tyranny, and certainly its serving as the home for the remnants of decimated European Jewry during the War. In that setting, tiny, fledgling and struggling Israel was perceived as the ideological peer of the West, seemed heroic for its courageous stand against the Arabs, and later as a bulwark against the Soviet penetration, and drew the almost unanimous support of the Western public opinion, which was itself struggling to restore the devastation of the War and to withstand the communist onslaught. In those years, Israel absorbed wave after wave of Jewish refugees, notably from the death camps in Europe and from the Arab and Muslim lands which they had to evacuate, and made remarkable strides in the construction of its economy, first in agriculture and then in industry.

In those heroic days, social solidarity in Israeli society was rife, the danger to its security drew people together, and the small Israel of three million people looked and felt formidable enough to repel all threats to its existence. Even though the PLO was born in 1960, which purported to annihilate Israel and replace it, neither Israel nor the world, nor even much of the Arab world which lent credence to that ambition, had much faith in the feasibility of that endeavor. Even the Arab minority of Israel, which at that point amounted to some 15% of the population (just over 400,000 out of three million), had so much reconciled to its status as a permanent minority in the Jewish state, that it was well on its way to integration, as evinced in the aid it lent to the state during the gathering clouds of the 1967 war. The feeling was that the Jewish state was a successful experiment, the Zionist endeavor a stunning victory, and it would be only a matter of time before the state stood on its own feet, Jewish immigration increased, settlement and economic development flourished, and Israel's temporary armistice boundaries were internationally and permanently recognized.

Optimism was born out of the recent twin miraculous acts of survival against all odds: residues of the masses of Jews who had been slated to extermination in Europe, were somehow rescued from the crematoria and could remake their lives in the Jewish state; and the 600,000 Jewish refugees who had made their homes in Israel somehow resisted the Arab attempts to uproot and exterminate them, and emerged as citizens of the Jewish state and its protégés. Yes, there were occasional bouts of depression, dissent and despair, like the economic austerity in the 1950's, the Arab waves of marauders who infiltrated Israel's borders and occasioned retaliations in the 1950's, the Lavon Affair and the economic depression in the 1960's, and the Eichmann trial and Ben-Gurion's retirement from public life, also in the 1960's. But everyone of those obstacles was overcome, and when overcome it was celebrated. So much so, that despite the depressing jokes about the "last to switch off the lights at the Lydda Airport" (before it was re-baptized Ben-Gurion), and the shrinking of Jewish immigration into Israel to a trickle, vitality and purposefulness were the driving forces of the country.

In the three weeks of anxiety which preceded the six-day war in June 1967, when the trauma of the Holocaust was only 20-some year old, and threats of extermination emanating from the Arab world filled the air, the Israeli public was horrified lest another campaign of elimination against the Jewish people was brewing while the world looked on, almost impassively. That was the last opportunity for Israel to break the siege and act unilaterally, bravely and decisively to shatter her enemies in six days and raise the marvel of the world and despair among Arabs and Muslims. That was when not only the 22-member Arab League assembled in Khartum to declare its three No's (No recognition of Israel, No peace with Israel and No negotiation with Israel), but the 56 Muslim countries (including the 22 Arab states), gathered in Cairo for an Islamic Conference, to account for the rout in the war. That was also when, in both instances, those two august gatherings decided to pool their resources and relaunch the battle of destiny against the Jewish state. A new element was invoked in that vow, namely the urgent need to erase the "humiliation" caused to the Muslim world by the combination of Israel and the US. Europe began at that point, through the theatric measures adopted by de Gaulle, to put an end to the great alliance of his country with Israel, to take its distance from the Jewish state and to weave a close relationship with the Arab world.

Thenceforth, and following the general trend in the Arab world, which sought solace in their faith, major doses of Islam were injected into the vocabulary and symbolism of the Arab-Israeli dispute, which had theretofore been treated as a clash between Arab nationalism and Jewish Zionism, and henceforth as a clash between Islam and its rivals, primarily Israel and its American supporter. It has then become typical for Israeli relations with the Arab world that the secular Arab leaders, who are themselves threatened by Muslim rivals domestically, like Sadat and his followers in Egypt, Arafat and his successors for the Palestinians, and Hussein and his heirs in Jordan, to seek accommodation with the Jewish state, while Muslim regimes and movements and their underlings, like in Iran, Hizbullah, the Hamas, Syria and Lebanon, have taken the lead of the front of refusal facing Israel. And it seems that not only the latter are gaining the upper hand, but that the former, who had the good sense to launch their countries on the avenue of peace, have been having second thoughts, aided by the renegade attitude of Turkey, who has been abandoning its secular moderate attitudes and embarking on an Iranian-like Islamic militant course.

It appears, then, that the course of accommodation adopted by Israel throughout its existence, which included good relations with Islamic countries like Iran and Turkey, and peace accords involving considerable territorial concessions to its neighbors, far from yielding the hoped-for fruits of peace, has, on the contrary, produced a polarization between the rival parties. It has turned out that whenever Israel has yielded, this has encouraged its rivals to seek its demise (consider current attitudes of Egypt, Jordan, the Palestinian Authority towards Israel), and only where it stood fast and demonstrated the unfeasibility of its demise, could it achieve any improvement in its image and any heightening of its stature. In other words, it can be said that Israel has paid the price of its moderation and of its policy of appeasement, but it would now require a persistent reversal of its stance in order to gain respect and inspire awe among its neighbors

In the process, the circle of the conflict was further widened. If at the beginning it was Israeli-Palestinian, immediately followed by Israeli-Arab, it now grew to the monstrous scope of western-Muslim. It abandoned the old moulds of conventional wars with armies pitted against armies, and adopted the amorphous patterns of terrorism, where faceless but murderous self-sacrificing combatants, in singles or in small squads, blow up indiscriminately citizens in their houses, in planes, buses, trains, public squares, restaurants or on leisure in beaches, bars, theaters and cinemas. There is no longer a battle front or a war zone, for the entire world has become one. Henceforth, the Islamikaze[1] can hit in Israel or on its frontiers, but also in the streets of New York, in

---

[1]Islamikaze has been coined by this author in his "Islamikaze : Manifestations of Islamic Martyrology" , Frank Cass, London, 2003. It is the combination of Islam and kamikaze, meaning the combatants that we usually, and wrongly, dub "suicide bombers".

the offices of Washington DC, in the commuter trains of Madrid, in the London subway, in the bars of Bali, in the housing projects of Riyad and on the streets of Casablanca, Amman and Jakarta, using civilian populations as their shield and target. In other words, local or regional wars, launched from land or naval bases, where territory was gained or lost, and dominance established or yielded, have been replaced by baseless but omnipresent skirmishes and hostilities. New patterns of response had to be invented, and the uphill battle to produce adequate remedies to this developing plight is only at its beginning.

These universal developments which have embraced the world over, and have been predominantly triggered and conducted by *Jihadi* Islam, have had a special significance as they apply to tiny Israel, for whom they do not merely constitute matters of national defense, as they do elsewhere, but relate to the very core of its existence. Being surrounded, indeed besieged, by a vast hostile Muslim world, which cannot tolerate impassively any act of Israeli self-defense, which by definition must be directed against members of its league, Israel is often abandoned to its own devices by a West all too often preoccupied by its own security and economic concerns, and little inclined to disturb its seemingly cozy relationships in the short term with a menacing Muslim world in upheaval, which also controls much of the world oil reserves and large sums of the capitals accruing therefrom, and whose presence in Europe has become a major and growing concern.

Jerusalem, Winter 2011-2012

Part One

The Dangerous Setting

Chapter 1

When the World Appeared
Sane and Predictable

Prior to the 1967 war, when friends and foes were well defined, borders were delineated and policies were pro or con, within the confines of the cold war, one knew whom to fear, whom to count on, whom to defy, whom to suspect and whom to respect, what and whom to prepare against, and what to expect in conflict and in peace, who was allied with whom, who was likely to aid whom. Upon the conclusion of the 1948 War, where the Arabs had hoped to nip the Jewish state in the bud but failed, Israel has engaged in building its armed forces upon the assumption that it can never match the Arab armies in manpower, resources, hatred and propaganda. So it resigned to cultivate good quality and highly motivated troops, better strategic plans, an edge in technology and one major power or more to provide strategic and diplomatic backing. Since its armed forces were based on reserve troops which could be rapidly mobilized in times of national crisis, an unfailing intelligence was supposed to provide the requisite warning systems to allow time to prepare for all-out hostilities, and an out of proportion large and effective air-force to help arrest a sudden onslaught of the Arab armies. Due to the tiny size of the country on the one hand, and its densely populated northern half on the other, it has become axiomatic in Israeli strategic thinking that any attack upon Israel had to be resolutely thwarted and then swiftly transferred into enemy territory.

The 19 years that elapsed until 1967 were lived under
the armistice regime between Israel and each of its neighbors, which was governed by an armistice agreement and
monitored by a mixed armistice commission[2]. It was em-
phatically regarded by the Arabs as a temporary agreement
"without prejudice to future permanent solutions", because
they hoped that rejected Israel would not be able to survive
without Arab acquiescence much longer. Border skirmishes
became part of Israel's daily routine, with all its four immediate neighbors: Egypt, Jordan, Syria and Lebanon continuing to deny not only the right of Israel to exist, but even
the fact that it did. They simply pretended it was not there,
and every time they needed to refer to it, they claimed it
was the "Tel-Aviv Government", the "Zionist entity", the
"alleged Jewish state" and such. Every time Israel retaliated
for the attacks against it, it was dubbed the "aggressor", *eo
ipso* rallying the Arabs against it. It is difficult to invoke any
other example in the annals of nations of an entire culture
which fed on, drew its inspiration from, and rallied its entire people around hatred of the other, as did the Arabs vis-
à-vis Israel. True, Communist China and Vietnam, and the
Soviet Union during the Cold War, tried to demonize the US
in the same fashion, but the continued underground sympathy to American culture and to the American people and
generosity among the populace, permitted a rapid mending
of the fences when the confrontation receded. In the case of
the Arab enmity towards Israel, born partly out of a rabid
and well-entrenched anti-Semitism, it seemed to stand all
the tests and defy all attempts to extenuate it. The domestic
policies of all Arab countries as well as inter-Arab affairs
were dominated by their aspiration to take revenge on Israel,
to "erase the consequences of its aggression", in the "next
round", and to launch the *coup de grace* against it when their

---

[2]For the Israeli-Jordan Armistice Commission, for example, see R. Israeli, *Jerusalem Divided: the Israel-Jordan Armistice Regime*, Frank Cass, London, 2003.

power was deemed sufficient for that "holy" task. For, the very existence of Israel was considered "aggression", and its genocidal and politicidal elimination was viewed by the Arabs as the only viable remedy to that plight. Arab nationalism both reflected and personified by President abdul Nasser of Egypt in those years, articulated those Arab ambitions.

In those years, Israel's strategy of survival was clear, and it was communicated to the Arabs and to the world, which signified that since the country was tiny, with indefensible borders and harboring a small population (three million or less at the time), it must cultivate a first rate intelligence service to provide early warning and allow a rapid mobilization of the reserves in case of sudden attack on its borders; the air force was particularly emphasized due to the rapidity with which it had to block any attacking army until land reserves were alerted, recruited and deployed; the war had to remain brief in order to permit the reservists to complete their task and revert to their civilian employment lest the entire economy were paralyzed; all the while, to maintain a small, but well-trained and highly-alert, regular army to hold the lines until reinforced by the reserves; and to transfer immediately the field of combat into enemy territory, so as to minimize destruction in the small and vulnerable Israeli territory. Underlying that strategic thinking was the realization in Israel that the cease-fire obtained in 1949 with all its Arab neighbors, which came to be expressed in a regime of armistice, was to be considered a more-or-less permanent state of affairs, since the Arabs rejected Israel's legitimacy since its inception, and vowed to eliminate it. While in Israel armistice was viewed as a way of self-preservation under international rules, the Arabs regarded it as their way to deny its legitimacy and to signify their intention to continue to reject it.

Thus, while armistice was supposed to be temporary, by definition, from Israel's point of view a transition towards peace, as indeed the texts of the respective armistice agreements expressly stated, for the Arabs it was a clear statement that their taking cognizance (not recognition, and assuredly not acceptance) of their rival was only temporary, and certainly not *de jure,* even not *de facto,* judging from their adamant refusal to acknowledge that such an Israeli entity existed at all. Therefore, while the polarity of war and peace usually describes the state of international relations between any two parties, even if allowing for middle ground situations like "cold war", "non-diplomatic" or "informal" relations, and various degrees of diplomatic relationships when such existed (Embassies, Ministries, Consulates, *Charge d'Affaires,* roving Ambassadors, Special Envoys, etc), the Arab-Israeli relations soon acquired their peculiar twists and their specially adopted vocabularies. Already during the 1948-9 War of Independence, two periods of cessation of hostilities, which elsewhere and at other times would be dubbed "cease-fire", were called the first and then the second "truce", after which war, violence and killings were renewed. That vocabulary also lent its name to the UN mechanism which was set up in Palestine under the appellation "Truce Supervision Organization" (UNTSO), which after 6 more wars, many cease-fires, two peace treaties and a never-ending "peace process", is still there doing who knows what.

But this sort of cessation of hostilities, which followed the exhaustion of both parties by that longest of wars, which lasted more than one year (not counting the acts of war between the UN Partition Plan of November 1947 and the declaration of Israel's independence in May,1948), necessitated yet another language. The regime which was to reign between Israel and each of its four immediate neighbors (Egypt, Lebanon, Syria and Jordan) was called "armistice", hinting at some reality of stability, even though its temporariness was read into it, to differ from the truces which had come and gone, and the various cease-fires which signaled flimsy, unpredictable and at times moody lulls along the various fronts of battle. More vocabulary had to be invented in order to create the policing mechanism of this new regime: Mixed Armistice Commissions (MAC) between Israel and each of its next-door rivals, presided over by "UN Observers", who soon took over the management of the whole affair in view of the generally usual miscommunication between the parties. But these creative, wasteful and intricate bodies, far from facilitating a transition to peace, on the contrary became a self-entrenched interest in themselves, geared to separate the parties so as to necessitate UN mediation and intervention between them, not an engine of promoting peace by encouraging the parties to meet, negotiate, agree and advance, along the lines envisaged by the Armistice Agreement, to progress towards a permanent settlement.[3]

Due to this dissonance between the parties as to their ultimate goals—Israel to gain legitimacy and recognition, the Arabs to eliminate it—it became inherently impossible for them to agree on anything (how can one agree on anything with an entity it wishes to obliterate?), and when anything was agreed upon, for example the Armistice Agreements between them, it was clear that sooner, rather than later, they would have to be violated, and that the job of the UN intermediaries was assured for generations to come. In any situation of conflict, which usually involves material assets, like territories or economic interests, and sometimes prestige and national pride, the parties wage war, but when one of them is defeated, or they are both exhausted, they negotiate to reach a settlement. A permanent peace between them is reached when there is a meeting of minds between them, which is translated into a treaty, and then usually respected by the parties who respect law and accept the limitations included therein. If there is no meeting of minds, like in Versailles, where one party was defeated and humiliated, the imposed "peace" terms do not constitute a meeting of minds, therefore the treaty is not an agreement but a *diktat* that is bound to be ultimately rejected and redressed. In all the armistice agreements there was no meeting of minds at any point, except for the need to control damage by ceasing hostilities, and then to regroup for the next round. Hence the lethal and

---

[3]R. Israeli, *Jerusalem Divided*, op. cit.

tragic cycle of wars which seemed to have no end, and the ephemeral nature of any interim "agreement" that could be reached, but everyone knew would be breached as it was being signed.

Indeed, skirmishes, usually accompanied by fire and casualties (in spite of the armistice, cease fire and truce) developed all the along the lines between Israel and its neighbors, save for the years between 1956 (the Sinai Campaign) and the Six-day War (1967) when the Egyptian border was monitored by UN troops. The incidents were generally provoked by the Arabs, who had no vested interest in sanctifying a status quo which they were afraid might take root and stabilize Israel. But, in cases like the Sinai War, it was Israel who colluded with France and Britain to attack Egypt, though for Israel it was a preventive war to thwart the Egyptian troops which were menacing its existence, and a defensive war against the *fidayeen* terrorists who ravaged southern Israel. But beyond border incidents which the Arabs wished to keep alive, there were contractual violations of the armistice agreements, when the parties (usually the Arabs) simply refused to comply, like the military occupation of demilitarized areas, interference by the Arabs in Israeli developmental projects or water plants, which could, in their eyes, help solidify Israel's rootedness into the land. But the most blatant of those violations was Jordan's flat refusal to implement Article VIII of its agreement with Israel which had stipulated free access by Israel to its humanitarian and religious institutions in Jerusalem, like the Hebrew University, the Hadassah Hospital, the Mt of Olives cemetery and the Wailing Wall, which had been left as enclaves in Jordanian-held territory. The UN and the Powers, rather than force Jordan to comply, acquiesced in this situation and further accustomed the parties that violation of the armistice could go unpunished. Worse, it instilled within the parties contempt to signed agreements, a cultural feature which was to pester and poison Arab-Israeli relations in years to come.

But the contours of the conflict could not be clearer. Is-rael was dreaming to turn its armistice boundaries into per-manent and recognized ones, while the Arabs were lurking for the day to undo that dream. Israel was struggling for its survival and growth, endeavoring for Jewish immigration, which dwindled to a trickle in the 1960's and stabilized when the population attained around 3 million after several massive waves of newcomers had exhausted themselves, and as the economic situation was severe, the armistice borders long and difficult to monitor, and the country still deeply plunged into its third world status, despite its few islands of excellence, in the military and in farming, precisely the two typically un-Jewish occupations, which were emphasized in Israel out of necessity, and particularly perfected to meet the pressing needs. The Arabs knew that for each encroachment on its territory, for every act of violence or for any incident on its borders, Israel would react violently and overwhelm-ingly, therefore they were usually deterred from escalating the conflict into full-scale war. Israeli society, conversely, was very tightly-knit, solidary and united in its yearning to survive and to preserve its forces for rainy days, in spite of the deep political divisions which splintered the politi-cal scene. The same historical leadership, under the domi-nation of *Mapai* (later Labor) which had founded the state and led all its battles thus far, was still holding the reins and confidently steering embattled Israel through its trials. Even the Arab minority which stood in the beginning at 15% of the population, and which had been cut off from other Ar-abs around, and was still far from any nationalistic upheaval, had become tame and was well in its way to integrating into Israeli society, well aware that their chances to ever re-link with their kin across the border of enmity, was very low in-deed.

Internationally, and following the ascension to power of De Gaulle in France, who gradually dissolved the alliance of his country with Israel after the Algerian crisis was settled, Israel was more or less abandoned by the Powers. Yes, the

American assistance had not yet assumed the importance of latter days, and the French previously steady stream of military supplies, which culminated under Prime Minister Mollet and defense Minister Bourges-Maunoury, suddenly came under close scrutiny and threatened to dry up, while the alternative avenue of the US was still far from opening up. It was then that Israel was compelled to begin developing its military-industrial prowess, which was to pay off years later. The Soviet Union, which had long embraced the Arab cause and served as their main source of military and economic aid, and certainly China, which was itself under siege by the US and most of the West, also adopted a more or less hostile attitude towards Israel. The American Congress, entreated by American Jewry and the Israeli lobby, demonstrated sympathy to Israel, but the disastrous American venture in Vietnam sapped the White House's energies, at a time when President Johnson was so bewildered and demoralized by his failure to win decisively that conflict, that he eventually opted not to re-run for a second term in 1968. He certainly had no stomach for adding the perennial Middle Eastern dispute on his brimful plate. At the same time, though the Egyptian border seemed deceptively tranquil, due to UN forces' presence there, the security along the Syrian and Jordanian boundaries were far from reassuring, and they were constantly on the verge of explosion.

It was in this fragile, sleepy, provincial, backwater and forlorn Israel, facing the prospects of an insoluble conflict with the Arabs which it confronted firmly, coolly and optimistically, in spite of the raging wave of the Nasserite nationalism which threatened to sweep it into oblivion, that the fledgling Jewish state found itself on the eve of the 1967 Six Day War, which catapulted it to international prominence and revolutionized its fortunes, both for the better and the worse. Whatever the case, one has to remember that in those years the wars that Israel was constrained to wage were all unquestionably defensive in nature, what was called "wars of no-choice", which almost never warranted a wide public discourse about their necessity or desirability. It was widely reckoned that Israel was attacked or about to be attacked, and therefore it was not only fully justified to react in kind, but even to pre-empt and strike first when conditions so dictated. So, when Nasser determined that time for the decisive and fateful confrontation with Israel had come, which he was sure to win, he precipitated the exit of the UN forces from the Sinai, declared the closure of the Tiran Straits to Israeli navigation, and in effect declared war. Anxious Israel, which felt abandoned even by its closest "friends", who reneged on their assurances from the post-Suez arrangements (1957) that guaranteed free navigation in the Straits if Israel withdrew from the Sinai, turned inward in a painful process of self-examination, questioning the honesty and sincerity of the powers-that-be who, as soon as the fire broke out, acquiesced in the withdrawal of the firemen from the burning spot. Especially questionable were Secretary General U Thant's motives, who instead of behaving like a Hammarskjold before him, and standing firm to calm the moods and avoid war, was to charter the new defeatist road of his successors, who preferred to complete their double-term without raising the anger of anyone over striving to avoid the risk of war. Nasser was delighted on how quickly the world system caved in, and mobilized the Arab world, including "moderate", "pro-American" and "peace-loving" King Hussein of Jordan, to ally with him, and the rest of Afro-Asia to rally to him. The rest is history.

One of the most remarkable developments following the crushing defeat of the Arabs and of Arab nationalism of the Nasserite messianic type, was the surge of Islam as an alternative to fill the void in the heart of the desperate masses who sought something to hang on to, to replace the sinking idol of Gamal abdul Nasser. That was perhaps the watershed which marked the slow 30-year transition in the Arab camp, from the political and military confrontation with Israel, to overwhelm it and diminish it, following the beaten path of a quantitative dispute aimed at gnawing at Israel and reducing its size and strength; to a more qualitative conflict of values, which demanded total victory and no compromises, with a view of wiping Israel out totally. But this strategy, which launched terrorist attacks, refused any accommodation with Israel and invoked Islamic vocabulary and symbols, thus driving the severity of the conflict one notch up, was also simultaneously directed against the pro-Western Arab regimes (those erroneously called "moderates"), who for the sake of survival, began to adopt more subtle demarches, for example announcing readiness to make "peace" with Israel if it only withdrew from Arab territories and established a Palestinian state. But the radically negative trend, led by Iran since its Islamic revolution, and its Hizbullah ally in Lebanon, and rallying the Muslim Brothers of the Middle East, who are in opposition to their own governments (in Egypt, Jordan and Gaza), not only continues to raise the banner of total rejection, but appears to make headway in widening its constituency in Sudan, Libya, Algeria, and support in the more distant and un-Islamic Venezuela and Bolivia.

The Arab stance towards Israel at that point could be summed up in three major issues:

First, since Israel sought recognition and acceptance by the Arab world in order to gain legitimacy in the Middle East, the Arabs were adamant to deny her exactly that. Even not recognition *de facto,* not to speak of a recognition *de jure.* Israel simply did not exist for them, they were fighting a phantom or a mirage which they had a difficulty to recognize, despite the airplanes of these makes which Israel deployed in its skies. That lay at the base of their refusal to meet, to negotiate, let alone to agree on anything with an entity which did not exist.

Secondly, there was a major territorial issue when Israel trebled her surface area in 1967, when it seized the Sinai Peninsula from Egypt (twice its own size), the West Bank from Jordan and Gaza also from Egypt (about one third of its territory) and the Golan Heights from Syria, which is a narrow strip of land, but of great strategic importance due to its dominating altitude over the Galilee in Northern Israel. As against the Arab claims of "aggression" and "expansion", and their categorical demands that Israel evacuate their lands forthwith unconditionally, under the famous Security Council Resolution of November 1967, Israel built up a stonewall of counter-arguments which deferred such a rendition of territory to a peace arrangement. It principally argued, that it captured that territory as a result of a defensive war when she defeated the Arabs and occupied their territory, not by invading them, but by repelling their attacks. Therefore, yielding those lands unconditionally and without any peaceful arrangements would simply encourage her rivals to use the same territory again to re-launch new attacks. That would be suicidal nationally and immoral ethically. Besides, it was claimed by Israel that there was no Palestinian entity involved in that war, therefore the claimant parties for any territorial demands were those which lost the lands in their war of aggression. Nevertheless that Resolution 242, whether accepted or rejected by the parties, immediately became a bone of contention due to the widely differing interpretations of its meaning, thus proving once again that those diplomatic "geniuses" who spend their lives inventing wordings and formulas to agree upon, in fact sacrifice clarity and real solutions for the sake of temporary and fleeting "agreements", thereby perpetuating problems instead of helping to resolve them. "Constructive ambiguities", as one of those geniuses called them (Henry Kissinger), do not stand the test of reality when the day of reckoning comes.

Thirdly, the Palestinian issue, which was often used by the Arabs as a pretext to perpetuate the war on Israel, was conventionally considered the "heart of the Middle Eastern dispute", and it was universally agreed among the Arabs and much of the world, that only its solution could produce peace. The problem was that until 1967 the Palestinian territories which were governed by Egypt and Jordan, respectively, seemed to settle permanently into that mold and did not arouse any demand for their independence. Suddenly their autonomous voice was heard, as the Palestine Liberation Organization (PLO) was founded just prior to 1967, and widely recognized by the world as legal claimants to the territories lost by Egypt and Jordan, which had themselves occupied them before. The sorry fact is, that Resolution 242, which does not even mention the word Palestine, nor even the Palestinians, and only alludes to the need to resolve the "refugee problem", with the appended commentary explaining that it meant both Arab and Jewish refugees, has strangely and inexplicably become the rallying slogan of the entire diplomatic arena when treating the Palestinian issue. The existing impasse during so many decades only points out to this persisting absurdity.

The rise of Islamic consciousness in the Arab world after 1967, which was further reinforced in the wake of the Iranian Revolution (1978), generated additional grievances and expectations from Israel, as if the basic Arab demands were not enough of a complication for anyone who sought a solution. They can be summed up in five essential points:

Firstly, the Jews, the "descendants of apes and pigs" in Qur'anic parlance, and in regular and perennial mosque sermons, who had attracted upon themselves the wrath of Allah and were therefore dispersed among nations, are an accursed people which does not have the attributes of a nation, therefore its very attempt to assemble and create a state is an affront, as it were, to Allah's will; they should revert to their original status of *dhimmis* under Muslim hegemony.

Secondly, the Jews are not only establishing an unworthy state, but by doing it they have lured the million or so Jews who had lived "happily under the protective wings of Islam" to move there, thus exposing the Muslim propaganda about its tolerance and protection of the Jews as a lie. Therefore Israeli Jews are often "invited" by Muslim rulers to migrate back to their countries of origin. That would again prove the "hospitality" of the Muslims towards Jews and also deplete Israel of half its population;

Thirdly, the Jewish state has dared to combat, and to emerge repeatedly victorious, against the "elected nation of Allah" (the Muslims), thus contradicting the rules of history, which have willed that Islam was born for conquest, expansion and victory. What is all the more humiliating is the fact that Israel has won in spite of the fact that it is vastly outnumbered. Therefore, only the elimination of Israel would restore history to its original channel and rehabilitate Muslim pride.

Fourthly, the land of Palestine had been a Muslim *waqf* (holy endowment) since its conquest (*fat'h*) by the Muslim armies in the 7th Century, and is to remain so for all generations to come. Its takeover by the Jews to establish their state has subtracted it from *Dar al Islam* (the Abode of Islam) and thrust it into *Dar al Harb* (the Domain of War), hence the urgent necessity to retrieve it via *Jihad*. The land of Palestine in this respect is no different from Andalusia, Sicily and Kashmir which have also fallen into Unbelievers' hands; and finally

Fifthly, Jerusalem is not simply part of the Holy land, but the pearl in the crown inasmuch as it was the place where the Prophet ascended to Heaven from (*Mi'raj*), the first direction of prayer (*qibla*), and the third holiest place to Islam after Mecca and Medina, due to the *Haram al-Sharif* in its midst, which encompasses al-Aqsa Mosque and the Dome of the Rock. Due to Muslim conviction that Islam is original and it supersedes Judaism and Christianity, there is no recognition of any previous attachment of the Jews to their Temple Mount, nor to its relevance to their religious life today.

In 1973 the combined armies of Egypt and Syria attempted, under the best circumstances of strategic surprise, of the scale of Pearl Harbor, to regain their territories by launching a simultaneous assault on the slumbering Israelis on the holy day of Kippur (hence the Yom Kippur War) which ended in a diplomatic draw, though once again in military defeat for the Arabs. The intensive usage of Islamic symbols and vocabulary during that war was evidence of the

Islamization that had permeated the Egyptian armed forces.[4] The mixed ending of the war, which was played and replayed in slow motion by the Egyptians as the "October Victory", permitted a series of Israeli retreats, codenamed "disengagements" from the Sinai which led, in 1977, to the peace accords between Israel and Egpyt, the first and largest Arab country to settle amiably with Israel. When President Anwar Sadat was condemned unanimously by the rest of the Arabs, he floated, in self-defense, his "triangular theory" which professed that his negotiations with Israel were his tactical apex of the triangle, which could remain mobile and flexible as long as the strategic base of the triangle remained firm and immutable and safeguarded the principles that the Arabs had agreed to defend and preserve, to wit: not to yield territory to the Israelis, not to conclude a partial or separate agreement with them, and to protect the rights of the Palestinians. He pleaded that his peace with the Israelis be understood and accepted in such light, because he gained territory without bloodshed, and he retrieved it in its entirety; he made his agreement conditional on a second framework agreement which obliged Israel to negotiate with or about the Palestinian issue, and he extracted from Menachem Begin a recognition of the "legitimate rights of the Palestinians". For him that meant Palestinian independence, for Begin-some sort of autonomy. This was another diplomatic ambiguity which was to cause bloody problems for many decades to come.

Sadat's ambivalence had another aspect to it. He explained that his deal was the best he could achieve in his generation: a peace treaty with Israel in return for a total withdrawal of Israel from the Sinai. In fact, he launched the peace initiative, which brought him to Jerusalem in 1977, only after he was assured in pre-negotiations that he would get all his territories back. He had realized, that the two Israeli townships of Ophira and Yamit and another score of booming

---

[4] Israeli, Raphael, "The Role of Islam in President Sadat's Thought", *Jerusalem Journal of International Relations*, Vol 4, No 4, 1980.

agricultural settlements, which were implanted in the Sinai, could grow and expand, if not uprooted forthwith, to populate hundreds of thousands of settlers which no ultimate, but too late, peace arrangement would be able to remove from the land. Therefore, he decided to press on, thus proving that settlements by Israel could act as an incentive for peace negotiations[5]. Namely, that any Arab party should hasten to settle with Israel lest any procrastination could lead to such a massive colonization that retrieval of that territory became more and more unfeasible. But the rest of the Arabs retained only the first part of that precedent, namely that peace with Israel meant compelling her to withdraw from all her 1967 acquisitions. In other words, while for Israel peace signified the realization of her dream towards recognition and acceptance, the Arabs understood peace as a price they were constrained to pay if they ever wanted to regain their territories. The lesson learned was, that without a solid and concrete pawn in Israel's hands, in the form of territory, the Arabs would not have any incentive to make peace. I.e., without the occupation of Arab territory, there could be even no trigger to peace negotiations.

The year this first peace treaty was signed (1979) was also the beginning of the Iranian Revolution, which put at loggerheads Egypt and Iran, who had been close partners under Sadat and the Shah, and now turned rivals, especially after Saddam Hussein of Iraq launched his eight-year war against Teheran, where the Sunni Arabs aligned with him against the Shi'a. That struggle continues to dominate Middle Eastern politics 30 years later. In the intermediate years, it was Iraq's hegemony which dominated Arab politics, and Saddam's threats against Israel qualified him among the Arab masses as the worthy successor of abd al-Nasser, or the "new Saladin", who would deliver the *coup de grace* to Israel and resolve the Palestinian issue via the long-promised victory. He

---

[5]See Raphael Israeli, *Man of Defiance:A Political Biography of Anwar Sadat*, Weidenfeld and Nocolson, London, 1985, esp. ch. 10, pp.216-247.

became the champion of the Palestinian cause and was the first Arab leader to budget $25,000 for each Palestinian Islamikaze[6] family which lost a martyr in action against Israel. Nevertheless, Saddam enjoyed American and western support, since they regarded Iran's Islamic threat as more imminent and more menacing. The mood turned around overnight when, in August 1991, Saddam invaded Kuwait and took over her prodigious petroleum reserves. The West as well as the Arabs, who had supported Iraq, were stunned by that demarche which they considered as a betrayal of their trust. Swiftly, in a reversal comparable to the Soviet deployment to a total all-out war against Germany, which until June 1941 was its "ally" under the Ribbentrop-Molotov Agreement; the US and its western allies, together with most Arab countries, who had until 1988 footed the bill of Saddam's horrendous war against the Iranians, with its attending gas war, got together to build the coalition necessary to beat the tyrant.

Only then did the contours of Saddam's strategy become understood in the west, though they had been made explicit before. Saddam's allies had simply refused to read the writing on the wall, and his threats to "burn half Israel" with the lethal binary weapons he was developing, were dismissed as rhetoric. I fact, Saddam, who succeeded in numbing his Arab allies and the West, which continued to deal with him, for fear that the Iranian Revolution might be a worse alternative, vied for hegemony in the Gulf, which he sought to achieve by taking over the Iranian Gulf coast, which could afford him safe havens for his Navy and liberate him from the strait jacket of the 30 mile sea-shore where his naval bases were threatened; and at the same time he thought that by taking over the Iranian oil, he would come to dominate

---

[6]This term was coined by this author, combining Islam and *Kamikaze*, the self-sacrificing Japanese pilots of the Pacific War , to counter the erroneous wording of "suicide bombers" adopted in the West, since there was nothing suicidal in those murders, as demonstrated by the author's book bearing the title *Islamikaze: Manifestations of Islamic Martyrology*, Frank Cass, London, 2003.

about one third of the world production. But when his invasion of Iran in October 1980 ended up in an interminable trench war which cost 1 million casualties on both sides, he obtained a cease-fire in August 1988, which permitted him to turn against his Kurdish population. As the West and his Arab allies continued to slumber, he launched a sudden attack on Kuwait, attempting to achieve on the opposite side of the Gulf, in August 1990, what he had failed in Iran, namely coast-line and petroleum, claiming that Kuwait was in truth an Iraqi province, and feeling certain that the Americans would not react. But President George Bush was swift to organize an international coalition to liberate Kuwait. His unstated war aim was to retrieve the oil wells of Kuwait which had been sabotaged by the Iraq invasion, but his stated war aims in his "Desert Storm" campaign were to "liberate Kuwait, to remove Saddam, to break the backbone of Iraq's forces, to democratize the Gulf states which had been invaded or threatened by Saddam Hussein, and to create a new world order.[7]

None of the declared "noble" war aims was fulfilled, however. Kuwait was freed from the Iraqi yoke, all right, but it was handed back to its emir, who treated it as his private property, ran away when the invasion began and did not lift a finger for its liberation. Neither Saddam was removed, nor his armed forced broken, both paradoxically, due to Saudi intervention which could not bear to lend a hand to the demise of an Arab country and of the glorious capital of the Abbasid Dynasty-Baghdad. Thus the job was left unfinished, and it would take the bold invasion of Iraq in 2003, under the presidency of George W. Bush, 12 years later, to finalize what his father had started, this time from bases outside of Saudi Arabia. At the time of dire crisis, when Saudi Arabia was threatened to be overrun by Iraqis, it asked immediately for relief from the US, and under duress consented not

---

[7]For details see Raphael Israeli, T*he Iraq War: Hidden Agendas and Babylonian Intrigues*, Sussex Academic Press, Brighton, 2004.

only to the stationing of foreign forces of its land, but also agreed, together with its satellites in the Gulf, to take measures towards liberalization of their absolute monarchical regimes, so as to make American interference justifiable on moral grounds. But as soon as Iraq was beaten, the Saudis intervened on their behalf to arrest the American advance on Baghdad, and demanded that the Americans evacuate forthwith Saudi soil, confident that the emergency had revolved. Its *'ulama'* (doctors of the Holy Law) who provide the ideological underpinnings of the regime, pressed the King to demand the removal of the "New Crusaders" from the holiest Muslim sites. The sheikhs retained their power as before, no democratization occurred, save for the King agreeing to install a *shura* (advisory council) which he appointed. Elections, though partly adopted in the rest of the Gulf, were a far cry from democratization, and the rulers continued to "dance sheikh to sheikh".

Among the pledges of war aims remained the "new world order", which could be attained, as usual, only at Israel's expense. So, while the Jordanians and the Palestinians were forgiven their embraces with Saddam during the crisis, and the rest of the Arabs were rewarded for their participation in the coalition (where they did not lift a finger in combat, save for Saudi Arabia which was directly threatened and actively defended its borders), Israel who suffered missile attacks but refrained from reacting at the American behest, was punished. Not only did the US, unlike Germany, refrain from according to it loan guarantees to repair the damages and to help absorb the massive waves of Jewish immigrants from the disintegrating Soviet Union, but it compelled Israel to make overtures towards Syria and the Jordano-Palestinians in the Madrid Conference, which were to complicate the situation even further. In fact, the new world order, being about the only asset that Bush could rescue from the list of his stated war aims, he opened the conference personally in July 1992 and then flew back on his Air Force 1 to Texas where the Republican Convention was to designate him for a second term (which he lost to Bill Clinton). That Madrid conference, which was only a show to bail Bush out, soon turned to a farce, when Israel refused to recognize the Palestinians as a separate entity, and they were incorporated within the Jordanian delegation, which everyone knew did not reflect reality on the ground. Elections in Israel in early 1992 brought Labor Party's Rabin to power, who was accorded all the favors previously denied to Shamir, in an attempt to mollify him. Clinton took over in the US, and the "peace process" acquired new actors and new contours, and instigated new hopes and promises.

All cards were reshuffled when informal talks with the Palestinians in Oslo in 1992-3 produced the Declaration of Principles (DOP), which the Israeli government was duped to sign with the PLO by a group of naïve ideologues, who believed that if they meant well, so would their partners. They enticed the government, under the false claim that the Palestinians had changed, to a series of major concessions without demanding reciprocity. In fact, the Palestinians under Arafat, had only changed their tactics, in order to extract concessions from those un-experienced, visionless, obtuse and mindless Israelis, while their strategy of gradually bringing to Israel's demise was not altered. In fact, the much hailed "peace agreement", which created euphoria in the world and exhilaration among the Israelis who had just emerged from a five-year *intifada,* was neither peace nor agreement. It was not a peace, because nothing substantial had been agreed between the parties, it was only an agreement to negotiate. The proof is that it soon collapsed and nothing of it survived 18 years after its signature in September, 1993. And it was not an substantive agreement because it carried no iron-clad sequence of events for implementation. There was no meeting of minds, which is a prerequisite to any agreement between parties. The DOP, instead of expressing that meeting of minds that never was, in fact used the agreed wording to cover up the deep differences that were and remained. So it soon dissolved under competing interpretations, claims and counter claims, and especially when the Palestinians ignored the principle clause of putting an end to violence during the negotiations, something that Arafat never had the intention to implement.

The Palestinians revolutionized their stature markedly in the world through that accord, which gave them legitimacy and a foothold in the territories, while the Israelis signed their own demise, unnecessarily, by never comprehending the goals of their rivals and foolishly showering on them one concession after another, without obtaining any major gesture in return. For example, on the major issues of recognition and of territories, instead of insisting on negotiating the final status of the territories **before** letting the PLO in, and running elections **before** handing the PLO the rule of those territories (and what if the PLO lost?), Israel ushered Arafat in, together with his corrupt bureaucracy, and handed them government in the major cities, allowed them to bring armed forces whom she herself armed, naively believing that Arafat would control terrorism and keep the peace and order. In return for the recognition by Israel of the Palestinian right of self-determination, no parallel and equivalent demand was made of them to recognize and accept the right of the Jewish people for self-determination, something which still stands as a stumbling block today due to the Palestinian flat rejection of that proposition. Those Israeli geniuses who led the negotiations and who would heed no warnings from others, were content with the PLO recognition of the state of Israel instead. In Palestinian interpretation, however, Israel with 20% of its population already Palestinian, and 4 million more Palestinians demanding their right to "return", would become another Palestinian-majority state. Thanks very much for that generosity.

Israel also recognized the PLO as the movement of national liberation of the Palestinians, which is fair and square, provided, once again, equality and reciprocity were invoked. But they were not, and the Palestinians did not volunteer to recognize Zionism of their own volition, and they continue to cry from all the rooftops of the world that Zionism is racism. Where else in the world could one find such foolish negotiators who would accept to recognize their enemy while the latter is spitting at their face in total rejection? This has had a far reaching reverberation on this so-called "peace process", because when the Israeli public rebelled against accommodating the PLO while the Palestinian National Charter vowed to eliminate Israel, Rabin and his government pledged that no signature would take place unless "all the anti-Israel clauses in the Charter are abrogated or amended". The problem is that such clauses do not exist, for that document only vows to eliminate "all manifestations of Zionism in Palestine". Having failed to read that document, or to comprehend what it stated, the Israeli leaders, with American support, continued to demand its amendment, but the PLO dragged its feet and tried all sorts of subterfuge and detours[8], but the Charter is still valid in its original formulation to this day. Had the Israeli negotiators insisted initially on reciprocity, the Charter would have been *eo ipso* abrogated and there would have been no humiliation caused to the US and Israel, that though no "amendment" ever took place, the two governments were fooled to accept that it was, and they gained only derision and contempt for their ill-comprehension of the process.

Even as the Palestinians engaged in the Oslo process, terrorism against Israel mounted, thus making a mockery of the entire process and exposing Arafat's strategy of deceit and continued warfare. But it was too late. The Palestinian Authority was established and recognized by the world, it had its armed forces which turned in 1996 against Israel, and an unrelenting terrorism activity, in which it allowed the Palestinian cities under its rule to serve as shelters to terrorists from Israeli reprisals. In 1994, a mere six month

---

[8]See Raphael Israeli, "State and Religion in the Emerging Palestinian Entity", Palestinians Between Nationalism and Islam, Vallentine Mitchell, London, 2008, pp.147-170.

after Oslo, when Rabin was still duped by the process and posed no serious objection to Arafat's manipulations, the latter urged Muslims in a speech in Johannesburg to rally to the Palestinians for a *Jihad* to "rescue Jerusalem from the Zionists". Rabin and his government refused to react in kind and to arrest the "peace", in order "not to let the enemies of peace win" and not to give them "the right of veto over the process". Encouraged by this spineless attitude of the Israeli government, Arafat mounted terror attacks at night and denied them during day time, increased his armed forces beyond the perimeters allowed in the DOP, smuggled prohibited weapons into the Palestinian Authority, and sheltered the murderers who killed Israelis and retreated to Palestinian-held territories. And when he arrested them for show, he let them out through the revolving door. In one case in 1994, a few months after the DOP was signed, 21 Israeli young soldiers were blown up, and when Israel showed signs of resentment, Arafat accused it of a "staged provocation" to discredit the Palestinians. All those abuses were not good enough reasons for the Rabin government to change course. If he admitted his major error and withdrew from his dramatic commitments in Oslo, he would have had to resign and recede into oblivion for the disaster he had ushered in through *naivete*, excessive self confidence in his ability to change reality and the American growing involvement, once Washington was brought into the process after it had been kept in the dark during the secret Oslo negotiations.

Rabin's demise, which was about to cause him the loss of the next elections in 1996, was spared him when he was tragically murdered by a lonely right-wing Israeli, who intended to put an end to that slow process of the peace recession, ended up, on the contrary, rallying the public behind the martyred and personally esteemed Prime Minister. Nevertheless, the right-wing Likkud won the elections, though Netanyahu was constrained to swear allegiance to Oslo, and to sign the Hebron and then the Wye Plantation agreements with the Palestinians. The signature of so many agreements in close succession, however, was evidence that there was no firm agreement about anything. The best proof was that precisely after those additional "agreements", the partners came to the end of the road once Netanyahu floated his famous slogan: "The Palestinians can only receive if they also learn to give", signaling the end of the "giving without taking" relationship with the Palestinians. The Israeli left, which accused Netanyahu of not having pursued the previous policy of generous giving, was again returned to power in 1999, under Ehud Barak's leadership, who held the promise of bringing the process to completion. He initiated the 2000 Camp David II in the final months of the Clinton Administration, also to no avail, since Arafat refused to acknowledge the finality of the conflict even if Israel withdrew from 95% of the territories, including East Jerusalem. That adamant stance showed once again, that the mantras of "occupation" and "settlements" were no more than pretexts to delay any definitive settlement under which Israelis and Palestinians would entertain no more claims from each other and live in peace.

The horrific acts of Islamikaze which accompanied the Second al-Aqsa *Intifada* after the Camp David fiasco, precipitated once again the swing of the pendulum in Israeli politics, which brought Ariel Sharon to power, as he was viewed as the man capable of fighting terrorism and bringing quiet and security, if not peace, to his embattled public. His first act when he gained the confidence of the public, was to launch a decisive assault against terrorism, daring for the first time reverse Rabin's Oslo axioms and treating the Palestinians of the West Bank and Gaza as enemies, not as partners immune to retaliation for their terrorism. The Oslo champions had invented the "suicide-bombing" terminology, signaling that those terrorists who defied Oslo by wreaking havoc on Israeli cities and sowing death and destruction, which came to average over 100 casualties a month, against the putative will of the Palestinian authority, were deranged individuals who could not be countered or defended against, therefore more devastation was expected on their part. For if they had the courage to admit that the Palestinian authority, their "partner in peace" was behind those individuals, they would have had to explain why they did not go after the Palestinians into their sanctuaries, for fear of "destroying the peace process" on which their entire political career was hedged. Sharon had no such inhibitions, he called the spade a spade, did not hesitate to enter Palestinian towns and clean them up one by one, thus ending their sanctuary status and subjecting them to scrutiny and punishment, and treating Arafat himself to the status of renegade, relegating him to a besieged and forlorn existence, instead of the honored partner he was and had enjoyed under Rabin.

Arafat died and was replaced by Abu-Mazen, a supposedly "moderate" leader, who obtained a doctoral degree in Moscow on the theme of Holocaust denial, continues to deny the right of the Jews for self-determination, and insists on destroying Israel as a Jewish state by returning to it 4,5 million Palestinians which would alter its nature. The irony is that those same Palestinians who complain against "apartheid" in Israel, and Israel's "oppression" of the Palestinians under "occupation", are the same who wish for their compatriots to suffer the same bitter fate if they were to "return" to Israel. Be it as it may, as the Palestinians and the Israelis were driven into an impasse, Ariel Sharon, who became an immensely popular Prime Minister, and was faced, together with his sons, by severe charges of corruption, which involved granting favors to wealthy foreign businessmen, decided in 2004 to execute a sharp *volte-face* in his politics, in an attempt to escape indictment. Suddenly, that life-time fighter who regarded the score of Israeli settlements in the Gaza area as every bit important as Tel Aviv to Israeli security, felt, at everyone's surprise, not least his own party, that Israel "could no longer control another people" and had to disengage, even unilaterally, from Gaza. In 2005, against the stance of his party, which he quit and founded a new one with his followers-Kadima, a painful evacuation of 8000

Israelis was effected from the Gaza area, and all the prosperous and flourishing settlements built there on barren land,
reverted to their arid status, where the ruins of the Israeli
settlements were turned into artillery and missile positions
to bombard Israeli settlements along the border. Sharon was
temporarily rescued from the indictment, though he was be-
fallen by a severe stroke which catapulted his deputy, Ehud
Olmert, to the Prime Ministership, but Israel has marked another major fiasco in her security and foreign policy.

The weak and indecisive Olmert government wasted
the years of unlimited support from President Bush Junior
(2001-9) in two disastrous wars in Lebanon and then in
Gaza, which apart from strong sanctions on Israel in the international arena, brought little succor to it. While September 11 may have been the watershed in American awakening
to the new dangers, the Gaza Disengagement has marked the
end of the era of sanity and national steadfastness, of strategic calculation and conventional military confrontations
with the enemy on Israel's borders, as the latter, voluntarily,
apparently due to Sharon's personal complications with law,
retreated from territory without even his party's consensus,
in fact against the majority of his own followers, and without any agreement or quid-pro-quo; and the inauguration of
the era of irrationality, where wars are thrust on the population of Israel, and no longer launched against its defenses;
where irregular armies, not even belonging to countries, are
involved; where civilian populations and not frontlines are
attacked; where targets for retaliation or prevention are difficult, if not impossible, to discern and attack; where one can
no longer line up diplomatic support, due to the inevitable
massive civilian casualties of the enemy when one acts in
self-defense; and where the exit from war cannot be clearly
defined by any treaty or agreement, or understanding, or
resolution, due to the lack of a formal partner who wishes
to negotiate.

Chapter 2

The New Asymmetrical Wars

Abu-'Ubeid Qurashi, one of the aides of Osama Bin Laden, published after September 11 in the Arabic press and in the al-Qa'ida site on the Internet, a stunning article regarding his organization's strategy in its unseemly confrontation with the US and western civilization in general. This article demonstrates that not only do those champions of evil do their home work adequately, and that they are equipped with the requisite patience, sophistication and methodical thinking, the fruits of which were seen in the deadly precision of their operation against the Twin Towers, but that western democracies have something to learn in the war against terror. For it transpires that the Muslim terrorist organizations which have been waging war against the West directly are inspired by al-Qa'ida war doctrine, and it is not too early to try to comprehend their schemes. Qurashi, who has obviously studied the most recent western research in matters of the future battlefields and war doctrines, has come up with conclusions that are alarming: first, that the era of massive wars has ended, because the three war models of previous generations have been eroded; second, the fourth-generation wars of the 21st century will consist of asymmetrical confrontations between well-armed and well-equipped armies, who have a turf, a way of life and material interests to defend, and therefore are clumsy—against small groups armed with light weaponry only, who have no permanent bases and are on the move at all times. Thirdly, in these wars, the main target is not the armed forces, but civil society that has to be submitted to harassment and terror to the point of detaching it from the army that fights in its defense; and forthly, that television is more important than armored divisions in the battlefield. The Twin Towers, the terrorist explosions in London, Madrid and Bali, and the Israeli confrontation with Hamas and Hizbullah on its borders, show how these doctrines can be rendered operational.

This war doctrine lies in the gray zone between war and peace. Namely those who initiate this kind of war, e.g. by wanton terrorism, would not declare it openly, and would leave it to the defenders to announce war and thereby become the "aggressors". The terrorists themselves would create atrocities that are sure to attract the attention of television so as to "strike fear in the heart of the enemy" (a Qur'anic prescription), and make them retreat to their bases. But when the victim strikes back in self-defense, television can again be counted on to show the "abuses" of the "aggressor" and create sympathy for the cause of the terrorists. On television, the huge armies which crush everything in their path will always look more threatening than the "poor", "frustrated" "freedom fighters" who are "oppressed" and "persecuted" by far superior troops. Thus, the author could show that small groups of poorly equipped *Mujahideen* have been able throughout the past two decades to defeat super- and lesser powers: the Soviets in Afghanistan, the US in Somalia, Russia in Chechnia and Israel in Lebanon and then in Gaza. According to this analysis, the three major components of modern warfare are: early warning, the ability to strike preventively, and deterrence—exactly the elements that were paralyzed by al-Qa'ida on 11 September. As for the early warning, the writer claims that the terrorists have achieved a strategic surprise, in spite of American technology, on the scale of Pearl Harbor in December 1941, or of the Nazi attack against the Soviet Union in June 1941, Suez crossing in the Yom Kippur War in 1973, and the assault on the *Cole* in Aden in 2000. On the basis of the above analysis, the terrorists were able to deliver a deadly blow on September 11, and levy on the Americans a very heavy economic and psychological price. The ability to deliver a preventive strike is linked, in the mind of Qurashi to the issue of early warning, because when the latter fails, then a preventive strike becomes irrelevant. But even if it had worked, there would have been no one to strike against in retaliation, as the terrorists are small groups, hidden and mobile. And finally—deterrence totally collapses in the face of the asymmetry between an institutionalized state which values life and a desire to live and prosper, and a group of *Mujahideen* who are indifferent to life, and indeed desirous to perish in the Path of Allah and attain the delights of Paradise. Thus, since nothing can deter them, they can always determine, against all odds, when, where, how, what, and whom to strike, without fearing that anyone will retaliate against them[9].

It is harrowing to reflect on how applicable this doctrine is in our daily lives, starting with the Middle East, but going to the periphery of the Islamic world, in places like Australia and Canada. For example, the Hizbullah in Lebanon, which is linked to al-Qa'ida, not only ideologically, has had some successes, but has also exported this doctrine to the Muslim terrorist movements in the Palestinian Territories, such as the Hamas and the Islamic Jihad. Moreover, Palestinian "secular" organizations such as the *Tanzim* and the *Aqsa Brigades* have been converted to these tactics, once Arafat's call for martyrdom, with himself at the helm, had become the favorite form of struggle against Israel. There is, however, a way to counter every deed or doctrine, with a view of reducing its effect, thereby immunizing western society from its deadly threat and eliminating the terror it imposes on all civilized people. For example, if the terrorists intend to detach Western societies from their armed forces, an area where they have been partly successful by inculcating doubts into the publics by supporting protest movements from within, perhaps it is time for these societies to realize that they have been unwittingly used by their enemies

---

[9]Al Quds al-Arabi (London), 9 February, 2002. In Memri 344, 10 February, 2002

to attain their ends, namely to dismantle national unity, to incite publics against their governments, and to play into the hands of the terrorist subversive doctrine. If television is a declared means to discredit Western societies and their systems of defense, perhaps the media should not be allowed to the battlefield until the end of hostilities. Perhaps it is better for governments to be accused of obstructing the media and freedom of the press, than to let them document the asymmetry between the established strong defenders of freedom and the weaker terrorists in the field, with the former more likely to be condemned and the latter considered as "victims" and sympathized with.

If terrorism has adopted the recourse of fighting by using *Islamikaze* "martyrdom", because there is arguably nothing to be done against "suicide-bombers", each of whom can terrorize and paralyze an entire public, then it is necessary to demonstrate, like President Bush, that we are facing not a war against individuals who are desirous of death, and whom we cannot bring to justice when they succeed in their task, but against those who train them, dispatch them, arm them, indoctrinate them, support them and finance them. And that as long as we keep them on the run, they will be less able to concoct and carry out their dark and cruel schemes against the West. That Muslim supporters of this doctrine pursue their campaign of intimidation against the West is not new, but what does seem surprisingly new, compared with the legendary fighting spirit of the British, for example, is the seeming capitulation of European capitals to their tormentors, and the baffling incomprehension they exhibit of the Islamic phenomenon which has repeatedly declared itself so clearly inimical to them. Just consider the spirit of *dhimmitude* which has inundated the entire West due to its much-cultivated dependence on Muslim oil and the humiliating consequences thereof. This state of mind, which dictates caution, surreptitious maneuvering in order to survive, and a self-humiliating sycophancy toward the Muslim rulers in the hope of gaining their favor, even at the risk of harming the juridical process (consider the scandalous release of the Lockerbie culprit), has been inherited from many centuries of Islamic rule on vast swaths of Christendom, from Sicily to the Iberian Peninsula, from the Balkans to the gates of Vienna. This aggressive Islam which attempted, but failed, to Islamize Europe in the past, had also subjected large Christian communities to the *dhimmi* regime in the Near East that was conquered by the emerging new faith of Islam, like the Copts in Egypt, the Assyrians in Iraq, the Maronites in Lebanon, and countless other Christian communities which first became subjugated majorities, and then systematically persecuted minorities, in their own countries. This amounted, after many centuries of oppression and contempt by the rulers of Islam, to a self-diminution of the *dhimmis*—a loss of their pride and confidence in themselves, that they did not stand up to the standards set for them by their rulers, and a total distortion of their self-image and the image of their oppressors. So much so, that many Christians and Jews, years after being liberated from *dhimmitude*, continued to think and act as *dhimmis*, namely to hold themselves grateful to their Muslim masters, who beat, humiliated, and mistreated them. Any observer of the international arena today would have noticed how Western policy-makers dangerously submit to Muslim demands even when they are not compelled to do so.

When the Americans took the lead in combating terrorism after September 11, realizing that that they had to meet their enemy on a battlefield different from the conventional one they had been used and prepared for, they could only slowly, and not always effectively, respond to the new Islamic strategy of asymmetrical war. President Bush indeed vowed to "smoke the terrorists out of their hidings", but this proved easier said than done. Ten years (thus far), of warfare in Afghanistan, and eight in Iraq, with the grudging participation of the rest of the West, have not done much to bring about the capture of Bin Laden or Zawahiri, or to weaken significantly their sponsors among the Taliban. Quite the contrary, the latter seem to have considerably increased their numbers and expanded into Pakistan too. While at least in Iraq there are some American successes, notably in handing the rule from a tyrannical Sunnite minority to a seemingly democratic array of Sh'iite groups and Kurdish and Sunnite minorities, Afghani social and tribal divisions, and the deeply entrenched systemic corruption there, did not allow yet such a development. In either case, if and when the Americans depart, as their allies get tired and do not possess the combative stamina to persist, there is no guarantee that those gains could be preserved. In fact, exactly according to the calculations and predictions of the asymmetrical warfare ideologues, the war on al-Qa'ida and the Taliban has degenerated into a war against the peoples of Afghanistan and Iraq. The American victory in both Iraq and Afghanistan was swift and decisive at the outset when regular forces were deployed, but then, in the uncertainty of guerilla warfare, the upper hand of "people's war" began to erode the western superiority and to cause manifold more casualties than in the initial conventional sweep. What is worse is that more and more common people in both countries, on whose backs the war is being fought, wish the American fighters and their allies to leave, even as these brave young men are sacrificing themselves for the future of their countries.

If this is so for the powerful and relatively remote westerners, who are not directly threatened by any of this, how much more so for tiny, more vulnerable and embattled Israel which is directly bordering on some of these irregular forces, which have constrained it to change its winning tactics of yesteryear, after they produced the 1967 victory, and the less spectacular draw in the battlefield of 1973. For since then, it is the irregular and non-state forces which seem to thrive. It is no coincidence that the leader of the Hizbullah, Hassan Nasrallah, the Shi'ite Lebanese cleric who professes a war of annihilation against Israel, in the service of his Iranian and Syrian masters, and stands in opposition to his own government, has been cited as the most popular leader in the Arab world. It is worth noting that well before September 11, some Arab commentators spoke out in favor of Bin Laden, claiming that he was not a terrorist but an "unfortunate man seeking refuge in the high mountains of Afghanistan", hiding from a "terrorist US who has taken over the world". Therefore they claimed that only attacks on US Embassies, such as those in East Africa in 1998, could resolve the problem of globalization as long as it remained impossible to defeat the Americans in direct combat.[10] One of the authors of these gratuitous words, is Bary Atwan, the editor of a major Arabic daily which appears in London, who is constantly sought by the major international networks for interviews and pretends to present Arab views on current affairs. Three months after the September 11 tragedy, the same journalist was invited by *al-Jazeera* to moderate a panel to comment on one of the video-cassettes released by Bin Laden. He lauded Bin Laden for his "good timing" when he chose to lash out at America's hypocritical policy which allowed "Ariel Sharon to act criminally against the defenseless Palestinian people"[11] and added, among others, his verdict against the American response in Afghanistan:

> The US issued its own judgment and carried out the verdict, and now it is seeking the evidence. It is like executing someone first and then looking for the evidence that he deserved capital punishment. The US is using huge B-52 bombers and bombs villages and towns. They also use Daisy Cutter bombs, weighing 15,000 pounds each on Tora Bora and the caves... I noticed that in the video-cassettes Bin Laden's left shoulder looked frozen, I hope he is all right and was not hurt...
>
> Whenever an American is killed in the war, they say it was "friendly fire", and when a helicopter crashes, they say it was a "technical failure". Americans never fall as a result of resistance

---

[10]Abdul Bari Atwan, in a talk show in *al-Jazeera*, 10 July, 2001. In Memri, *Terror in America*, No 45, Feb 2002.

[11]*Ibid.*

or Arab and Muslim fire. We have already observed the lies in these statements when we saw the Taliban and al-Qa'ida exhibiting the downed helicopters with their registration numbers... In Iraq too the Americans tried to reduce the numbers of their casualties, and no one tells us the true numbers to this day... The US bombed and killed 65 tribal chieftains in Afghanistan... but America continues to insist that they were members of al-Qa'ida. This is a lie, a disinformation. Why can't she admit that she killed them erroneously? Errors are always attributed to Arabs and Muslims, but the Americans are always supermen who cannot do wrong, who always hit their targets, and whoever kills them is a terrorist and criminal...

The fact that Bin Laden is still alive has spoiled the celebrations of American victory in Afghanistan... The fact that he is alive has caused the postponement of American aggression against other countries as Syria, Iraq, the Yemen and Somalia. The fact that he is alive and smuggled this cassette to al-Qai'da, which got it to Pakistan and Qatar, means that our brothers in Iraq, Syria, Hizbullah, the Yemen and Somalia, must be grateful [for his survival]. Had Bin Laden been killed at the outset of the war, as the Americans, and some Arab regimes, May Allah forgive them!, had anticipated, it is well possible that the war would have moved to these countries and we would have witnessed bombings of Iraq, Syria, Lebanon, Somalia and the Yemen ...[12]

This is a mere one page from exactly the same wording and propaganda which have been poured on Israel by its Arab neighbors, whenever it tries to pre-empt, retaliate or prevent the murderous attacks against it in this asymmetrical war where words in the media are no less important than moves in the battlefield. Not only are the enemy troops evasive, hiding behind civilians and caring little about the civilian casualties they cause as a result, but they thrive on such consequences which are part of the media war to blacken the image of the enemy, the way Bary Atwan, who

---

[12]*Ibid.*

lives in the comfort, security and freedom of London, has been doing with regard to America. Paradoxically, at the same time that more irregular forces are getting involved in the current and future wars, so will their lethality increase manifold, so predicts the OC Ground Forces Command of the Israeli defense forces (IDF), Maj.-Gen. Avi Mizrachi. As a result, the future battlefield the IDF will face will be more difficult, lethal and uncertain, said he during a military conference at Latrun. He was speaking at the third annual Latrun Conference on Maneuver in Complex Terrain, co-hosted by the IDF, the US Joint Forces Command and several leading Israeli defense industries. Over 100 military officers from close to 30 countries were present at the conference, attesting to the universal awakening of the new battle conditions. He emphasized that in any future conflict, Israel would have no choice but to use its ground forces. "A war cannot be won without moving forces on the ground," he said. "Even today there are people who believe that it is sufficient to threaten to use the forces, but in the Middle East this is not enough. Only a ground maneuver will end the conflict and win the war." The future battlefield, he said, would be more lethal due to Syria, Hamas and Hizbullah's continued investment in underground infrastructure and ability to minimize its signature, to the point that it does not need to maneuver like a conventional military, but only use its firepower from pre-planned bunkers. Mizrachi revealed that Syria has taken civilian trucks, loaded them with weapons and scattered them in different villages along the border with Israel, ahead of a future conflict. "This is why we need to split up our capabilities between a conventional war scenario and one that we are fighting against a non-conventional force," he said.[13]

Later in the conference, a disagreement erupted between the head of the Armored Corps, Brig.-Gen. Agay Yehezkeli and Chief Infantry Officer Brig.-Gen. Yossi Bahar. Speaking

---

[13] Jerusalem Post, September 4, 2009

after Mizrachi, Yehezkeli said that in a future conflict with Hizbullah in Lebanon the IDF would need to launch a quick ground operation, heavily depending on tanks, deep into Lebanese territory in order to curb the rocket attacks against the Israeli home front. During the second Lebanon War in 2006, the IDF hesitated before sending large ground forces into Lebanon, and for the first part of the campaign mostly relied on the Air Force to try and stop the Hizbullah Katyusha rocket attacks. In both cases the civilians, among whom weapons and guerilla fighters were hidden, bore the brunt of the casualties, bringing upon Israel a cataract of blame and condemnation, regardless of the fact that they had triggered the war. The media dispatches of civilian casualties and destruction, and of some UN and other international charitable organizations, which by nature operate among civilians, won public opinion to the aggressors in the war, and those who fought back with their hands tied, ended up being condemned, exactly like the Americans and the British in Iraq and Afghanistan. The only difference is that the West has the option to disengage and go home, but the Israelis have no option but to stand and fight for their own turf and survival. The next speaker, Bahar said that he disagreed with Yehezkeli and that a deep penetration of Lebanon was not needed immediately at the outset of the war. He said that several brigades would be capable of conquering southern Lebanon and taking control of the 165 villages south of the Litani River[14]. The ultimate result, in any case, will be paralyzing the efficacy and speed of IDF troops who, instead of cutting through military forces as they did in 1967, will have to watch their step as they advance through civilian populations, which can attack, every bit like the guerillas behind them, but cannot be touched when it comes to defending against them.

The last three major fiascos of Israel in this asymmetrical confrontation will have to be analyzed, in order to explain

---

[14]*Ibid.*

Israel's dilemmas and the new challenges that its armed forces have to face. The first of them is the 2005 "Disengagement" in Gaza, the greatest foolishness done by an Israeli leadership since Oslo. Since it is itself a derivation from Oslo, which has been already discussed above, it is necessary to add some background before we proceed. As the Arabs saw it, Oslo was the means to repatriate, via the main gate to Palestinian territory, the remote, exiled and forlorn leadership and armed forces of the Palestinians, based in Tunis and elsewhere in the Arab world, which had consistently failed to infiltrate, through the back window, by three decades of guerilla warfare against Israel. Implicit in Oslo was the mutual realization by both parties that the pre-Oslo situation had become untenable, and that Israel's Labor government had become so desperate that it would seek and accept any accommodation at almost any price. That meant for the Arabs, for the first time in the history of Israel and Zionism, that the *Intifada* had worked where conventional warfare had repeatedly failed, and that Israel, if properly and continuously lured by "peace" offers, which were made explicit throughout the world, would have to yield to the international mood of peace and make the necessary concessions to the Arabs to regain their lost territories. The Arabs also noticed that instead of gaining more territories through conflict, a soothed Israel, through negotiations and pledges for recognition, peace and accommodation, could be led to yield territory, as had so dramatically happened under the Israel-Egypt peace agreement. Following that paradigm, then, "peace" did not satisfy a deep and widespread philosophical desire to live in peace, but a newfound conviction that it was the only way to retrieve without wars and defeats their lost land. A similar idea had been floated in the early 1960s by Habib Bourguiba, the French-educated Tunisian President, who counseled the Arabs to reduce Israel to size and weaken it by accepting it in their midst, instead of strengthening it and hardening its fighting spirit by warfare. That same idea was adopted and elaborated by Egyptian intellectual and official

Butrus Ghali, who advocated the idea of "assimilating" (*in-dimaj*) Israel by accepting it and then melting by dilution its tiny population (at the time some three million) into the vast surrounding and dominant Arab culture. Paradoxically, Ghali, who later became Egypt's Secretary of State for Foreign Affairs, and then the Secretary General of the UN, was part of the Coptic minority in Egypt, which was itself under the constant threat and pressure to lose its identity among the surrounding Arab and Muslim masses.

The Egyptian-Israeli peace accords, and then Oslo, had indeed demonstrated to the Arabs that land, a concrete asset, could be obtained from Israel by just uttering the word "peace", though for them it was code-word for achieving their strategic goal of diminishing Israel, not accommodating it. And so, the rejectionist Arab stance of the Khartum Conference after 1967, which had vowed no peace, no recognition and no negotiation with Israel, was suddenly replaced by a "burning desire for peace", under conditions which could not guarantee Israel's security, and therefore were not accepted until verified and tested by Israel. That permitted the Arabs to blame Israel for "rejecting peace" while they had become its "fervent champions", causing a dramatic reversal in public opinion in the world, who, naturally, sided with the Arab "peace seekers" and sanctioned the Israeli "war mongers". Those processes, which seemed to the Arabs not as a conciliatory measure on the part of Israel to attain peace, but as defeat for the Jewish spirit, which was now constrained to retreat, raised Arab expectations that with more demands, terrorism, pressure and peace sloganeering, they would achieve more and more. They were encouraged by what they considered as the beginning of Israel's downslide, which will gain momentum as the "peace process" went on, resulting in its loss of territory, of its unbeatable image, of its deterrence and of its legitimacy and international support. The Israeli-Egyptian peace accords became a precedent for the rest of the Arabs that if they make peace they can obtain all what they claim as their territories to the last inch, and they would not be content with anything less, as we have learned from negotiations with Syrians and Palestinians. The Arabs also learned that there are no consequences to aggression. They could attack and threaten Israel as repeatedly as they desire, for every time they lose the war, the retrieval of their lands in full is guaranteed, so what would deter them from trying again and again? Germany has learned from its aggression that it can lose territory to Poland, the Soviet Union and other neighbors, because war is not a picnic, and the attacked victim should be compensated for its casualties and destruction, while the aggressor must be deterred from ever attempting again, knowing what it costs. It is immoral to restore any aggressor to its original territorial possessions thus encouraging it to attack again.

But the "cold peace" which prevailed between Israel and Egypt after Israel restored to Egypt all the Sinai, thus demonstrating that Cairo was interested in its territory, not in peace, was mindlessly repeated in 1994, when Israel signed another peace-accord with Jordan, which rushed to pre-empt an Israeli-Palestinian settlement after the Oslo process had begun. In both instances, Israel signed peace with the rulers, Sadat and Hussein, respectively, while strong anti-Semitism, the boycott of Israel and of Israelis, championed and led by the Muslim Brothers in both places, continued unabated in their countries. It is those elements, that also encouraged the rise of the Hamas among the Palestinians, which triggered the gratuitous unilateral Israeli withdrawal from Gaza in 2005 and the ensuing Gaza war in late 2008 and early 2009. Prime Minister Ariel Sharon, who was at the height of his popularity in 2003, after having beaten terrorism in the West Bank, and despite the worldwide accusations against him that Israel had committed a "massacre" in Jenin in that context, which started with accusations of 5,000 Palestinian dead and ended up with 50, half of whom were armed fighters, made the stunning announcement that Israel should retreat unilaterally from Gaza. The same man who had insisted a few months earlier that Gaza was as important for Israel's defense as Tel Aviv, with the unlimited support of the 8,000 Israelis settlers there and much of the Israeli public, who were ready to take the hardship of daily bombings, suddenly made that *volte-face*. In view of the rebellion within his party, which saw the looming danger of such a move, many observers attributed it either to his advanced age and his ailing health or, more probably, to an attempt to instigate the attorney general of Israel to close the dossier of his impending indictment for a major act of corruption. That calculation was bluntly simple: the Israeli population would easily be swayed by a promise of a peaceful arrangement with the Palestinians, when it came from Mr Security, who was elected on a platform of defense, and had done so well in the war against the infrastructure of terrorism in the West Bank. In order to satisfy Israel's yearning for tranquility, the public would be inclined to forgive personal violations of the law for the sake of attaining "peace". And the gamble worked. The dossier was closed down under strong protest from eminent jurists, but with the encouragement of the media and public opinion, and the marketing of the idea of unilateral withdrawal which was put on the table, in order to overcome his party, his government, parliamentary and public objections. Even the Chief of Staff, General Moshe Ya'alon, who objected to that step, was dismissed, and a more docile one, Air Force General Dan Halutz, was appointed in his stead to carry out that divisive order.

As it was marketed to the incredulous Israeli public, that unilateral withdrawal was to remedy the suddenly untenable Israeli rule over the unruly million Palestinians in Gaza; it was to "end the friction" between those multitudes and the 8,000 Israeli settlers distributed in a score of settlements, mostly rural and some townships; it was to reduce the security burden over the Israeli army, which had to provide protection round-the-clock to all the comings and goings of the settlers; and, most importantly, would bring tranquility to the border areas around Gaza, under the assumption that if Gaza is handed to the Palestinians, they would have no incentive to pursue their clashes with Israel. Connected to that was the envisaged improvement in the image of Israel abroad, when it relinquished one-sidedly "occupied territory". Indeed, the announcement of the plan instantly drove Israel in general and Sharon personally, into a loop of popularity unknown for decades, which not only was conducive to dropping the corruption claims against Sharon (who was in those crucial days termed a "citrus", referring to the citrus fruit which Jews use for prayer during the Feast of Tabernacles and is carefully preserved in a soft cotton wrapping and within a hard ornate box), but brought him an unprecedented wave of praise throughout the world. Enamored by his "citrus" status, as the darling of the media, he was blinded to believe that the shift in the eyes of public opinion was permanent, and became oblivious to the fact that Israel and its leaders have always been praiseworthy in the eyes of world public opinion and the media only when they made a concession of any sort, but as soon as the retreat ended and time came for self-defense, the floodgates of recriminations were opened against both Israel and its leaders. The "disengagement" was carried out in 1995, amidst heart-tearing scenes of removing entire families by force from the homes they had built and cultivated, from the fields and hot houses they had tilled and expanded, from the neighborhoods and communities they had come to familiarize with and to love. And all that, not for the sake of allowing other disinherited people to take root or improve their living, for as soon as the Israelis left, and following the jubilant celebrations of "freedom" by the Palestinian mobs, new military positions and missile and mortar emplacements were constructed on the ruins of the abandoned Israeli houses and villas, which began shelling the environing Israeli villages and ushering in the next war. Most disconcerting was the fact, that as the Israeli hot houses, which had provided employment for thousands of Palestinians, were purchased by American Jews in order to be handed intact to the Palestinians for the pursuance of peaceful farming activity, were immediately dismantled and looted by the crowds, they returned the once flourishing villages which provided fruits and vegetables for export, into barren and desert land, and launchers of destruction and hatred, as they were before.

It did not take long before the disaster became apparent. True, in return for the mindless Israeli unilateral withdrawal, the Bush administration yielded to Israel a letter of assurances that the new realities of the ground would be taken into consideration when the permanent boundaries between Israel and the Palestinians would be decided. In Israel, the elated Israeli government took that to mean, that the "major blocks of settlements in the West Bank", similar to the one that had been just evacuated by Israel in the Katif Bloc in Gaza, would remain within Israel in the eventual permanent settlement. But as soon as the Obama team was inaugurated, doubts and suspicions were voiced by his administration as to the validity of this pledge. But the whole situation was absurd in the context in which it was shaped. For it was a contradiction in terms to agree to evacuate an entire block of settlements in Gaza in the name of recognition of other similar settlement blocks in the West Bank. You cannot introduce a principle and persuade others to accept it by creating a precedent to its very contrary. Indeed, not only did the Palestinians, other Arabs and Europeans take the unilateral withdrawal as a "triumph to Palestinian resistance" and refused to contemplate to give anything in return, even not an agreement acknowledging it, but it was considered as the standard setting yardstick to all future Israeli withdrawals, namely to be total, unconditional, and unrewarded, thus making any peace accord unattainable in the future.

The trauma of uprooting 8000 diligent, productive and creative citizens, who provided work for thousands of Palestinians, grew into anger and despair when the outcome of that gratuitous withdrawal became apparent. Sharon, who soon suffered a stroke and went into a coma, did not live to see the dire consequences of his renegade conduct vis-a-vis the very principles he had defended and fought for all his life. For not only were the evacuees not entirely compensated nor resettled properly in Israel, and Israel lost tremendously in its agricultural export, but a devoted and idealistic part of Israeli society, backed by a large public in Israel, became dispirited and lost confidence in the very government it had helped bring into power. Exactly what the Arabs had heralded had begun to unfold, as the beginning of the end of Zionism, which had been folding up and giving up territory since the peace with Egypt, and then the Oslo agreement with the Palestinians. The right wing in Israel viewed this as the beginning of the implementation of the Arab dream. None of the other "advantages" of that disengagement worked out either: the security hazard against Israeli villages and towns, especially the township of Sderot, only increased, as they began to be systematically and continually shelled and bombarded, the friction between Israelis and Gazans went one notch up and did not disappear, necessitating a defense apparatus on no lesser scale than before. The peace process was not pushed forward but damaged, and the Palestinian public, far from appreciating that conciliatory measure by Israel, on the contrary hardened its position and clamored for the *coup de grace* against bleeding and weakened Israel. The result was the take over by Hamas in the Palestinian general elections of 2006, which led a year later to Hamas' toppling the rule of the PLO-dominated Palestinian Authority in Gaza in 2007, and to its expulsion from there. The creation of two mutually exclusive Palestinian governments in Gaza and Ramallah, one representing the PA and the other the Hamas, poses a problem to whoever wishes to deal with a credible, valid, effective and legitimate representative of the Palestinian people. Some have asked Israel to deal with both simultaneously, as if any foreign diplomat were asked to negotiate in parallel channels with President Sarkozy, who was officially and legitimately installed as the elected President, and his Socialist rival, Segolene Royal, who lost and graciously moved into the opposition.

The removal of Israeli troops and settlers from Gaza did not satisfy the Hamas there, which regarded Israel's withdrawal as a first step towards its defeat. Apparently under direct Iranian and Hizbullah guidance, the Hamas in Gaza began to plan the next step. Following the preceding unilateral, calamitous and unnecessary retreat of Israel from Lebanon in 2000, after Ehud Barak ascended to the Prime Ministership of Israel, which was also taken by Hizbullah as a victory on their part, the latter sent their messengers to Hamas in Gaza to persuade them to adopt Hizbullah tactics in order to oust Israel from all Palestinian territories, as they had done in Lebanon, so as to diminish Israel's stature. That advice was enthusiastically embraced by the Hamas, though at that point it had not yet taken control of Gaza from the PA. The two then concocted the plot which was to trigger the Second Lebanon War of 2006 and then the Gaza War of 2008-9, both asymmetrical wars which put into the test the war theories of harassing Israel by border clashes and skirmishes, sapping its morale by bombarding and shelling its villages along the border, irrespective of the counter-damages that Israel's reprisals might cause, and then confronting it by unconventional wars and methods. These methods consisted of operating in the name of movements, not countries which could be pinned down, punished and retaliated against; mixing among civilian populations and launching attacks from their midst, so that any retaliation would by necessity be viewed as a "brutal attack against innocent civilians"; avoid frontal confrontations with large-scale military formations, which cannot be won; and make sure that supportive media like *al-Jazeera* be present in the battle field in order to ensure an early, and sometimes preemptive, coverage of any "defensive" measure taken against the "genocidal" death and destruction that the "cruel and blood-thirsty enemy" is waging against its "poor, peaceful, defenseless and innocent victims". In both cases it won a great success inasmuch as it showed that in the confrontation of a man with a tank, the man will always win; in a clash of soldiers with women and children, the latter will always win; and in the competition between squadrons of airplanes and destroyed houses or mutilated casualties, the advanced hardware will always lose.

For months since Israel evacuated Gaza and the Philadelphi Corridor which separated Gaza from Egypt, the Gazans built an impressive underworld of tunnels where prohibited weapons under the Oslo accords were stored, or through which they were smuggled from Egypt, contrary to the latter's commitment under the peace with Israel to prevent such hostile acts from its territory. One of those tunnels was used in June 2006 to undermine an Israeli border position and blow it up, killing some of its occupants and kidnapping Gilad Shalit, who was to become a worldwide *cause celebre* in successive years, for the failure of Israel to gain his release. That unprovoked act, which was jointly crafted by the Hamas and their Hizbullah advisers, under Iranian instigation and Syrian inspiration, to deflect world attention from the prosecution of Syrian officials for the Hariri murder in Lebanon, and from the Iranian determined effort to pursue its nuclear program, would a month later, snowball into the second Lebanese War of July-August 2006. Had Israel taken the immediate steps of removing the Hamas government, of arresting all its leadership and of imposing a siege on all Gaza, the Shalit crisis might have been solved immediately, and both the Lebanon and then the Gaza wars could have been spared. But Israel hesitated, taking piecemeal measures for fear of world public opinion which was bound to sanction it and pressure it to allow "humanitarian assistance" to the "poor innocent Palestinians", thus playing into the hands of the Hamas which precisely relied on such a state of mind to avoid any punishment in its asymmetrical war. Had it been made clear that Shalit's incarceration was also a humanitarian issue, and if it is not resolved by his immediate release, then no humanitarian consideration would be given to the Gaza problems, which would have been caused by the Hamas itself, then that emotional blackmail of the entire population of Israel could have ended soon after it began. Encouraged by the hapless inaction of Israel, the Hamas pursued its shelling of Israeli villages, secure from any retribution and protected by world public opinion from any harm. And so, the UN and world bodies, and the international and humanitarian organizations, instead of helping put an end to hostilities as is their call, on the contrary unwittingly encouraged it by immunizing the aggressor from any risk, and shackling the hands of the victim in any attempt of his self-defense.

Sure enough, a month later, in July 2006, calculating that helpless Israel was paralyzed, Hamas's ally, Hizbullah in Lebanon, which acts as a state within a state, but does not bear any international responsibility which the Lebanese state had also abdicated, decided to strike exactly along the lines of the Gaza blueprint. Under the watching eyes of an impotent Lebanese army which was supposed to guard their country's borders, they ambushed an Israeli patrol, killed some of its members and kidnapped two of them, again confident that Israel would not dare to escalate the situation for fear that deterioration could trigger Israeli massive retaliation which would kindle fire in the vulnerable north of the Galilee. In both cases, the kidnappers made clear that they would release the kidnapped soldiers only in return for thousands of their members who had been convicted for murderous acts of terror in Israel. Still ailing from the Shalit kidnapping, and humiliated and intimidated by Hamas' intransigence, Israel decided to react, but this time mindlessly, immeasurably and inefficiently, once again playing according to the scenario of asymmetrical war that the Hamas and the Hizbullah had envisaged. In immediate reprisal for the massive Israeli air bombardments, which flattened the Hizbullah neighborhoods in southern Beirut, and caused much death and destruction, enough to precipitate world wrath against Israel for hitting "innocent civilians", Nasrallah ordered his batteries of thousands of missile launchers to pound indiscriminately all towns and villages in northern Israel. But no one could be blamed there, because the

Lebanese government dissociated itself by assuring itself and others that it was not "its war", and Hizbullah could not be disciplined by any one because it was "not a state". The asymmetrical war strategy could not have been better illustrated. Instead of launching an immediate and massive land operation, landing at the Litani River and squeezing the Hizbullah south to the Israeli border, on the way destroying the missile bases, the COS, Air Force General Halutz, who had been selected to carry out the Gaza disengagement, decided that the Air Force could do it alone. But it could not, and every time it bombarded a village in south Lebanon where the missiles were being dispatched against Israel from, villagers were inevitably hurt and a world cry rose against Israel and in favor of the "poor, innocent Lebanese victims of Israel's cruelty". No one wished to remember who triggered the war, nor to see the damage and casualties caused in Israel by the missile attacks.

So, once again, Israel's hands were tied, and its leaders too hesitant to deal the military blow necessary to defeat the Hizbullah on the ground and end the war rapidly. An absurdity soon developed on the diplomatic front as well. When the Security Council discussed the matter, ending it in that disastrous Resolution 1702, Lebanon whose territory was the origin of the war, was spared any sanction, because it was not involved in the war, it just suffered its consequences; the Hizbullah, which was the fighting element against Israel, could not be blamed, nor charged with any obligation because it was not a state. So that UN circus could only implement to the letter the Hizbullah strategy of "hitting and complaining", achieving precedence over Israel, which had to withdraw its forces without achieving its goal of releasing its kidnapped soldiers, even though it shouldered no responsibility for anything. Again, had Israel conditioned the withdrawal of its troops on the release of its soldiers, which appeared in the preamble of the resolution, that might have exerted pressure on the Lebanese to comply. But the Israeli government foolishly accepted to yield to international pressure and withdraw first, and it took many more months of emotional blackmail and suffering of the families of the kidnapped, until Israel could obtain the two corpses of its soldiers in return for an exorbitant price which was beyond the requirements of the resolution. The other requirements of the resolution, such as disarming the Hizbullah or preventing the flow of weapons to them from Iran and Syria, were not implemented. True, the UN presence in south Lebanon, has had a calming effect, and save for a few incidents that were not the work of Hizbullah, no major clashes have happened since. But just like in Gaza, where EU observers withdrew from the border crossings when threatened by Hamas, relinquishing their duty and the "guarantee" given by the US and Europe to Israel to coax it to withdraw from there and facilitate "peace", so will UN troops probably ply to Hizbullah threats when hostilities renew.

In the meantime, while Israel (and Hizbullah) were licking their wounds from the war that led nowhere, the Hamas completed its takeover of the Gaza strip, attributing to itself the credit for the Israeli total withdrawal and vowing to revive, in effect, the old Khartum decisions of never recognizing Israel, negotiating with it or making peace with it. In that frame of mind, the stale arrangements of cease-fire, truce, armistice were no longer applicable to contain this new situation where war was vowed, but the Islamic government which rejected the Oslo framework, had to manage a more-or- less bearable existence to the masses under its control and responsibility. That terminology, which was invented in the era of sanity and conventional wars, which were concluded by international agreements, had to be superseded by the vocabulary of asymmetrical wars, where battles never ceased, not nations but movements were involved therein, and intervals in the battle were unofficial, temporary and non-committal. *Hudna* was revived from the ancient Islamic arsenal of legal jargon, which the Hamas invoked due to the unbearable losses it suffered at the hands of Israel and its urgent need to "normalize" in some ways the situation along the border until it devised new ways to pursue the struggle. *Hudna* basically means quiet, a pause in hostilities, the very term the Arabs used for their armistice regime with Israel in the years 1948-67. Many Israelis, including government officials, were so enthusiastic about the new wording that it seemed that only the right lexicon was missing to achieve the quantum jump towards peace. The first and second truces during the 1948-9 War were also qualified by the Arabs as the first and second *hudna,* respectively. In the Arab and Muslim mind, *hudna* is undoubtedly a transient situation, with a short-lived cessation of hostilities pending the reinforcement of the Muslim armies and their capacity to renew the battle. That means that the *hudna* is not an internationally binding contract but an expedient and provisional measure to avert total loss in battle, to control the damage, and to gather strength to violate it as soon as feasible, as long as this is viewed as Muslim interest.

Had the Hamas wished to come to a genuine cease fire with Israel along the Gaza borders, it was not the lack of appropriate wording which would have prevented it. There were many *hudnas* before between Israel and all adjoining Arab countries, and none of them either prevented wars or led to peace. And if pursuing the hostilities against Israel is Hamas' vision, it would not be the wording which would stand as an obstacle in their way. For the Hamas *hudna* has a very specific significance that cannot be detached from the historical Islamic context. In their worldview, which was repeatedly voiced after the Oslo mishap, first in Arafat's speech in Johannesburg, and then as a routine reference in his repeated addresses to Palestinians, the Hudaibiya comparison was invoked. To wit, exactly as the Prophet Mohammed had been compelled to conclude a *hudna* with his enemies in Mecca, primarily due to his military inability to overwhelm them, he concluded a ten-year *hudna* with them, which he violated two years later, he, Arafat, suggested that Oslo was a transient necessity, until the Palestinians were able to beat their enemies. Indeed, a mere few months later,

well before the ascending to power of Sharon and Netanyahu, who are now blamed for "arresting the peace process",
Arafat mounted a series of murderous terrorist attacks in an
attempt to destabilize Rabin's government, his heroic "partner for the peace of the courageous". The precedent set by
the Prophet for a maximal *hudna* of ten years, unless it was
violated before, suggested to Arafat and his audiences that
Oslo must be viewed as a provisional measure. If of all the
historical precedents for conciliation and peace between any
two rivals, he singled out Hudaibiya as the relevant analogy,
that means that it looked to him as the most appropriate to
mention to Muslim audiences. Many faint-hearted Israeli officials and intellectuals counseled their government to accept the *hudna* offer as if it were a favor, while behind it
stood the rationale of numbing the Israelis by temporary
breaks in the succession of hostilities, to allow the Hamas
to gather power and then attack again. Accepting that pattern meant also accepting that the initiative and the decision
to go to war would always depend on the Hamas, and Israel
would have to follow suit, since it could only respond, but
not in the time and place of its choice. This is the essence of
asymmetrical war, which Israel was not obliged to reconcile
to, but it mindlessly did.

Indeed, while Israel was deluding itself that the *hudna*,
which has no root in international relations and was only
geared to serve the Hamas, was affording it some tranquility, be it for a moment, the Palestinians in Gaza were dig-
ging more tunnels, smuggling in more prohibited weapons,
spreading hatred and propaganda against their neighbor and
delegitimizing the Palestinian Authority by replacing it in
Gaza for all intents and purposes. What is worse, instead of
Israel's sweeping the Hamas out of the area, it allowed a permanent base for the dispatch of rockets and missiles against
Israel, on almost a daily basis, thus turning the life of hundreds of thousands of Israelis into hell: Children were star-
tled in the middle of their sleep or on their way to school by
falling missiles or by the alarms announcing their launching;

businessmen could not maintain their shops open, and when they did no shoppers ventured out of their houses to purchase their needs; the old, the weak and the disabled abandoned their villages and townships, and the future seemed gloomy to many of them. That impasse lasted 7 years with no relief in sight. The candidate for the presidency of the US, Barack Obama, who visited the area as part of the ritual of visiting Israel during the elections campaign, clearly hinted that he would not tolerate without reprisals if his daughters were constantly threatened as were the children of Sderot. But the Israel government continued to profess restraint as if that were rewarded by a similar conduct from the other side. What broke the deadlock was the Israeli elections, declared for May 2009. Only then, realizing that during its three year term it brought a disastrous war upon Israel without resolving the Hizbullah menace, and that it stood no chance to win if the Hamas fire was not ceased, it decided to move into action. All that while, as part of its empty promises to bring peace, it carried on an intensive dialogue on the levels of the Prime Minister and the Minister of Foreign Affairs, with the top echelon of the Palestinian leadership, addressing all the core issues, but to no avail. According to both the Israeli and Palestinian negotiators, the gap between the parties did not shrink much, and the maximum offered by Israel still stood miles away from any minimum acceptable to the Palestinians. Having negotiations was not the issue, but the extent to which the parties were ready to narrow the gap yawning between them.

The Hamas knew that the war was impending, because it understood that no country could endure without retaliation the exposure of its civilian population to arbitrary bombing and shelling. So, they prepared for war, ever devoted to their asymmetrical war theories: they dug more tunnels to conceal their activities and to store their weapons; they turned every house, alley and street into a military position, recruiting the civilian population, children and women included, into part of their defense system; they fortified every public building, like hospitals, schools, mosques and public institutions, ready to declare any counter-attack against them as a breach of "rules of war"; they mined and trapped every passage way to maximize Israeli casualties; and they set up hundreds of rocket launchers to torment all Israel if they were attacked. Furthermore, as the radius of the shelling of Israeli territory continued to grow, due to the smuggling in of longer-range missiles into Gaza, more and more cities and townships in southern Israel, like Ashkelon, Qiryat Gat, Beersheba and Gedera, came within their range, and the endurance and tolerance of the Israeli population were stretched to their limit. Fresh from the bitter lessons of Lebanon, the Israeli military, under General Ashkenazi, had had the time and the wisdom to ruminate over the fighting of asymmetrical wars in urban areas, where civilians were part of the battlefield, and the defenders did not show any concern for civilian casualties. Quite the contrary, the more civilians hit, the more Hamas interest stood to be served. Just prior to Xmas of 2008, Israel finally struck, much to the relief of the public, which was ready to endure more shelling and more casualties for a while, provided the problem is resolved once and for all.

All the scenarios of the asymmetrical wars were played out as if choreographed before hand. Despite the many limitations put on the Israeli troops, as far as the civilian population in Gaza was concerned, clashes became inevitable. Operating from underground tunnels, from basements of houses and mosques or from UN buildings, and from regular apartments which were all mined and readied for killing, it is no coincidence that many Gazan civilians (innocent or not is quite another issue) were killed or wounded and many of their houses were destroyed. It was immediately claimed by the media, by humanitarian bodies and all manner of peace people, who woke up only when the "poor people" of Gaza were hurt, and cared little to raise their voices against the constant bombings in Israeli villages across the border, that the number of casualties on the Palestinian side was much greater than that on the Israeli side, and that was "evidence" that Israel attacked "disproportionately", "cruelly" etc., thus shifting the blame to the retaliation rather than insisting that the Palestinian bombardments triggered that reprisal. It was like claiming that because the numbers of Germans killed in Dresden were superior to the casualties in London, Coventry and the rest, the British were to be accused as "aggressors", "disproportionate" etc. Or, in general, since more Germans and Japanese were killed during WW II than Allies, the latter must be considered the culprits. In the case of the Gaza war, where the Palestinians were clearly the aggressors, the practical reasons for the gap in the numbers of casualties emanated from many other sources too: first, Israel invested tremendously in the defense of its citizens, while the Palestinians did not, for it was part of their strategy that civilians be hit. Their own troops were entrenched in underground tunnels. Secondly, the Israeli soldiers were better trained and better equipped, therefore they suffered less hits. Thirdly, the Israelis kept the initiative in their hands, deciding the timing, the intensity and the pace of the battle, taking in the process all necessary measures to reduce their own and the enemy's civilian casualties. At the end, Israel, which took many bombardments and not a few civilian casualties herself, had to arrest the advance into Gaza under international pressure, in view of the death and destruction sown during the battle, without attaining its goal of putting an end to the bombardment of its towns and villages. No better application of the asymmetrical war could have been imagined.

Predictably, the Hamas declared victory over the Israelis, who soon retreated, but the worldwide condemnations of the Israeli "excess of power" did not, indeed could not, compensate for the large scope of destruction, which forced the Hamas to reinstall the *hudna* in practice along the border, in order to allow for the continued flow of humanitarian supplies from Israeli territory. This was followed by the notoriously anti-Israeli Human Rights Commission of the UN's inquiry into the Gaza War, headed by Justice Richard Goldstone, which found Israel and Gaza both guilty of "war crimes" and "crimes against humanity", though the emphasis was predictably on Israel's guilt, it being the powerful state, which had signed international treaties which obligated her to obey war rules and other Geneva agreements dealing with the conduct of war[15]. Conversely, the Hamas, being a declared "terrorist movement" and representing no government, which can be shown to be responsible, and had no international obligations, emerged relatively unscathed, just like in Lebanon 18 months earlier, when Hizbullah waged the war and could not be held responsible. Thus, just like the US of America, who by counterattacking in Afghanistan, killing many civilians, could also have been accused of "war crimes", while al-Qa'ida could not be officially condemned for September 11, the blame ultimately went to the victims of terrorism, the US and Israel. The countries which nourished the terrorists or were unable to arrest them, like Afghanistan, Lebanon and Gaza, remained blameless, and this is obviously a recipe to encourage more terrorism and more violence. What is there to stop the culprits, if their victims bear the blame while they get world sympathy?

Everyone knows that this situation is temporary, pending the gathering of forces by the terrorists and the implementation of works of restoration which were promised by various Arab and international bodies. The stakes are high, because everyone understands that amidst the "humanitarian" rhetoric surrounding the huge task of reconstruction, there is a clear danger that Hamas will use the building materials, especially cement, ironically paid for by outsiders who supposedly oppose terrorism, to reinforce its military positions at the expense of dwellings for the victims of the war. Iran pursues its support of the Hamas government and instigates it not to return to the fold of the Palestinian Authority, nor to join its "peace efforts" championed by the US and the Quartet. More extremist elements, of *Jihadi* inclinations and

---

[15]The Commission published its over 500pp. report on 15 September, 2009. See all the papers of 16 Sep., 2009.

inspiration, have tried to break the *hudna* in order to inflame the border anew, but the ruling Hamas has been reining them in, for now, for fear of losing control. In any case, it is clear that this state of affairs cannot endure and that sooner, rather than later, one of those militant groups who have their fingers on the trigger, will lose patience and pull it. One conclusion it is safe to draw, which is that asymmetrical wars have increased the pace of hostilities in the vicious Middle East cycle between war and peace. In the previous era of sanity, a punishing defeat of the Arab Armies gave the area the respite of a decade or so until they reorganized, rearmed and retrained their troops, or a new leader like a Nasser or a Saddam emerged. Now, any militia or tribal chief or religious or gang leader, can pull the trigger at will, either encouraged by his country or in spite of it. This is asymmetrical war at work, that no more spectacularly successful examples of it could be cited than in Lebanon and Gaza of recent years. They are bound to repeat themselves and to engulf the Middle East again and again, in blood and tears, UN whining notwithstanding, and UN reports like Goldstone's providing the "moral" underpinnings for the continuation of terror and war.

Even more worrisome is the wider issue of the domination of the UN in general, by the Islamic bloc of 57 countries, who have no regard for truth, fairness or law. We remember how in 1975 they mobilized the UN Assembly to condemn Zionism, the movement of national liberation of the Jewish people, one of the most constructive and successful in modern history, as "racism". Muslim and other tyrannical regimes voted for the motion, but democratic countries opposed it, in vain. Until President Bush initiated in 1992 another vote which repealed that odious resolution, to which Muslims continued to be opposed. Then two rounds of Durban (2001 and 2009), purporting to condemn racism, under the UN aegis, ended up singling out democratic Israel and liberal Zionism as racists, and introducing "islamophobia" as a new concern to the world in order to dilute the rabid anti

Semitism which is promoted by Muslims, while the countries of tyranny and terror emerged unscathed. The Human Rights Commission of the UN, which has been dominated by such "champions" of human rights, democracy, liberty and legality as the Sudan, Iran and Libya, has mastered the manipulation of the human rights discourse to demonize Israel and to single it out for the majority of its condemnations, like the appointment of the Goldstone Commission with the mandate to "investigate Israel's war crimes", as if the conclusions were known before the investigation began. This is not a new tactic, merely a repetition of the 1975 condemnation of Zionism as racism, the 1997 accusation of Israel at the Human Rights Commission, for "injection of Palestinian children with AIDS"[16,] and now blaming Israel for war crimes by the Goldstone Commission. The organ that is ironically called the Human Rights Commission, has become a major tool for the pursuance of the asymmetrical war against Israel by demonizing it, isolating it and denying it the right of self-defense from terrorism, which if allowed to continue will cause more damage than terrorism itself.

---

[16]R. Israel, *Poison: Modern Manifestations of Blood Libel*, Lexington Books, 2002, pp. 65-6, 106-8.

Chapter 3

The Psychopathology of
the Islamic World

To defend tiny Israel during her fateful period of infancy, surrounded by indefensible borders, defended by a negligible population which grew from half a million to about three million in those nineteen years which preceded 1967, constantly menaced by the combination of 22 Arab states which numbered then between 40 and 100 million people as the years wore on, and financed by an unending flow of petro-dollars, seemed an un-surmountable task. Nevertheless, the faith was great and confidence was unshakable in the capacity of the revived people, whose vestiges had just emerged from the ashes of Auschwitz, to stand up to any challenge. No doubt was entertained as to the survival of the nation, which attracted universal sympathy from the western world, governments and public opinion alike. To them it was evident who was the free nation, the pioneer, the democratic, the enterprising and creative, the innovator, the builder, the absorber of refugees, the human, the peaceful and the positive; and who threatened those efforts, attacked and harassed the builders, sought revenge, perpetuated poverty, backwardness and tyranny, refused to absorb refugees and elected to prolong human misery, provoked war, and shunned peace and precipitated instability and chaos in this part of the world, which was so crucial for the equilibrium of tranquility, due to both its reserves of oil and its weight between the rivals of the Cold War. But both Israel and the western world which supported it had failed to diagnose the problem at its root, and they treated its aggressive symptoms in terms of the jeopardy it posed to their perceived immediate interests, rather than in terms of its socio-psychological engines which moved it. Exactly as the humiliation of Germany at the Versailles Conference is cited as one of the reasons for the rise of Hitler, so one might today invoke the armistice agreements of 1949 between Israel and the Arabs, as the genesis and the precursor of the present day impasse in the Middle East.

Concomitantly with their expectations and their combined war potential, the Arab countries which invaded Israel the day it was declared, in defiance of the UN Partition Resolution of 1947, had expected an easy victory on fledgling Israel, whose tiny size, poor equipment and seeming flimsiness, did not augur well for her ability to withstand that onslaught. Instead, Israel was not only able to survive, but it also ended up controlling at the end of the war larger territories in Palestine than assigned to her in the Partition Plan. The depth of the frustration and humiliation for their defeat in the war corresponded to the summits of their arrogant self-confidence on the onset of the hostilities. Contrary to the 1967 war where they recognized their rout and undertook to redress it, in 1949 it was their refusal to take cognizance of the facts, and their persistent avoidance of the consequences thereof, which blurred their view and distorted their reasoning. Their world of thinking was often overtaken by the hatred they entertained towards Jews and Israel, and their capacity for observation and analysis was diluted by their sense of humiliation, at the hands of Jews to boot. On the one hand, they demonized the Jews and Israel for the "injustice" they caused to the Arabs in general, the Palestinians in particular, but on the other hand they had to account for the inexplicable fact that those "cowardly" Jewish *dhimmis*, who had lived from time immemorial in submission under Muslim rule, should now demonstrate, once and again, their military prowess, in spite of their vastly inferior numbers. Hatred and humiliation would then become the key concepts guiding their complex emotional makeup, and the chief engines governing their mode of action.

In matters of hatred, Arab children, and many other Muslim infants for that matter, are imbued with large doses of it with their mothers' milk. The infamous passage from the Book, which is cited in sermons in the mosques throughout the Muslim world, and which depicts Jews as "descendants of pigs and monkeys", a-priori lends justification to any monstrosity attributed to Jews. We understand today that Muhammad had pronounced those derogatory words of the Jews when they rose against his authority in Medina at the outset of his political career there. But today, when they are repeated *ad nauseam* throughout the Muslim world in Friday sermons, by journalists and politicians, out of any context, they serve no other purpose than disparaging the Jews and insulting them. What is that if not anti-Semitism, irrational as it may be? That derogatory reference, which is seconded by many others[17], has had a profound and lasting impact on Muslim thinking, behavior, social norms and the education of their children, and not necessarily in areas of conflict with Israel or adjacent to it, sometimes even in parts of the world which have never seen a Jew. Ayaan Hirsi Ali, the now famous Somalian refugee, who immigrated to the Netherlands and was instantly catapulted to prominence there when she was elected to Parliament, recounted in one of her many press interviews about the religious indoctrination process she underwent in her country of origin in her youth. Her history teacher, Sister Aziza, used to take the class for an outing to the Iranian embassy and to promote a Muslim revolution. Gradually the girls in her class started to physically cover themselves. She herself took to wearing the *hijab* and to admire the Muslim Brotherhood. Aziza started to use the '*yahud*' (Jews) word. One day she said: 'You all sit up and listen.' She showed the girls a magazine from Iran (a Muslim, not an Arab country) with pictures of dead people, piles of

---

[17]See eg. Suras 2:61, 4:44-46, 4:160-61, 9:30-31, 5:64, 5:82 and more.

bodies and blood, and said: 'look what the *yahud* have done to the Muslims.' The pictures were Iranian propaganda. They were taken from the Iran-Iraq war, showing Iraqi soldiers killing Iranian citizens. 'This is what the Jews have done, and Saddam Hussein was an agent of the Jews', Sister Aziza taught. She instructed the kids how to pray: "You hold your hands together, and you say: 'Allah please protect us from evil, Allah please keep us healthy, Allah please take care of my mother and my father, Allah please destroy the Jews.'" Hirsi Ali pursued her tale:

For me, '*yahud*' [Jews] was not the same as human. It's the enemy. It's Satan. I remember a joke, well, it wasn't even a joke, from the time I was a very little girl. We were in Riyadh and Jedda when the oil boom started. They were trying to build an oil pump; the construction project went on forever. At last, when the project was done, they opened the top of the pump, but instead of oil, water came out. And I remember my mom saying: 'See, the Jews are at it again.' And I think about the three most horrible insults you could think of in my world. The insults were '*yahud*', '*shuri*' and '*hanis*'. 'Shuri' means a communist. 'Hanis' means gay. You guys are used to laughing at it, but it's really not a laughing matter. Because it's no longer just the Saudis who think like that. These ideas are spreading throughout Islam and all over the world to people who never met Jews, who know nothing about Israelis or what Israel represents. In 1993 I went to Antwerp with a friend. The friend said, 'We are now in the Jewish neighborhood' and pointed at an Orthodox Jew. And I lost my breath and said: 'Jewish?! Is he Jewish?! Wait, where? Where?' You see, I needed to visualize this huge fantasy of evil that I had in my head. And then he showed me a few people walking around and asked, 'What exactly were you expecting?' I looked around and said, 'Can you tell me, if a kid has two hands and two legs and he's walking, are there children who are Jewish as well?' And my friend responded: 'Yes, there are Jewish children as well. At that moment I felt something else inside me, that said it was shameful to voice what I had felt. I had to suppress that. So in 1993 I didn't talk about it again. It was in 1994, during history class, when I first saw pictures of what happened in the Second World War. I was coming from Somalia, and similar things started to happen in my country, along with Rwanda, Sudan, Liberia, Sierra Leone... There are many things I learned at that time in history class, but the story of the Holocaust made the biggest impression on me. I went to all the Holocaust museums. I've been to *Yad Vashem* twice. As I understood it, the Holocaust wasn't just the story of the Jews ... I don't know if this goes for everyone, but knowledge enlightened me...As a Muslim, I belong to the universal tribe. Every human individual, regardless of his beliefs, faith, sex, deserves to live and is equal. My criticism is of religion, especially Islam, and not of Muslims. Therefore, my criticism of Islam is not a rejection of Muslims. It is the idea of race that makes us destroy each other. You have to change your mind and learn to accept the other. My case is to convince fellow Muslims. I call myself Muslim not because I believe in Allah any longer, but I come out of that culture, and I want to fight to modify that culture, and create a culture of love and human rights...[18]

If this was the case for remote Somalia, which has had other more serious problems to tackle and many more important values to impart to its miserable children, how much more so for the Arab children who are exposed, day in day out, to the bombardments of hatred in their schools, among their families, on their media and in their streets. Hirsi Ali's enlightenment after her move to Holland, puts in perspective much of the education to hatred to which those innocent children are exposed in the Muslim world, and which bears no necessary relationship to deprivation or poverty (Hirsi was from a well-to do background). Add to that the universality of anti-Semitism in Islam (she heard the same derogation of the Jews in Saudi Arabia and then among European

---

[18]Gitit Ginat, " Freedom fighter", www.haaretz.com - 18 May, 2006

Muslims); the power of stereotypes and cultivated myths (Hirsi had never seen a Jew in either Somalia or, even much less likey, in Jedda); the fallacy of attributing these attitudes to the Arab-Israeli dispute (Somalia never was a party to it); and the lumping together of Jews and Israel as an insepa- rable entity, Muslim protestations to the contrary notwith- standing, and one begins to comprehend what we are talking about. Hirsi later also understood the systematic Holocaust denial current among Muslims, became a perennial visitor to Israel and to the *Yad Vashem* Holocaust Memorial in Je- rusalem, and grew to castigate Muslims for the atmosphere of Jew-hatred that they cultivate in their midst. Much of the virulence against Jews in the Muslim world, is attributable to the constant flow of hatred propagated among Islamic so- cieties[19].

In the Arab and much of the Muslim worlds, there has been no let up in this regard. Their publics are permanently inundated by biased information and one-sided propaganda emanating from their authoritarian governments, who have not educated them to think freely, to gather information from many sources, and make judgments for themselves. And the official version of news universally, exclusively and constantly transmits and diffuses the versions crafted by the governments in place, which invariably demonize the Jews-Israelis-Zionists, impute to them the most horrible monstrosities, heap on them the most horrible accusations and attribute to them the most evil intentions. History is also re-written and tailored to suit the evil nature of the Jews, in daily columns, in "scientific" books, encyclopedias, not to mention Friday mosque sermons and political speeches made by unscrupulous clerics, "scholars" and writers. Ci- tations are invented which have no source to draw from, without concern for the false reporting to the readers or the distortion of the minds of children and youth who will

---

[19]See R. Israeli, *Muslim anti-Semitism in Christian Europe: Elemental and Re- sidual anti-Semitism*, Transaction, New Jersey, 2009.

grow in error, be bereft of intellectual curiosity and forti-
tude, and get accustomed to their "narrative" instead of to
the truth. Arab media have no compunction about distorting
reports, inflating negatives and attenuating positives when
Israel or Jews are concerned, lest the stereotypes they are
harnessed by their governments to propagate be corrected.
Rumors and accusations that Israelis are killers of children,
spread diseases around, undermine governments and diffuse
corruption, are quick to travel in the Islamic world and adopted, lock stock and barrel, without critique or verification.
Confirmed reports about a scientific invention by Israelis or
Jews, an Israeli sports team which won a medal or a cham-
pionship, or any international distinction awarded to Israel,
like a Nobel Prize, or aid brought by Israel to Arab patients
and children, are sure to disappear from the Arab news reports lest, Allah Forbid, Jews might appear in a positive light
and contribute towards the attenuation of the Arab hatred towards them.

No wonder then that children in kindergartens in Gaza are
prone to vow for *Islamikaze* careers when they grow up, and
for their mates to watch television programs of the official
Palestinian Authority, or of Hamas Television, in which even
popular international cartoon figures render Palestinian kids
heroes who devote their lives to fight the "Zionist enemy",
and the latter are dubbed the "scum of the earth" whose sa-
cred duty of all Palestinians it is to blow up. The infamous
Muhammed al-Dura case, which became *cause celebre* in
France, after it was proved in court that it had been jointly
staged by a French Television channel and the Palestinian
Authority with a view of demonizing Israel, provides am-
ple evidence of this manifestation of hatred. In Arab lore,
Jews and in consequence Israelis and Zionists, are accused
of racism, bigotry, corruption, undermining the world order, wielding international power on the media and finances,
desecrating Muslim holy places, occupying Arab lands, discriminating against their own new immigrants; their leaders
as devious monsters, their foreign policy as aggressive and

expansionist, threatening the peaceful Arabs; accumulating a dangerous nuclear arsenal, and striving to the demise of the Arabs. As regards the Palestinians specifically, not only usurpation of their rights is invoked, together with the claim of their occupation, their exploitation and their persecution, but even genocidal accusations are occasionally raised against Israel. In the meantime, Israel and Zionism are routinely charged of eliminating Palestinian culture in order to replace it by the Jewish-Zionist one, and of diminishing the Islamic prevalence in Palestine and other occupied territories.[20]

This image of the Jews, Zionism and Israel, which is cultivated in the Arab, and many Muslim, media worldwide, at the exclusion of anything positive which may be said about them, naturally channels public opinion towards a very deeply-seated hatred towards those entities, which is becoming gradually irreversible, even in the countries which have signed peace with Israel, like Egypt and Jordan, or used to be Muslim moderates, like Turkey, Qatar, Morocco and the Emirates, who sharply shifted their openness towards Israel the moment the first reports of Israel's "atrocities" in the Gaza War (2009) started to filter out. It seemed that the infrastructure of hatred entrenched in the Islamic world towards Israel was there all the time, and all it needed was a trigger to re-launch it with ever greater vigor. Admittedly, even in many European countries where that same sort of anti-Israeli hostility was aired on the same occasion of the Gaza War, it was connected, at least in part, with the wrath of the Muslim minorities in the West which are fed by the same disinformation, hallucinations and hatred that they brought with them from the Islamic world, and continue to "update" their background "education" from the Arab media or from the anti-Semitic European media. In sum, the Jews, who were traditionally depicted in despicable terms in

---

[20]For details of such accusations, see R. Israeli, *Peace is in the Eye of the Beholder*, Mouton, Berlin and NY, 1985.

Islam, continue to be portrayed stereotypically in Arab writings, in cartoons and in the electronic media.

These perceptions of Israel also dictate the choice of items that the Arab press publishes about the Zionist state as well as the interpretations they lend them. Political controversies as well as political factions in Israel, for example, are seen not as arising from political conflicts within a democratic system, but rather as a sign of dissent, disintegration and failure to achieve unity. Former generals serving in the Israeli government do not signify a normal and legitimate way for people to move from one sphere of activity to another, like Generals Marshall, Eisenhower, Haig and Powell in the US, but are "proof" of the militarization of Israeli society or the "martial mentality" of its leaders. The careful screening of "facts" and outright fabrication of "data" that fit their negative image of Israel, sometimes generate contradictions which the Arab media choose to ignore. For example, while the Arabs keep repeating that neither Arab or Muslim tradition ever called for hatred of Jews as such, their verbal and graphic depictions are the most contemptible one could imagine; while they assert that the Jews in their midst have "always enjoyed equal rights", their leaders are exhorted to improve the treatment of their erstwhile Jewish minorities to allow for their return to their native lands, which they had abandoned in favor of immigration to Israel. When Israel develops industry in the Arab sector under her rule, she is accused of scheming to alienate Arabs from their lands, but Israel is also accused of preventing industrial development in that sector in order to keep it backward. When Israel takes a firm stand against Palestinian terrorism, she is accused of oppression, but when she shows leniency and flexibility, the Arabs claim that this was a maneuver to gain world sympathy for the occupation.

The second axis of continued and aggravated Arab hostility to Israel since 1948, in addition to the scrupulously preserved hatred towards Jews, Zionists and Israel, which has been elevated to the degree of an icon, has been the sense of humiliation which their rout at the hand of Israel had occasioned. Humiliation, which has been also invoked by Muslim movements like al-Qa'ida, in the context of their struggle against the West, has two aspects to it: the first is the military defeats they have suffered, hence their permanent urge to take revenge, and the second is the exposure of their incompetence and backwardness when compared to the achievements of the West and Israel. Humiliation is born out of the sense of injustice done to them, which is another way of stating that defeat is undue to them, because justice would have justified their victory. Hence the Arab permanent clamor for justice ("peace with justice", a "just solution" to the conflict), as if justice were absolute and not in the eye of the beholder. Justice ('adalah in Arabic), which is also, incidentally, the name of an Arab civil rights group in Israel, is linked in Arab parlance to the notion of balance between the saddlebags on the camelback, short of which the camel cannot march at length to cross the desert. Justice is also connected to honor, and the maintenance of one's honor hinges on one's ability to protect one's property, including one's women, and on one's proven capacity to retrieve them if they are violated. Otherwise, one's reputation is irretrievably compromised. Thus, one's honor is constantly on the line, and it is always tested by one's daring in the service of one's honor. An Arab will not rest until the wrong done to him is redressed and his property is recuperated. Only then is justice done and the offended party can revert to functioning normally. There are no objective criteria to examine the feeling of right or wrong, or what constitutes an encroachment on one's honor; they hinge upon the subjective sense of the wronged individual. Only when the wronged party feels satisfied does he feel that justice has been redressed.

When the Arabs demand justice, they mean their justice, i.e. the retrieval of their rights and properties as they perceive them, regardless of whether, what arguments and how others might advance as disclaimers in historical, legal, logical or human terms, for all these are irrelevant from their point of view. First, the Arabs must get full satisfaction, in accordance with their sentiments and convictions, their rights must be recognized and stated, and only then they might show generosity and give back out of their own volition, not as a result of coercion or force. Thus, the whole notion of compromise does not come into play, because if something is yours, you must obtain it first, regardless of what others may claim. Sadat in his speech at the Knesset in November, 1977, and the Syrians in their various negotiations with Israel, the Hizbullah in Lebanon, and the Palestinians in their two factions (PLO and Hamas), have all demanded a total Israeli withdrawal of forces before negotiations can proceed, or at the very least an Israeli commitment to retreat at the end of the day. Not because, as some diplomats have thought, the Arabs wish to obtain the end results of the negotiations before they even begin, but in order to signal that what they regard as their property is not negotiable. It is theirs, period.

The Palestinians, like the rest of the Arabs, sense in their deepest consciousness that the Holy Land in general, and Jerusalem in particular, with its innermost *sanctum,* the Temple Mount, have been the exclusive patrimony of the Arabs/Muslims, since they were included in the *futuh* (conquests of Islam), and were bequeathed to them by Allah, for all generations to come, as a *waqf* (holy endowment), never to be parted with or negotiated away. Hence, their "right of return" is not only a human and political need, but also a religious duty which imposes on them to struggle and pay any sacrifice so as to snatch the land from its usurpers who have subtracted it from Islamic dominion. This is valid in particular with regard to the *Haram- al-Sharif* (the Temple Mount) which was the very site of the Prophet's mystical nightly journey (*isra '*) and ascension to Heaven (*mi'raj*). Thus, only after this right of theirs is recognized, as a matter of course, worldwide (what they call "international legitimacy"), may they evince *ex gracia* generosity and allow others to collect some crumbs from their table. Until then, all measures are allowable to retrieve the loss by peaceful means if possible, through violence if necessary, for in any case its holy character prescribes *jihad*.

As long as matters are not settled to their tune, the Arabs feel humiliated. This is the reason why every time they are close to the conclusion of a set of negotiations, after Israel has made far-reaching concessions to the Arabs for the sake of peace, but short of total surrender to their demands, they back down and retreat. Israeli negotiators, and many a Western observer, are stunned in disbelief, unable to comprehend how their interlocutors have once again missed another opportunity. Instead, they would rather wait to obtain the whole thing, without concession or compromise on their part, for the sake of satisfying their honor and sense of justice, rather than bend to the humiliation of accepting the part, which would signify that they have reconciled themselves to injustice. Justice is for them whole and indivisible, therefore they educate their children to claim it all and to deny their rivals any part of it. When they report to their own people about their clashes, debates or arguments with Israelis, there is never an understanding of the other's pain, sensitivity, loss or ambition. Conversely, there is in Israel a whole political camp which sympathizes with the Palestinians and even supports them, diffuses their grievances and expresses them in the media. No trace of that is found on the Palestinian side, and if there should be one "saint" who would dare, he would be condemned, arrested, or even gunned down or executed as a "traitor", so uniform is the wall of hatred and so unacceptable is the understanding of the rival. In "moderate" Egypt and Jordan, who have signed peace with Israel, anyone who maintains links with it or comes out in favor of peace and normalization with it, is excommunicated by his community and, more ominously, excluded from his trade union, which means in effect that he is denied the right to make a living, due to the "unforgivable sin" of reconciling with the enemy, who should have no longer been considered an enemy after the peace was signed.

After every incident, Palestinian spokesmen are allowed to voice their grievances in the Israeli media, where the damages and casualties inflicted on the other party are reported and debated, while the Palestinian media never interview any Israeli or anyone critical of them, and they disregard the casualties and damages inflicted on the others, or rejoice in public when they learn about them. They always present Israel as the aggressor who pesters the life of innocent Palestinians for no reason, and cultivate the feelings among Palestinians that they are the eternal victims who can do no wrong. The very notion of being a refugee, which is perpetuated by Palestinians for generations as if it were a permanent status, became a state of mind which reflects their sense of victimhood. As they are the poor and eternal victims, the whole world owes them everything. They make children, but the UN has to feed them. The poverty and density of their camps, from which they make no effort to exit, are for the US and the rest of Western world (not the Arabs, not even the rich among them) to resolve. The Palestinian Authority has built 13 different security apparatuses, and the separate Hamas government is building many more, but it is the donor countries of the West which have to finance them. They are dipped in corruption and in inefficient government, but it is the rest of the world which has to foot the bills. It does not occur to them that if they had rolled up their sleeves and applied themselves to work, to pursue the road of construction and peace, they would have solved all those problems in the past decades, instead of perpetuating them and throwing the blame on others. Nor does it occur to the donors that if they had refrained from sustaining the victimhood with their donations, the refugee status would have been obliterated. Donations and humiliations go hand in hand: the recipient depends on the donor, but aches and hates him for that dependence and is humiliated by it.

The theme of humiliation widely reverberates throughout the Arab discourse with the world as well, especially the US, which is considered Israel's main sustainer. For some Arab writers and thinkers, Israel is considered a launching pad for taking over Muslim holy places, Judaizing Muslim land, killing, maiming and imprisoning innocent Muslims, and conquering more Muslim territories, so as to form a western base to "diffuse Jewish corruption, westernization, humiliation, enslavement and exploitation of Muslim society"[21]. Conversely, a Kuwaiti columnist, Ahmed al-Baghdadi, while lashing out at Arab regimes who persecute their own *intelligentsia*, and positing the Arabs and Muslims as "masters of terrorism", justified the aggressive reactions of the West, which "has turned to humiliating Arabs and Muslims and rejecting them from its midst ... Islam does not tolerate others' opinions and even undercuts its own intellectuals at a time when the "heretic" West and Israel do not practice that kind of terror"[22]. In a "letter to America", published in the Hamas' *al-Risalah* in Gaza after September 11 (2001), the message is clear:

> Oh America, the sword of oppression, arrogance and crime!!! Do you remember how you smashed man's humanity? Do you remember how you mistreated the Blacks under your aegis? Can you describe for us the humiliation, disgust and contempt you meted out to those unfortunate people, whose only sin was that they were born to black parents?... They were born free, but were enslaved in your virgin land...
>
> America, re-examine your decisions to cast hundreds of veto votes [at the Security Council of the UN), with a view of denying humanity its rights. Look at your humiliated face, and check whether it is not due to those votes. This will teach you to stand by justice and by the righteous, even if they are weak,

---

[21] *Qira'a fi Fiqh al-Shahada*, (Readings in Islamic Martyrology) was published in 1988 as a special addendum to *al-Islam wa-Filastin* (Islam and Palestine) that appeared in Nocosia, Cyprus, and has been the ideological supporter of the Palestinian Islamikaze operations against Israel. See ibid. 5 June, 1988, p. 7.

[22] *Akhbar al-Yaum (Kuwait)*, 3 November, 2001.

and then perhaps the dust of humiliation will be removed from your sad face...[23]

Thus, in a fascinating reversal of projecting their own feelings which justify their *Jihad* against the West "even at the price of misery and humiliation"[24], their yearning is revealed of humiliating the West and Israel in return, because only counter-humiliation can remove the traces of humiliation. These manifestations of humiliation and the constant need to remove them by retaliation in kind, have been part of the Arab psyche since their defeat of 1948. But then, they were also cognizant of their inability to inflict defeat and to humiliate others in their turn. It is noteworthy that since the 1973 War, when they construed its results as a "victory", and more so in the two Lebanese wars (1982, 2006), and with the rise of the oil prices, the terrorist attacks that they inflicted on Israel and worldwide, their smashing victory against the Soviets in Afghanistan (1979-89), and the Israeli withdrawals from Lebanon and Gaza (2000 and 2005, under the pressure of Hizbullah and Hamas respectively), they perceive their ability to inflict humiliation as having gained the upper hand. But there is also another kind of humiliation, self-inflicted by those Arabs who have sought accommodation with Israel and the West. In a popular song sold on audio- and video-tapes throughout the Arab world, to celebrate Islamikaze acts of martyrdom, and savor the humiliation they have caused to America on September 11, such Arab leaders and their Israeli allies are castigated in harsh terms :

> [Referring to Israel and to peaceful Arab leaders in humiliat-
>   ing terms]... Your history is black and covered
> Your ancestry is a tree whose branches are corrupt...
> And the Arab rulers in this homeland
> Lie in a perpetual sleep

---

[23] *Al-Risalah*, (Gaza), 13 September, 2001, cited (in Hebrew) by MEMRI, *Terror in America, No 1*.

[24] *Al-Gumhuriyya*, 7 October, 2001. See MEMRI 289, 19 October, 2001.

> Eating from the fruit of your tree
> And drinking of your humiliation
> As if they were not Muslims.[25]

An exiled Egyptian cleric, Abu Hamza al-Masri, who found refuge in London and stirred Muslim extremism until pursued in justice and incarcerated after the underground bombings of 2005, pitched in his feeling of humiliation by connecting it to his understanding of violence. For him, the term "violence" had become a weapon used by the world media to dub anyone defending his faith and honor in the face of the Arab regimes who rule "through oppressive legislative measures". Therefore, he says, the very term "violence" is deceptive and incompatible, in his eyes, with Islamic religious law and the struggle for the survival of Islam. He said that *Mujahideen* have never recognized that term, because it was used to sustain the monopoly of those regimes in the usage of terrorism, and conversely to eliminate the religious precept of "doing good and prohibiting evil", thus alluding to that Muslim terrorism, of which he is a champion, enters in effect the category of good, and anyone fighting it falls automatically in the category of doing evil. This thinking also helps explain why, for Muslim radicals, the western definition of terrorism is not acceptable as long as it addresses itself to the means of combat and its targets (namely acting against innocent civilians to attain a political goal), instead of addressing the core theme of the struggle, that is Islamic good against Western (or Israeli) evil. This too is linked to humiliation:

> As a rule, Islam teaches that those with opinions different from one's own should be treated gently and with flexibility, provided that they are willing to listen and comply, and provided that one's tolerant efforts do not lead to a blurring of rights and boundaries... Treating gently anyone who blocks his ears and

---

[25]By Ayman, a poet, in *Al-Istiqlal* (the Weekly of Islamic Jihad in Gaza), 13 December, 2001.

forces perversion, heresy, abomination and humiliation on the Muslims in their own countries, by armed force, is a kind of stupidity involving the loss of rights and religious precepts... [26]

Ultimately, for the Muslim world, humiliation should be the fate of the Jews, as prescribed in the Holy Qur'an, not of Muslims, and the present situation where these norms have been reversed, ought to be addressed and redressed. Saudi clerics, who usually deride Arab nationalism and pan-Arabism[27], insist that there is no way to defeat the "descendents of monkeys and pigs", namely the Jews, unless the road of *Jihad* is embraced. They say that as long as the Palestinians fight for their orchards, namely their material belongings and false nationalism, they will not achieve much, and therefore they ought to go back to their Islamic faith and fight in its name. They counsel their audiences to learn from the ways of the Jews:

> We have to realize that our defeats by the Jews are due to the fact that they did not let the Islamic *umma* confront them... These were defeats of Arab regimes which did not raise the banner of Islam... Should our lost [sons] revert to the Truth, then the Jews shall return to their wretchedness and humiliation that they were doomed to [by the Holy Book]. Then, when the ignorant wake up, nothing can rescue the Jews, they will never see victory, as long as they profess mistaken notions, heretic curricula and a humiliating peace...[28].

There is nothing which exemplifies and advertises the humiliation which the Arabs- Muslims painfully experience more than Israeli, Western and other non-Muslim presence in what they regard as "occupied" territory, be it Palestine, Iraq, Afghanistan, Kashmir, Andalusia and the like. Hence the urgency of expelling the occupiers from those lands in

---

[26]*Al Quds al-Arabi*, 21 July, 2001.

[27]Cited in R. Israeli, Islamikaze etc... p. 290.

[28]*Ibid.*

order to cleanse the spot of humiliation. *Jihadi* movements, like al-Qa'ida, Islamic Jihad, Laskar-e-Taiba and others, emphasize the recourse to *Jihad* to achieve this goal. The way Islamic ideology gave rise to the Islamikaze, and more so the way Islamic society rose to the defense of Islamikaze attacks, first against Israel and then against western countries and some Islamic countries deemed too supportive or docile towards the West, counsels us to try to understand the psychological make up behind them, beyond the themes of humiliation and hatred discussed above. Also in need of explanation is the fact that at the same time that there is great delight felt in the Muslim camp, in spite of the many expedient attempts to hide the phenomenon and explain it away, when Israelis or westerners are murdered *en masse,* there is a sense of a great shock and consternation in the face of the vigorous US or Israeli counter-attacks. Because when Muslims attack and sow death and destruction, that is mere defense against the aggressors, therefore, no counter-attack is deemed justified, and it would always be deemed aggressive by definition, thus deserving retaliation, and so on *ad infinitum.*

In its own lands, where it feels weaker materially, though it boasts its moral superiority, the Islamic world shows awe, if not respect, towards the West, and at the same time feels humiliated by it technologically, militarily, economically, and culturally. The frustration at the Muslims' inability to match up to the strong, especially since they were themselves the prevalent culture in the past, creates elements of confrontation between the two. This is a confrontation because, unlike Western culture which, at least in theory, accepts others for what they are, frustrated Muslims are eager to destroy the bearers of strength rather than try to lift themselves to their level. Frustration generates shame, and aggression is used to displace the shame. Several areas of comparison may be suggested, which point out the differences between the two cultures and can help explain why Muslims and the West do not perceive the world in the same fashion, and therefore it is so difficult to devise ways to compromise and co-exist. Israel used to be isolated in its understanding of the Islamic enmity towards it, but now that the confrontation has widened and grown global, more and more civilizations are drawn into the circle of those who try to crack the genetic code which characterizes Muslim societies.

The Attitude towards Human Life and Death

While Islam does not permit suicide of the faint-hearted individual who runs away from the difficulties of life, and enjoins him to face up to his fate and count on Allah, the Muslim fundamentalist champions have found a way to sanctify death as "martyrdom," and to idolize it to such an extent as to turn it into a desirable pursuit, sanctioned by Allah, Islam, the precedents of the Prophet and his *tabi'un* (followers). Gradually, on the footsteps of the medieval *fida'iyun*, the revived ideas of sacrifice and the Shi'ite ideal of suffering under the Khumeini Revolution, and their application in the Iran-Iraq War and then, by Hizbullah in Lebanon, against the U.S. and Israel; and then through the adoption of those ideas by extremist Muslim radicals, such as Hamas and Islamic Jihad; they developed as a popular, effective, and universal strategy of warfare among other Muslim fighters, especially the Palestinian nationalists of the *Tanzim* and the Aqsa Brigades in their Intifadah against Israel. Finally, Muslim women and children were brought into the widening circle of Islamikaze, which, though still limited to hundreds, and potentially appealing to thousands, finds wide support among tens of thousands of clerics, columnists, political leaders, and professionals, including some "enlightened" (by their standards) intellectuals; and hundreds of thousands, if not millions, of sympathizers who cannot contain their adulation for them and express their sentiment openly in public. For this reason, one can no longer speak exclusively of the war declared by "militant Islam" against the West and the Jews, but of a growing circle of support in the Muslim public in general for the radicals, especially when they can show "positive" results to their credit. The most harrowing and callous manifestation of this attitude to human life has been the dragging of teenagers and women, by Palestinians and Hizbullah, into their relentless battles of terrorism against Israel. More recently, in the second Lebanese and the Gaza asymmetrical wars, extensive use of civilians as human shields has become a linchpin of Hamas' and Hizbullah's strategy as we have shown above.

This attitude toward human life has other dark aspects to it, both internal, within the Muslim community, and vis-à-vis the enemy. During the Intifadah of the Palestinians, or the insurgency of the Islamic Groups in Algeria, for example, we have seen massive slashing of throats of other Arabs/Muslims just for belonging to the "other camp," or for suspicion of "collaboration with the enemy," be it domestic or external. This was done without any concern for human life, for the families of the murdered or for the destructive impact on the minds of innocent civilians and children who grow up to accept, as a matter of course, massive use of murder and hanging in public squares before their eyes, which blunts their human sentiments. How much more so when the victims are the hated Jews or Americans, as the repeated celebrations of their death, or the mutilation of their corpses have shown. This is accompanied by a sadistic display of wounds, blood, lynching, abuse of the bodies of the dead, dragging corpses in the streets, and the chants of the onlooking crowds, who watch maddened by this orgy of cruelty, violence, and inhumanity. Funerals for their own favorite dead in combat, or as a result of targeted elimination by their enemies, or of the remains of Islamikaze bodies, are also accompanied by shouts, mass-hysteria, shootings in the air, huge processions where the body of the dead is arraigned by the masses out of control, and tossed from hand to hand; vows of vengeance for the life of the departed martyr, and for his replacement by many others who would volunteer in his footsteps, and the like. Compare that to the funerals of the victims of terrorism, in the U.S. or Israel, or any civilized society, which are silent and dignified, intimate and inward-turning, and you have one of the keys to comprehend the difference between the two cultures. If this is the situation with regard to Muslims-to-Muslims, how much more so when foreigners-enemies are concerned! We have seen the chilling scenes of indiscriminate blowing up of unsuspecting civilians in restaurants and cafes, the cold-blooded murder of passengers in buses, airplanes, and check-in counters; the shooting of passers-by in streets and of hostages, on a scale and with a frequency unknown in other times and other cultures, save the Nazis.

What is more disconcerting and harrowing is the jubilation of the masses of Muslims in support of such massacres, and the "learned" rationalizations that many clerics, intellectuals, and public opinion makers produce to justify them[29]. But that is not all: enemies can be abducted, killed, murdered, tortured, and jailed indefinitely, and no information about them is given to the families, no access to them is allowed to the Red Cross or anyone else, and expensive prices are extorted for just releasing any piece of information about their whereabouts or their putative fate. No other culture in modern memory has behaved so cruelly, so inhumanely, and so obtusely with captured enemies and their loved ones. They know the sensitivity and concern in the West for human life, therefore they exploit them to the maximum, either by keeping silent, thus raising the price of the extortion, or by hiding behind non-governmental organizations such as the Hizbullah in Lebanon or the Hamas in Palestine, or the Islamic Jihad in Syria, or anonymous captors, such as those who abducted and executed Daniel Pearl in Pakistan, just because he was Jewish, in order to escape responsibility. We have also witnessed live on television, the use of bare hands to tear Israeli soldiers to pieces and then the exhibition of the blood-soiled hands of the murderers to

---

[29]See R. Israeli, *Islamikaze etc.* Chap. 1, pp. 11-32.

boast before an approving public seized by inhuman frenzy and demanding more cruelty. We have seen Israeli teenagers ambushed by Arabs and their skulls appallingly crushed by rocks or against boulders, and left laying in the open. The worst part of all this is that when the Arab authorities are confronted with these inhumane situations, they "condemn these acts of murder of innocent civilians on all sides," as if there were two sides to this story, and as if these were natural calamities without murderers that could be identified, called to task, and prosecuted by justice. Quite the contrary, the murderers are often celebrated by their authorities and the public which supports them.

This callousness in the attitudes of Muslims towards their victims is supplemented by the horrendous reenacting of scenes of murder, as if they were sublime human experiences worth replaying and memorizing, and models with which to educate their public and for their young generation to emulate. This, of course, goes a long way to demonstrate how cold-bloodedly these murders are planned, and that they are not the spur-of-the-moment act of "frustration" by some ill-fated or "desperate" Palestinian or al-Qa'ida member. For, when the scene of an Israeli café or a paper-model of an Israeli bus is carefully and meticulously reconstructed in a public place at the heart of an Arab or Muslim city, and flying paper-limbs of Israeli children, dripping with blood are hung around as part of the scene, and explosions are replayed, and whines of dying victims are amplified for the impact of their despair, and all this to the frenzied cries of joy of the assembled masses, including children, then something is decidedly sick in the psyche of this society. If no amount of explanation or justification can excuse the horrible acts of murder themselves, where the murderers become hallowed martyrs, how much more so the sheer madness of reproducing those acts, once and again, as if a recorded reel is replayed in a slow-motion to satisfy the sadism of its producers. There are reports of Nazi murderers who delighted in projecting on screens to their private audiences their "feats" of mass murders, but even they did not stoop so low as to screen them, let alone replay them in detail, to the wide public. Only now do we understand that those reenactments are akin to, and a possible extension of the terrible *ta'zia* ceremonies celebrated by the Shi'ites at large during the 'Ashura day, where the Believers relive the suffering of Imam Hussein in Karbala by inflicting pain and injuries on their bodies. But while the Shi'ites exhibit a masochistic sense of identification with their Imam and their own kin, out of their own volition and without inflicting pain or damage upon others, the Hamas scenes express their hatred towards, and sadistic joy at the suffering of, their enemies especially if they are Jews.

A new addition that threatens to descend on the civilized world, is the Muslim radicals' menace to use non-conventional weapons for mass extermination, as if the mass-killings of satanic proportions, by their hand-made mechanical means, were not sufficient to quench their thirst for blood. Palestinians and Hizbullah, al-Qa'ida and Ansar al-Islam, are known to have experimented with gas and poisons contained in the shells and bombs they use against Israeli civilians. The best sign of what is coming is when they begin, in a process of projection, to impute to their enemy what they plan to do. The massacres that they perpetrate or plan against others, which for them are licit and to be expected, become in their minds the "crimes, atrocities and massacres" that the enemy did or will do. As they were experimenting with gas and poison, they spread the rumors about Israeli use of depleted uranium in the territories, "like NATO in Kosovo," or of "poisoned sweets" and "HIV positive virus" contamination of Palestinian children. This means that before they use those material for mass killings, they wish to inject in the minds of the world that they were not the first and that they only responded to the "massacres" carried out by Israel and the Jews with American connivance. The eyes of the Arab world were for long hopefully directed to Saddam Hussein until his defeat, to see what kind of arsenal he could deliver against America and Israel. No public voice was heard in the

Muslim world, attempting to dissuade him from that folly, for any moral reason, with a view of restricting the loss of human lives, and even not for the practical reason of avoiding a devastating loss to his people. More recently, the genocidal threats against Israel and the Jews, by Iran's President Ahmadinejad, at the time that he is preparing his nuclear arsenal to achieve that goal[30], does not arouse any objection or condemnation in the Islamic world, except in the context of the dangers posed to their own regimes by Teheran. For if the Twin Towers constituted for Muslims a "big success", so much more so the lesson that Saddam was about to teach the West, and after him Ahmadinejad. Hamas and al-Qa'ida, as well as Egyptian Muslim radicals, have actually been adding their voices to those in Iran who threaten Israel and the West with poisoning their waters or infecting them with viruses.[31] It is only hard to see who will be left to be brought under Muslim dominion, in accordance with the fundamentalists' dream, if and after the nuclear, chemical, and biological annihilation of the enemy is complete.

Intolerance Built into the Culture

Bernard Lewis has made the point that, unlike other civilizations which are essentially regional, Islam and Christianity have, by their very pattern of expansion, become universal, and exclusive in the sense that not only do they consider themselves the "fortunate recipients of God's final revelation to mankind, and therefore it is their duty to bring it to the rest of humanity," but that the clash between them becomes inevitable.[32] However, while Western culture has generally

---

[30]Former President Rafsanjani spoke of using a nuclear bomb against Israel. See *Iran News, Kayhan and al WIfaq*, 15 December, 2001. Memri, 325, January, 2002. See also *al-Sha'b* (Egypt) 23 September, 2001.

[31]Al-Qa'ida Spokesman, Suleiman Abu Gheith, in an article titled "In the Shadow of the Lances", and also Ayman al-Zawahiri's article in *al-Mujahidin*. For both, see *Memri*, June 12, 2002.

[32]Bernard Lewis, "How did the Infi dels Win?," *National Post*, June 1, 2002.

forsaken the use of violence to spread its message (unless it feels directly threatened), and pursues it by ways that the Muslims regard as devious (mission, the pop culture of jeans, fast food, pop music and coca-cola, television, cinema, alcohol, etc.), militant Islam and its supporters do not shun violence, as the Islamikaze phenomenon has been dramatically evincing. In other words, the humanistic idea of tolerance of the other in western culture, which has come to mean that the other is accepted as is, without value-judging him, has become predominant, and has paved the way to the free market of ideas that prevails in the West today. That thinking has not only permitted the renouncing of force, at least in principle, to spread Christianity, democracy, free trade, and other Western ideas, but has also allowed for Islam and other creeds to compete on its turf, without ever suspecting that the competition would ultimately become over the turf itself. Moreover, since the West accepted the idea of separating the Church from the modern secular state, the faith has become the domain of the individual while the public square was made impervious to it. In the Islamic world, practically all the "secular" governments, which for the most part lack legitimacy, must pay lip service to Muslim militants, at times by even including them in their governments. Even so, the militants appear as the most popular claimants of power, and if allowed to operate as political parties, like in Lebanon and Palestine, can often show their mettle and gain access to government. Therefore, no Muslim turf can be made neutral towards other faiths, and the frequent use of violence against them goes a long way to prove that, day in day out. To this day, while Islam can build its houses of prayer anywhere in the world, other faiths are prevented from doing so in some Muslim territory. And while tens of thousands of Europeans have freely converted into Islam, any Muslim who would entertain a thought to convert is considered a heretic or apostate and dealt with accordingly by capital punishment.

Furthermore, Muslim radicals regard the defeat of their own illegitimate governments at home as a prelude to their restoration of the universal Caliphate of all Muslims, and therefore treat the Western governments who protect, aid, and sponsor the dictators in place as the direct enemy of the Muslims. From their point of view, then, not only is Western culture despicable in its own "right" and faulty due to its own deficiencies, but it invaded their turf in order to subvert it and undermine it from within, until it falls off like a ripe fig. It is the West that came to them, not they to it. This creates a paradox nevertheless, for while Muslim militants decry the Western cultural invasion, which is "worse" in their eyes than the physical invasions of the medieval Crusades, they and their less militant coreligionists at the same time crowd the queues in front of American, Australian, and European Embassies and Consulates across the world, to gain visas of entry into those bastions of Western values that they love to hate. Some explain their quest as a simple will to study in the West, especially value-free technical professions, which are not "soiled" by Western thinking, ignoring the fact that Western learning and protracted sojourns in the West by necessity will have an impact on them, to the point that they would at the end elect to stay and become Western; others, wish from the start to improve their economic lot by immigrating to the West, but once they get there they congregate around their kin and constitute fertile grounds for Muslim *da'wa* (Call, Mission); still others, the likes of Sheikhs Bakri and al-Masri in Britain in previous decades, who have declared their intention to alter the West rather than adapt to it, have migrated to the West as "refugees," because there was no other place left as a safe haven for them in their countries of origin, and the West was generous enough to accommodate them, ultimately to its own detriment.

Paradoxically, it is the adherents of the latter category who place themselves at the forefront of Muslim radicalism in the West and who, benefiting from the hospitality and social welfare arrangements in their host-countries, recruit local converts or already naturalized Muslims for training abroad, for indoctrination at home and for activities in the Path of Allah. It is they who were tolerated by societies against whom they are operating ideologically, who are the least tolerant towards their hosts. Their objective is loud and clear: to Islamize their host societies and let Islam take them over. If until now, under the decisive impact of the integrationists, namely Muslims who wished to assimilate into society, fit into its political, economic and social institutions and become part of it culturally if not religiously, the penetration of Muslim radicalism into the West has begun to change these trends around. More and more Muslims "rebel" against their host cultures and demand, as full-fledged citizens, that their original culture be recognized as a component of the national make up; that state symbols (for example the cross in Scandinavian national flags) be altered to become inclusive of them, and that mosques, foreign Muslim languages, and Muslim education should be subsidized by the state, thus changing the social and political make-up of their host countries. All this emanates not only from the absolute conviction of the Muslims that Allah's message to them, being the most recent is also the most "updated" as it were, but also that their way to Allah is the only valid one.

In contrast to Christianity, the other universal monotheistic religion that claims the same, however, the Muslims did not preclude force to enforce their beliefs and to "save the Infidels from themselves," by their own volition if possible, and by violence if necessary. Therefore, when they speak of "tolerance" they mean some sort of temporary measure of accommodation towards the Infidel, who has clearly been born into an inferior creed, until Islam is strong enough to prevail. The miscalculation of al-Qa'ida on September 11, and before and after that of the Hizbullah, the Hamas, and the Islamic Jihad, was that they thought Western societies, including Israel, were so ripe for their demise that a shocking trauma, or a series of smaller but frequent and consistently growing blows, would in the end overwhelm the enemy. Thus, every time the enemy responds forcefully, or in more unconventional ways than expected by Muslims, like the Americans in Afghanistan or the Israelis in the West

Bank or Lebanon, or Gaza, they cry "Foul game!!" This is
not how the enemies of Islam are supposed to behave, their
very resistance to their subjugation by Islam is regarded as
"blasphemous" for its failure to recognize the will of Allah,
and their retaliatory strikes against Islam are seen as "signs
of distress and despair" which augur their approaching end;
hence the stepped-up activities by Muslims to speed that
process up, and bring it to its conclusion, and so on and so
forth. That point of view does not recognize the right of the
attacked "for the sake of Allah" to self-defense. The Muslims can, and indeed are called upon, to expand, conquer,
kill, enslave, dominate and rule, for the entire universe is
theirs to be included in *Dar-al-Islam*, but woe to those who
resist that "noble" process that is entrenched in the Will of
Allah, and if they do, they are decried as "aggressors," "killers of civilians and children," "arrogant," and as perpetrators
of "massacres."

Thus, any hideous attack upon Western enemies, even
when it involves innocent lives, as in the Twin Tower case,
is "inevitable", "blessed", "well deserved," a "great success," and causes masses to jubilate and writers to sing its
praise throughout the Muslim world, while every retaliation
is lamented, condemned, and blasted as "unjustified," "out
of proportion," "cruel," "wanton massacre," and "proof," if
proof was needed, of the enemy's inherent evil. The idea of
fair play, of attack and counter-attack, and in consequence
of casualties inflicted on both parties to a conflict, is misun-
derstood in Muslim circles. Even the issue of aggressive and
defensive warfare is foreign to them, because the Muslim
definitions of warfare do not follow the accepted objective
norms prevailing in the West, but strictly abide by the subjective rules drawn by Muslim jurists who have formulated
Muslim political theory and international relations[33]. According to these rules, any attack by non-Muslims on Muslims is

---

[33]For the most comprehensive and authoritative study to date, see Majid Khadduri, *War and Peace in Islam*. Johns Hopkins, 1969.

inherently illegal and immoral, and therefore it is incumbent upon all Muslims to assist their co-religionists, regardless of what they did to provoke the attack. Conversely, any Muslim attack on the West, for example, since it can be justified as a "defensive war" against the heretical West, or as an act of self-defense against the spiritual invasion of the West, or as a battle to repulse the enemy from *Dar-al-Islam* (for example Palestine, Andalusia, Kashmir, and Southern France), is *eo ipso* a just war that all Muslims are called upon to sustain. In other words, once a war against the enemy had been entitled "Jihad," and any of the latter examples justifies a Jihad, the arena is wide open for war. Guerilla warfare, or Islamikaze terrorism and the like, which are the tools of the asymmetrical wars, are means of warfare that are hallowed in Islam, with all the attending ideological and doctrinal elaborations attached thereto.

The West has no standing in these definitions and what it says or thinks does not matter, because the Islamic position is Allah-inspired and *Shari'a*-dictated, which means that it is beyond discussion, compromise, debate or concession. Therefore, while external wars in the West are considered quantitative issues (over territories, interests, assets), and when they are terminated, then compromise, concessions and negotiations are led until an agreement emerges; and when it does, it is binding on the parties who signed the treaty, cease-fire, or convention; in Islam the wars are qualitative (over ideas, doctrines, "justice," "redress of wrongs", "retrieval of rights", "Allah's *Jihad*" etc), are never terminated until the victory of Islam and the imposition of its rule is brought about. And when an "agreement" is signed under duress (like after a military defeat), it always derives from the precedent of Hudaybiya that was established by the Prophet, namely that the agreement is temporary (*hudna*=armistice), and it is to be violated at the first opportunity, when Muslims feel they have regained superiority, or have found new ways of warfare that the enemy is unable to counter (like the Islamikaze). *Sulh* (peace-cum-reconciliation) can be concluded only under the terms of a *Pax Islamica*, when the non-Muslim has accepted the hegemony of Islam and submitted to its rule[34].This is the reason why Muslim authorities in Egypt and Saudi Arabia justified the Camp David Accords of 1977, as well as the Oslo Accords of 1993, in terms of a temporary Hudaybiya-like truce, which is open-ended and reversible, if and when the circumstances so allow. Like the Prophet's precedent, these "agreements" were only necessary in order to extort concessions from the enemy, but once they are made and cashed, they no longer necessarily bind. "Islamic interest" is then the key concept in that culture which does not include respect for the Roman law of contract, and the international treaties and conventions which derive from there. This was exemplified once again during and after the asymmetrical wars of Lebanon and Gaza which were initiated and led by Muslim militants. This worldview, where rules of war and peace do not apply equally on the belligerents, and clearly benefit the Muslims while they are expected to obligate only the non-Muslims, is the very reason why the Muslims see themselves free to violate their "agreements," while they constantly accuse their adversaries of "violating all agreements and commitments," at a time when they themselves faced no reproach because they had never expected to live up to their "commitments" in the first place, while their adversaries, who were truly obliged by them, were expected to keep them to the letter.

Thus, when the Palestinians, for example, committed themselves in Oslo (another Hudaybiya, in the words of Arafat), without reserve or qualification, to end terrorism and violence in general, not to introduce to their territory any category of un-allowed weapons, to maintain their armed force at agreed levels and under one command, to put an end to incitement against Israel and the Jews, to arrest terrorists and pursue them in justice or extradite them, as a prerequisite to

---

[34]See Moshe Sharon, *"Hudna and Sulh in Islam"* (Hebrew), *Nativ*, Summer 2002

receiving more territory from Israel and advancing into the peace-process, they remembered only the Israeli part of the agreement, and when not fulfilled they heaped all the blame on Israel, while their consistent violations of their main commitments did not matter. They became accustomed by the Rabin Government to the fact that they could break their commitments, but that Israel, for fear of arresting the "peace process," would swallow all violations and proceed with its one-sided concessions, and so it was. But when a new Israeli government came in, which made further Israeli concessions in accordance with the peace accords contingent upon Palestinian parallel implementation, they cried "Foul game!" once again,and that brought the process to a dead end.

Intolerance based on a concept of superiority, whereby the superior does not have to conform like the inferior, is apparent also in the daily conduct in the Muslim world towards other religions. Rampant are the instances where Christian churches are burned down in Egypt, Nigeria and Indonesia, and synagogues are attacked and destroyed by Palestinians (notably the Joseph Tomb in Nablus and the Jewish Synagogue in Jericho during the Intifadah), and by Muslims throughout the Western world since the outbreak of the second Palestinian insurgency in late 2000, but rare are the occasions where Muslim mosques are attacked by anyone anywhere. The Muslims do not take this, and the fact that they can build their mosques anywhere in the West, as an indication of Western tolerance and acceptance of the other, but as a sure sign that no one dares to resist Islamic expansion while they, in their countries of origin, can curtail or totally prevent the construction of any Christian, let alone Jewish, houses of prayer. Muslims can be the inhabitants of any country in the world, including the Christian world and Israel on whose doors they knock for immigration or "right of return," but they would not, by law, allow any Jew into Saudi Arabia or Jordan. What is more, they still dub the countries to which they wish to immigrate as "racist" for not completely surrendering to their will, while Jews and Christians are severely restricted in various areas of the Muslim world. That suggests to them, once again, that while the whole universe is their domain as of right, other faiths are not, by their very nature, entitled to the same rights in the lands of Islam.

No country in the West witnesses its citizens following the shameful scenes, current in the Muslim world, where American and Israeli flags, and the effigies of their leaders, are burned ritually as a matter of routine, save when Muslim communities in the West practice that same ritual. But no sustained burning of Arab or Muslim flags or effigies is known as a phenomenon in the West or in Israel. Once again, the inability of the Muslim world to accept as their equals the national symbols of others is striking, at a time when the West respects theirs as a matter of course, and when it does not Muslim violence ensues as it happened with the Cartoon affair of early 2006. This, far from awakening the consciousness of the Muslims to their own intolerance, in contrast with the publicly advertised and exhibited Western tolerance towards them, on the contrary has confirmed them in their belief in the hegemony of their faith and symbols that no one dares to challenge, at a time when they openly defy, with impunity, other creeds and symbols. This has encouraged the Muslim communities in the West and in Israel to demand the right to construct their mosques, or to perform their Friday rituals, in places known as holy sites to other faiths. On Temple Mount in Jerusalem they built their mosques on a site that they knew was the holiest for the Jewish creed, they transformed many churches and synagogues into mosques during their conquests and expansion, and turned every occupied land into a *waqf* (Holy Endowment) that cannot revert to non-Muslims[35]. But woe to anyone who dares to turn a mosque into another house of prayer, or to occupy land that is or was Muslim, for that is intolerable. More recently, new challenges rose when Muslims began to illegally construct a mosque on the grounds and in defiance

---

[35]See repeated references to this in the Charter of the Hamas, See R. Israeli, *Islam and Israel*, University Press of America, ch. 7, pp. 123-170.

of, the Basilica of the Annunciation in Nazareth, to squat for the Friday prayers near the main cathedral of Florence, and to deny any historical rights to the Jews over Temple Mount, thereby declaring to Christianity and to Judaism, in Lewis' memorable words: "Your time has passed. Now we are here. Move over."[36] This is not exactly tolerance.

Incidentally, and significantly, the verse from the Qur'an that Bernard Lewis mentioned in connection with the inscription in the Dome of the Rock, to wit: "He is God, He is One. He does not beget, He is not begotten," which was meant to reject the basic dogma of Christianity about God and His Son, when the Muslims took over Jerusalem in the seventh Century, was also inscribed on the temporary tent-mosque in front of the Annunciation that awaited the building of the permanent mosque, obviously with the same intention and meaning. Coupled with the denial of Jewish rights on Temple Mount, this signifies, in the eyes of the Muslims, that they intend to indeed supersede both Judaism and Christianity, as Islam had taught them of old; hence, the hatred of the Muslims to the construct "Judeo-Christian tradition," which they regard as a passing episode in history, once the Seal of the Prophets, Muhammad, had dispensed to humanity the latest divine message that is Islam. "Your time has passed. Now we are here" is not only the statement of a factual chronological sequence, but also a declaration of mastery, dominance, hegemony, and exclusivity, backed by the will and the power to make it happen in the real world. For, a creed that was designed by Allah to replace all others and to bring all humanity under its aegis, cannot be expected to tolerate other faiths, let alone competitors for the same world constituency on the same sites.

The Eternal Victims

In stark contradiction to the dreams of world dominion that they entertain, Muslims tend at the same time to regard

---

[36]See Bernard Lewis, op. cit.

themselves as eternal victims of the West that they hate and want to displace, but whose help they need and implore; and they rationalize this contradiction by the plots and conspiracies constantly woven around and against them, as if the West had no other concerns than them, or could not do very well without their lachrymose complaints. First and foremost for them is the need to explain to themselves and to the world why and how they, who had pioneered civilization and sciences in medieval times, and had caused Europe to tremble and fear their successive mighty empires, found themselves, without preparation, warning, or transition at the bottom of the civilisatory heap and of the hierarchy of world powers when the modern era dawned. For a shame society like theirs, it is difficult, nay impossible, to take responsibility for their deeds and to devise a policy of adaptation that could help them pull out of the quagmire, for that would amount to admitting the deficiencies of their culture, the stifling restrictions of their faith, the pipe-dreams of their leaders, and the insufficiencies of their social systems. Thus, rather than admit their inabilities and seek succor elsewhere, it is easier to project their own ill-will on others, masquerade their jealousies and bigotry as "revivalism" and accuse the all-powerful West, the colonizer and imperialist of yesteryear, of all their ills, including their demise, suffering, backwardness, population explosion, dictatorial rule, corruption, and what not. They do not want to recall that when they were the powerful, the conquerors, the colonizers and the imperialists, they did not stop one moment to ask themselves what they were doing to their conquered peoples and civilizations that they gradually decimated.

Arabs and Muslims have resources, human and mineral, a great tradition of learning and a vast ambition to restore themselves to where they were before they began slipping in the modern era. But their self-inflicted deficiencies in government, economics, and antiquated social structures do not permit them to take off. Perhaps most stifling of all is the array of dictatorships of all sorts, monarchical and republican, one-party and military juntas, rulers who were never elected and self-imposed Presidents for-life. Illegitimate rule spawns corruption, helplessness, and hopelessness, and the near non-existence of civil society and non-governmental organizations and voluntary associations with the necessary clout to fill in when the government is deficient, make change difficult and nearly impossible. Uncontrollable poverty and population explosion are hardly the requisite processes to arrest these trends. When allowed to operate, Islamists often step in to fill the gap, but they are closely monitored or harnessed to the regime's goals, and therefore their operations are often circumscribed and cause them to become part of the problem instead of the solution. In this state of affairs, where the Western world, and Israel at their doorstep, advance and increase the gulf between themselves and the poor Muslim world, an eye-poking gap is observed on television screens and in neighboring Israel daily, which prompts people to find refuge in self-victimization: it is not their fault, it is the fault of others. This state of mind is aided in those societies by the dependence of the commoner on his corrupt government for food subsidies, for employment, for education and social services, for development, and for the individual's well-being. But the governments are incompetent, illegitimate, bent on staying in power and lacking in a blueprint for resolving the ever-aggravating problems of their countries and societies.

The stronger the regimes, by virtue of the modern weaponry, which affords them a superior power of enforcement, the more disaffected are the populations who sense that their government's interests are not theirs; all the more so, since the maintenance of the rulers in place is often made possible by their Western "allies" who provide the money, the economic aid, the weapons, and the food that keep this explosive situation from getting worse and from blowing up in the West's and the regimes' faces. Another paradox develops: because when they are dispossessed, unemployed, and hopelessly classified as have-nots, the masses in those countries not only are victims of their rulers and their Western "allies," and, therefore, feel "entitled" to demand that both provide for their needs, but the more they receive to sustain themselves and ascertain their survival, the more humiliated they become for that dependence, the more enraged they are by it, and the more violent-prone they grow as the only way to air their frustration that only keeps increasing. In other words, the West and the local governments, who are held jointly responsible for the poverty and frustration of which the masses are the victims, not only are expected to alleviate the burden of the impoverished and the disadvantaged, but when they do so are all the more resented and likely to become the targets of the frustration. This is a no-win situation which *inter alia* causes massive departures of immigrants to seek their livelihood or the implementation of their revolutionary dreams elsewhere, notably in the West. Bin Laden, for example, was no less enraged against his own Saudi government, which is sustained by its alliance with the U.S., than against America and Israel. If it is so with a Saudi system, which is not needy, and a Bin Laden who is not impoverished, how much more so with other Arabs and Muslims where both government and people are in dire poverty!!

The eternal victims also believe not only that everyone owes them everything, and they themselves are exempted from any self-strengthening effort, but also that they can use violence to redress the wrong done to them. So, for example, Palestinians who have been living on UNRWA's handouts and sacks of flour for the past sixty years, and where their population in the squalid refugee camps has quadrupled since then, believe it is the duty of the world to continue to feed them indefinitely. They make children and the West has to take care of them. They have resisted all attempts at resettlement in their host countries, which are also Arab and Muslim, but prefer to leave the refugee problem seething, and to continue to depend on the world's goodwill for survival, rather than force the refugees to take up a constructive life and end their refugee status. They maintain the illusion of the "right of return" in their refugee standing, which is the ultimate victimhood, and they are not about to relinquish it. What is more, the U.S., and other Western countries that shoulder the brunt of the UNRWA budget, are also the most hated and threatened by the Muslim radicals who feed from their hands. If they had learned, if they had been willing to learn, from Western nations and Israel, how to absorb refugees in their own territory and put them on a productive track, rather than to implant in them hatred and the mentality of the eternal victims, much of the bitterness and frustration that engender violence and terrorism could have been spared. And this is not only a matter of money or of development (Bin Laden and Saudi Arabia being the ultimate example), but a matter of culture. If one is educated to not accept any handouts, to rise on his feet and help himself, to shed the feeling of victim and be proud of a self- made and self-sustaining livelihood, then one's dignity is restored, the humiliation effaced or diminished, and the paralyzing jealousy and stifling apathy replaced by aspiration, ambition, and striving.

No wonder then that among Palestinians a high ratio was found to support terrorism, which is for them, to be sure, the "right" of the eternal victim to both avenge his situation and to have it redressed. How exactly this will happen, they do not say, unless they think, as part of their world of delusions that we shall address below, that they can bring the West to submission or destroy Israel and replace it. There is also no wonder that al-Qa'ida, the Hamas, Hizbullah, and the rest rationalize their wild terrorism as "retaliation" for their humiliation and victimhood by the strong, the arrogant, and the powerful who had rendered them victims. Therefore, while their terrorism is to be "understood" in their eyes, and justified as the cry of the desperate victim, any Western counterattack or defensive act, must be construed as "aggression" against and "massacre" of the eternal victim. They insist that for every one of their orgies of killing, one must seek the "roots" and comprehend the "reasons," and address the "causes," exactly as for every burning of a church or a synagogue; however, if a mosque is hit, or Muslim children are injured, even incidentally, that is intentional "murder," "desecration," and "blasphemy." For that reason, they do not recognize the difference between intentional damage and collateral casualties. It is the result that counts, no matter what the intention of the enemy planners may have been. America and Israel are always "children killers," "heretics," aggressors, arrogant, and perpetrators of massacres. Americans "killed" Iraqi children by "preventing food and medicaments from reaching them," even if it was Saddam who preferred to purchase weapons or compensate the families of the Palestinian Islamikaze, rather than import food and drugs for the sick. The dead corpses of the Iraqi children were there for display, for if they are clearly the victims, then the Americans must be their killers.

Thus, a reversal of roles is effected, whereby the West and Israel become the "terrorists" and the Muslims the victims thereof; it is the West who terrorizes the Muslim world and is arrogant and condescending towards it, and the Muslims merely act in self-defense. Hence the failure of Muslim countries, including in their Kuala Lumpur Islamic Conference of June 2002, let alone in international gatherings, to accede to the Western definition of terrorism, which is, in essence "the use of violence against innocent civilians to attain political goals." They refuse to relinquish the mantle of victimhood to others, therefore terrorism is what is done to them, not what they do to others. They struggle at all international forums to show that the Palestinians and Hizbullah cannot be considered terrorists, no matter what they do, because they fight for "liberation" from "occupation"; many of them also rationalize the Twin Tower horror as "liberation" from the choking American tutelage, or a "message" to the "real terrorist," which is America (or Israel for that matter), or a "lesson" to the arrogant, or a new "mode of warfare" against the threatening and aggressive West; or the "desire for death" of the audacious Islamikaze martyrs, matching up to the "desire for life and comfort" of the cowardly and decadent West. That is also the reason why they remind America of its own "terrorist attacks" against Hiroshima and Nagasaki, proof that what matters is not what is done, to whom and under what circumstances, but who does it. "Victims of the world, Unite!!!,." if, of course, America or Israel is the reason of your misery.

Other victims, such as the Americans murdered on September 11, or Indians obliterated in Kashmir, or Israelis who are blown apart in pizza parlors, or in the bus on their way there, are not victims in the eyes of Muslim radicals, and more and more in the eyes of plain Muslims in general, even when Muslims are the recognized and avowed perpetrators of the terror in all those cases. The victims of terror do not deserve compassion, because they "had brought that upon themselves," or better, "have concocted it themselves" in conjunction with the CIA or the Jews, or the Mossad. The wide acceptance of those theories of conspiracy, including among intellectuals and opinion makers, adds to the universal sense of victimhood that is rampant in the Islamic world. Another important corollary of this attitude is that, while in the Judeo-Christian tradition martyrs are usually the victims of external aggression inflicted on them in the pursuit of their faith, in Islam it is the perpetrator of the aggression, who also immolates himself in the process, who becomes the Islamikaze martyr. In other words, it is not he who suffers death or torture or misery on his way to martyrdom, since he had chosen that course avidly and advisedly, but he who must kill in order to gain his place in the hierarchy of martyrdom. This dramatic shift, from those who were killed in battle or by accident and thereby became martyrs in classical Islam, to the Islamikaze intentional mass-killing of others in order to go to Paradise and enjoy the seventy-two virgins promised by the Qur'an, is the mind-boggling thought that baffles the West today.

Self-Delusion, Fantasy and the Real World

The proverbial Arab enamoring with words, to the point of ecstasy, has been studied by scholars, such as Gibb and Patai, and found to be related to the strength of the Arabic idiom, as exemplified in the Qur'an, in the ancient Arabic poetry of the time of the *Jahiliyya,* and in the subsequent Arab and Muslim literature. The ability of the word to move people and to incite them to action, a key element in the training of the Islamikaze, is supplemented by a rich world of fantasy, which defies rational analysis, and in which wishful thinking replaces facts, and mantra-like slogans supersede policy ("Jerusalem will be liberated by one million *shahids*"; "if the Israelis do not like it, they can drink the waters of the Gaza Sea/the Dead Sea"), and the unpleasant is denied as if it did not exist (No Muslims have committed the Twin Tower murder; the Israelis/Jews did). For that reason, commitments are ignored, as if they had never been undertaken (Oslo, smuggling in weapons by Palestinians, arresting terrorists), promises are forgotten the moment they are made (to stop incitement and terrorism), slogans are coined and repeated (Israelis inject HIV positive to Palestinians; Oslo is like Hudaybiya), propaganda and incitement thrive (the Karine A and Suntorini weapons smuggling never took place; Israelis and Americans are children killers), boasting one's exploits (Egyptian democracy is more authentic than Israel's) and denigrating the enemy are rife (the Jews are cowardly, the descendants of monkeys and pigs), lies are made up to cover up deficiencies (Palestinians' economic suffering is due to Israel's policies, not to terrorist activities by the Palestinians), and denial is exercised when one is faced with facts(No Karine A existed, no blowing up of the Twin Towers took place). History is invented (Palestinians are the descendants of Cana'anites), false analogies are made (Palestinian leaders are comparable to the founding fathers of America), facts are denied (the Holocaust, or involvement in terrorism), and self-embellishment and self-aggrandizement are sought (The future belongs to Islam, the West's demise is imminent) for consolation. Palestinian and other Arab and Muslim textbooks for children tell the entire story with such eloquence that not much needs to be added[37]. But enough examples will be cited, especially in connection with Islamic terrorism, incitement to it, and its praise after the acts of murder, to illustrate the main assumptions of this chapter.

Each of the fantasies undergoes several stages: first the fabrication of a web of lies that has no relation to facts, and which Muslims think that if repeated often enough, it becomes a reality, in which they begin to believe themselves, even when they cannot prove it. Because no rules of evidence apply to them, and what matters is the manufacturing of "facts" and the diffusion of such in their midst and across the world, which swallows the stories, unsuspecting that hoaxes of that dimension can be invented, and out of belief that even if the Israelis or the Americans did not "do it," it is likely that they would, because "it is in their nature". A classic case in point is the blood libel against the Jews, which was repeated by the Minister of Defense in Syria (Mustafa Tlas), and reiterated by nearly all Muslim media, without criticism. In the same vein, the Palestinian delegate at the Commission of Human Rights in Geneva, of all places, could stand up and accuse the Israelis of injecting the AIDS virus into Palestinian children, or Arafat could lambaste the Israelis for spreading poisoned sweets to kill Palestinians, or the Saudis and Egyptians could claim that Israel had distributed an aphrodisiac among Muslims which increased the sexual appetite of women in order to corrupt their morals, or that the Israeli armed forces used depleted uranium bullets to harm the Palestinians. During the battles of Jenin in April-May, 2002, for example, a Palestinian father was produced on television cameras, crying and weeping for his nine children who had "perished" before his eyes and whom he "had

---

[37]e.g., Raphael Israeli "Identity and State-building: Educating Palestinian Children after Oslo," Journal of Terrorism and Political Violence, Spring 2002.

seen with his own eyes" under the rubble. That was in line with the Palestinian claims of "5,000" and then "500" "massacred Palestinians". A very horrible and heart-tearing experience indeed, except that all nine children were fortunately found safe and sound. Perhaps the most chilling hoax that was fabricated by the Palestinians, actively supported by all Arabs and Muslims, and passively accepted by much of the European press, was the "Poison Affair" of 1983, when the Israelis were blasted for "poisoning Palestinian schoolgirls in Jenin," and then in other areas of the West Bank, with a view to "sterilizing them before their age of reproductive activity" and thus "battle against Palestinian demography." These condemnations were made throughout the press of the world, and even when it was proved that the "poisoning" was a case of mass hysteria, what professional medicine recognizes as "hyper-ventilation," the accusations did not recede.[38]

Any condemnation goes, and when the accuser is not held responsible for providing evidence or spreading lies, accusations and libel become cheap and risk-free, and everyone can indulge in them at will. Self-delusion operates on other levels as well. Convinced in the righteousness and exclusivity of their Islamic universal message, Muslims cannot understand why the West and Israel pursue them, do not let them act with impunity in the Path of Allah, or wage war against them. For the message of Allah is clear and unambiguous, it declares the Jews monkeys, it forbids Muslims to befriend Jews and Christians,[39] enjoins the Muslims to "kill Unbelievers wherever we find them,"[40] to "murder them and treat them harshly," "fight and slay the Pagans, seize them, beleaguer them, and lie in wait for them in every stratagem"[41]; so, then, what do the Infidels complain about? That word of Allah was intended against

---

[38]See R. Israeli, *Poison: Modern Manifestations of a Blood Libel*, Lexington Books, Lanham and NY, 2002.

[39]Qur'an, Sura 5:51.

[40]2:191.

[41]9:123

them, and they cannot deny or resist it, because Allah him-self said it, and that is written, word for word, in His Divine Message—the Holy Book which applies to all humanity. They also believe that Allah and His Messenger had announced that it was acceptable for Muslims to go back on their promises and obligations with Pagans and make war on them whenever Muslims find themselves strong enough to do so[42]; or that Allah had taken away the freedom of belief from all humanity and relegates those who disbelieve in Islam to Hell,[43] calls them "untouchable and impure,"[44] and orders His followers to fight the Unbelievers until no other religion except Islam is left,[45] and more and more. Then, why should they spare non-Muslims, make any agreement with them, or honor any of their commitments to them?

The hard-core Muslims are therefore shocked that the West battles them and resists them, instead of submitting to them and recognizing that Islam is their only salvation. We have seen appeals to President Bush to convert to Islam and astonishment at his procrastination to do so. They cannot comprehend how and why Westerners are failing to see the light and do not hurry into the fold of Islam. In their world of delusion, they already see "thousands of Americans" repent-ing for their previous obdurate misunderstanding of Islam, and their "coming to tears when they listen to the Words of the Qur'an recited to them." Their worldview, which cannot accept a plurality of creeds, cannot also understand why they themselves, the disseminators of the good of Allah and His message, should be held in low esteem, feared and perse-cuted by the West. All they did on September 11 was the fulfillment of the Word of Allah:

> "For them [the Unbelievers], garments of fire shall be cut and there shall be poured over their heads boiling water, whereby

---

[42]9:5.

[43]9:3.

[44]5:10

[45]9:28.

whatever is in their bowels and skin shall be dissolved and they will be punished with hooked iron rods"[46].

Unbelievers will not only have to live in "disgrace in this life, but in the Day of Judgment He Shall make them taste the penalty of burning."[47] To have precipitated the Day of Judgment upon the victims of terrorist massacres, was therefore nothing anomalous, just the early fulfillment of the Word of Allah. Then, the stage of denial sets in, as Muslims realize the outrage they caused and the havoc that their delusions have impelled them to commit. Be they acts of terror against Israel, the Karine, a weapon smuggling, or the September 11 horror, Muslims first of all denied they ever did, intended, knew, or participated in those acts, paradoxically while at the same time evincing unrestrained jubilation about them. In their stage of denial, they wish both to dissociate themselves from the atrocities they had committed and to "enjoy" their results at the same time. The first major terrorist act against Israel, committed at the height of the Oslo euphoria in mid-1994, for example, when twenty-one young Israeli soldiers were murdered, was immediately denied by Arafat, who "had no knowledge" of it, and as "proof" of his innocence, denounced the "act." In an interview to Israeli media, he speculated that it must have been the "deed of the Israeli security services" who "were interested to wreck the Oslo Agreements." Why wreck them, when the Rabin government who signed them was in power, full of goodwill and leniency towards Palestinian violations, and eager to show to his suspecting constituency in Israel that they "worked," Arafat did not explain. His conspiracy theory and instinctive sense of denial was stronger than any rational consideration he might have invoked. When the *Achille Lauro* was hijacked by Palestinians in the Mediterranean in 1986, and an American citizen was murdered on board and callously tossed into the sea, the sea-jackers retired to Port Said where

---

[46]22:19-22

[47]22:9

they were arraigned, but President Mubarak denied that he had any knowledge of the mastermind of that terrorist act, at the same time that he gave him shelter in his country. The affair of the ship Karine A, which in early 2002 was seized by the Israeli Navy in the Red Sea, illicitly carrying weapons to the Palestinians, under the command of one of Arafat's associates, was totally denied by Arafat and the Palestinian Authority as an "Israeli plot." Then when presented by the facts and when he shipment of weapons was exposed to world media, Arafat said that he "had no knowledge of it personally," and only when he was confronted with the documents he had personally signed, did he have no choice but apologize to President Bush.

In the aftermath of September 11, similar patterns of behavior were detected in the Muslim world. In spite of their joy that they could not contain, Muslims from Pakistan to America, from Egypt to Afghanistan, denied that any Muslim could "commit such horror," because it was patently against "the compassion and tolerance of Islam," and verses were cited in support of that contention, such as that Islam "was opposed to compulsion in faith," or to the execution of "innocent civilians," unless they challenged Islam or "humiliated it." (Since the perpetrators claimed that they were humiliated by America, their acts were then justified). They also contended that an act of terror of such proportions could not possibly have been planned, let alone executed, by any Muslim state or organization, thus exonerating themselves in advance, even if that implied their admitting their incompetence in carrying out operations of such a scale. Even as the evidence was being gathered and divulged of the Qai'da involvement, and demands were mounting for its indictment, they continued to insist that "unless America provided decisive and undisputed evidence for Muslim involvement," it was wrong on the part of the West to "smear the entire Muslim world," (which was "opposed to terrorism", as we know, in any case), on account of the "yet unproven" deeds of the few. And so, the roles were again reversed: the

Muslims, who needed no evidence for their delusions, and never stop to reflect on the irrationality of their accusations against the West and Israel, suddenly became scrupulous about "evidence," when the accusations are laid at their door. And so they found themselves pledging that should any evidence emerge of Muslim involvement, the culprits ought to be pursued to "Muslim justice," and dealt with according to Muslim legal procedures, which meant in effect exonerating Muslims altogether.

But the facts kept pressing at the door, and when the Muslim claims of "innocence" became ludicrous in the eyes of world opinion, the stage of projection and laying the blame on others began. As in the cases where Israelis were accused by Palestinians of "provocations" in mounting terrorism against their own citizens in order to blame the "innocent and peace-loving Palestinians," or of concocting the Karine A arm smuggling in order to smear the Palestinian "impeccable reputation" of "law-abiding" and of "respect for its commitments," the Muslim world orchestrated a campaign of projection on others of the evils of September 11. First, it was claimed by Muslims in Egypt and Pakistan, America and Saudi Arabia, that the Jews, the CIA or the Israeli Mossad "did it," with countless "indications" indicting, successively or simultaneously, either or all of them. Again, becoming suddenly meticulous about "data gathering" and the provision of "conclusive evidence," they began to fabricate piecemeal fantastic stories about Israelis or Jews who "had been pre-warned and evacuated the premises of the Twin Towers prior to the blast," or the takeover of control towers by "suspect elements," also presumably Jewish, who "collaborated with the hijackers," or other hoaxes that never cease to raise our admiration for the boundless imagination of their inventers. Indeed, even though the reality of Muslim day dreaming is not itself limited by imagination, it proves to us to be more fantastic than their fantasies. From the concept of imagination we often use the positive derivative of the "imaginative," but they are bent on the "imaginary," which seems to fill their world and satisfy their emotions. In this Kafkaesque world of the unreal, only non-Muslims are supposed to be sinful, and therefore anything projected on them is either true, or could be true even if it is not proven.

This is the foundation of the vicious and sustained campaigns of denigration and diminishment of the West and the Jews in Muslim circles, countries, and societies, that we commonly call incitement and that is the prerequisite for terrorism against them. Incitement often means delegitimation of the enemy, making them look corrupt, decadent, an inherent enemy of Islam and Allah, and therefore deserving of annihilation through terror. To that end, any means is suitable, even inventing lies, making up false quotations from non existent sources, like the "citations" by Palestinians in their text books of "passages" that never were, which "prove" the Jewish conspiracy, its "evil," and its ill-intentions against Islam and the rest of humanity; or the ritual repetition of the blood libel as a fact of history, or liberal quotations from the forged *Protocols of the Sages of Zion* as true documents, etc. It seems amazing to us that they care little not only for the truth as long as it serves their goals of libeling Israel and the West, but even less about educating their children on falsehoods and training them to consider imaginary texts as "citations."[48] In May 2002, when the Israeli armed forces launched their Defensive Shield Operation against terrorist bases in Jenin, which was led extremely carefully and sparingly with regard to civilians, the Palestinians immediately shouted: "Foul Game!" They had conducted a series of murderous attacks against Israeli civilians, and blown up one hundred of them within one week, including during the Passover Seder in April 2002, where entire families were wiped out (29 killed in all), and that passed in the Palestinian public as a matter of routine; but when Israel decided to root out the bases of terror in the West Bank, immediate accusations

---

[48]e.g., Raphael Israeli "Identity and State-building: Educating Palestinian Children after Oslo," *Journal of Terrorism and Political Violence*, Spring 2002.

of "aggression" and "massacres" began, echoed by the Arab and Muslim press, (and also by the European press, and the numbers of "massacred" people kept increasing, reaching the peak of 5,000 according to Saeb Arekat, the Chief Palestinian negotiator. Then it turned out that "only" 50 Palestinians were killed in that center of terror, and for the most part amid very heavy fighting where 22 Israeli fighters lost their lives. There was no massacre, in short.

Similarly, when the Americans opened their counterattack against the Taliban, and thoughtfully attempted not to harm civilians, to the extent possible, in the process, and even dropped significant quantities of food to sustain them during the fighting, it was the stories of "massacres" of "innocent civilians," "poisoning of the dropped food parcels," the "intentional bombing of schools and food depots," the "cruel arrest of Taliban POW's" and their transport to Guantanamo where they were treated "inhumanly" like "the Nazis would," that dominated the Arab and Muslim reporting of the operation, not the intentional atrocities committed by the Taliban themselves and their supporters. Like in the "Jenin massacre" that never was, in the second Lebanese war of 2006 and the Gaza war of 2008-9, never were the acts which the Hamas and the Hizbullah did to trigger the fighting mentioned. For the Arab and Muslim audiences in all these cases, the story was not about reporting a balanced truth, where the evils, intentional or incidental, and motivations of both parties were recounted, and where the cause and effect sequence had to be explained, of horrendous terrorist attacks against civilians which had to be retaliated against and rooted out, but only about the "callous and senseless American and Israeli aggressive attacks against civilians," without reason or cause, just to satisfy the evil instincts of Bush and Sharon. For them, vilifying, debasing, calumniating, and libeling their enemies was the only way to delegitimize them as inhuman predators, so as to pave the way for future additional terrorist attacks against them. Projecting on the enemy, by heaping lies and pipe-dreams against him, by the way of pure and primitively simple incitement, however, does not only permit his delegitimation and encourages more attacks against him, but also, more significantly, belies and exposes the hidden dreams of what the Muslims would do to the Americans and the Israelis, if they could. Projection-cum-incitement, therefore, reveal to the West what fate is awaiting him, should the Muslim world win this confrontation. Wasn't it the Secretary General of the Arab League, 'Azzam Pasha, who declared on the day the Arab armies invaded nascent Israel in 1948 in order to eliminate it, that a "massacre would ensue that the world had never seen since the Mongols"? He meant a massacre of the Jews, exactly as the Muslim terrorists mean and implement today, but instead of piecemeal by terrorism—in one big stroke.

Thus, while Americans and Israelis, in their reprisals in self-defense, have espoused the strategy of saving civilian lives to the extent possible, and would rather fight surgically, at the risk of their own casualties, to minimize the enemy's civilian losses, rather than blanket-bomb entire cities or population centers, Muslim terrorists act differently. Their stated aim is to maximize civilian casualties in the enemy's ranks, as evidenced in the Twin Towers and in the massive explosions in crowded civilian places in Israel, where nails and bolts are added to the bombs for maximal effect, and sometimes poisonous substances are tucked on to the bombs for added damage. In other words, while the West operates with a considerable restraint of its forces, for fear of their devastating impact, Muslim terrorists act with the maximum unleashing of their power, something that leads to the fear in the West that they would not hesitate to use unconventional weapons if they laid their hands on them. That is exactly the soft-belly of the West, which ties in with its concern for human life, for due process of law and restraint in using power, which the Muslim terrorists who are not shackled by those limitations seek to exploit and strike at. To make that happen, roles are once again reversed: "We are not the terrorists!!!, You are!!!," they shout at the West. For, what Muslim martyrs do in terms of wanton killing, is not only justified, because it is in the Path of Allah, but by delegitimizing the West as terrorist itself, the fight against it is called for, and to be fought by all means available to the Muslims, precisely those that the West has restrained itself from using.

Dialoguing with Others

Some naïve minds in the West have come to believe that dialogue and negotiations with Muslim radicals can and will alter those attitudes and lead to coexistence between Muslims and their rivals. The problem is that dialogue has been treated in the West as if it were a real policy, whereas it is in fact a non-policy, designed only to fill an awkward vacuum and to make royalties, like Prince Charles, and legislators feel virtuous for "doing something." But while Europeans have regularly entered a "dialogue" with Muslims in good faith, fully intending to find common ground with their often unruly Muslim interlocutors—for the Muslims, "dialogue" means something else entirely. For them, it signifies the submission of a lesser culture and religion to their own superior one. Muslims hope to inspire in the Westerners and Israelis conversion to an Islamic view of the world. Anything short of that is regarded by them as an abject "failure of dialogue," and a signal to resort to threats of violence or acts of terrorism. They are well practiced at both, while the Westerners have literally become pushovers at this stage in their history. Except for the U.S., they hardly believe that anything is worth fighting over. Nor do they have a stomach for a fight of unlimited duration. They would rather capitulate than investigate in depth the meaning of tolerance, understanding, dialogue, and peace to Muslims. The problem today lies in the juxtaposition of a resurgent Islam on the one hand, and a self-deprecating West on the other, unsure of itself, its values, or even what it stands for. Its people have made a virtue of instant self-gratification, and therefore they invest next to nothing in the future—hence they have stopped having children. Their preferred way of life amounts to a "credit card culture." They want everything, and they want it instantly. Never mind that their governments no longer raise sufficient funds from taxation to cover exorbitant welfare entitlements, or that a bleak financial future awaits tomorrow's pensioners. In short, the West has become a disgrace to its own heritage, in sharp reversal of its fortunes when at the turn of the twentieth century the Muslim Ottoman Empire was considered the "sick man of Europe," and was therefore no match for a confident West.

U.S. Defense Secretary Donald Rumsfeld was onto something apart from the obvious when he distinguished between "old" and "new" Europe—except that in their eagerness to grab some (necessarily short term) economic benefits after emerging from Soviet control, the headlong rush of "new" Europe to join the EU will inevitably contaminate them with the prevalent Western disease. There is another drawback to this constant resort to "dialogue." It lulls the Western populations into believing that their governments are doing something constructive to avert violence or threats of violence in the future. In reality, nothing could be further from the truth, for this non-policy simply serves to embolden and concomitantly empower those Muslims whom Western governments have chosen to act as intermediaries with the wider Muslim community. Invariably, Western governments have elected these Muslims largely because they are the activists and therefore are prominent in the community, while the governments comfort themselves with the injudicious belief that these figures represent "moderate" Islam, or that dealing with Muslim governments can justify departure from the standard norms of justice, as the scandalous release by the Scottish authorities, in mid 2009, of the Lockerbie culprit has illustrated. However, these Muslims have known Europe long enough to have learned to tailor their vocabulary precisely according to whom they are facing across the table. They speak the language of peace, reconciliation, and goodwill to Westerners, and reserve their true thoughts and beliefs for fellow Muslims. In other words, they have learned to "work the system," admirably so.

In effect, these "moderate" Muslim leaders gradually extract one concession after another from Western policy-makers, rendering "dialogue" a one-way street. They enter each session with the full intention of testing the limits of the concessions they can extract, and it is a rare western government minister who would risk disappointing them— or else the headlines in the papers the following day would be sure to inflame the Muslim community. Herein lies the value of the worldwide Muslim penchant for overreacting to every perceived slight, real or imagined, by demonstrating their "rage" loudly and violently. Temperament comes into play here too (watch the shifting moods of Qaddafi as he was courted by the West and the concessions he got from it), for unlike other peoples who experience anger or humiliation, many Muslims are either unable or unwilling to contain those sentiments. One has only to recall the Arafat-orchestrated "days of rage" in the early stages of the *Intifadah* against Israel to understand that, in sharp contrast to Westerners, Muslims make a fetish of celebrating their anger. Such an uncontrolled behavior is unthinkable in the West, but not because of lack of provocation against it, particularly since September 11. Funerals too are manipulated to vent wrath and fury, emotion, general mayhem, and impromptu rifle-shooting. The total and shameless lack of dignity, even at what should be a somber occasion, is jarring to western eyes. Bodies are held aloft and bounced along the route, in a manner that would be regarded as disrespectful to the deceased in other cultures. Bodies have been known to fall off the stretcher amid the melee, and other processions turning chaotic as was recorded for posterity in the case of Iran's Ayatollah Khomeini's funeral. Iran's ambassador to Copenhagen, Ahmad Danialy, making his first public appearance in Denmark since being recalled by the Iranian Foreign Ministry in January 2006, following the Cartoon affair, addressed a public gathering and noted that the crisis had hurt the feelings of the Muslim world and caused a great deal of concern. "Now after the lapse of this period of unpleasant and bitter experience, I am very pleased to witness a beautiful and jovial gathering of the erudite and learned here in Copenhagen.... The conference is a step in the right direction for improving relations. The truth of the matter is that the world needs to direct new attention to one fundamental principle and that is: Respect for the sanctity of religions in all places and at all political, cultural and social levels...."[49]

And this happened when the Ambassador was aware that the damage, killing and destruction was caused by Muslim violent demonstrators worldwide, not by the cartoons, and of how his President speaks about eliminating Jews and Israel, how his clerics deprecate Christianity and other faiths, and how the Iranian regime supports the burning down of Jewish synagogues in the West Bank and in European cities. But if the purpose of the conference was not to elicit a mutual reconciliation but only "to introduce the Prophet (the Muslim one, not all the rest), the proper way," then why should we expect any care or concern, on the part of Muslims, for any faith except the Islamic one? The following conference in the United Arab Emirates, organized by the Tabah Foundation, brought sixty young people from Denmark and the Arab world together, under the banner of "The Search for Mutual Understanding," namely that the Danes should learn to respect Islam, never mind their own beliefs and culture. The delegates discussed a range of issues that the Cartoon crisis revealed as sore points between religious Muslims, and secular Western culture, such as freedom of expression and the role the media can play in hindering or facilitating global understanding. The four-day conference, held in Abu Dhabi, "exceeded the expectations of Jeppe Bruus Christensen," chairman of the Danish Youth Council, who naively and prematurely declared: "I

---

[49]Cited in R. Israeli, *The Islamic Challenge in Europe*, Transaction, N. J. 2008, p. 39.

don't think we should underestimate how important this is in the Arab world. It has gathered a great deal of attention." What he did not realize was that his statements were interpreted throughout the Arab world as a desperate attempt by Denmark to apologize for its "horrible" deed, and as a capitulation to Muslim demands. It did not earn Denmark any credit, but only scorn and contempt. Christensen felt that the two groups managed to "understand" each other and "accepted" mutual criticism, but he failed to comprehend that the Muslim goal was to assert its victory, not compromise, because its system cannot recognize that it can be at fault, unlike other (lesser) faiths. Thus, his feeling that the whole exercise "has been very constructive and positive", and that "we have been able to agree upon common values, such as having the right to criticize each other," would have been in vain had he read the Arab reports of the conference. Other participants from Denmark and the Middle East were more sober and realistic when they merely agreed that the conference "underscored the need for bridging the gaps that the conflict had revealed," and that "We have to accept that there are areas where we remain distant from each other." Moreover, to illustrate the depth of that gap, some Muslims continued to consider Denmark, which is one of the most open, tolerant, and hospitable countries of the world, to be "a racist and closed country."

Much closer to the reality was the evaluation by some Danish participants who heard their country being deprecated, albeit that it could be the model of tolerance for the entire Islamic world, when they said that "we have to acknowledge that that's the way it's going to be for some time." The conference also gave young Muslims the chance to meet their Danish counterparts and test the images presented by the media in their countries. "It's been very important for me to obtain the human aspect. To meet people and hear their opinion instead of seeing it in the media," said a nineteen-year-old Egyptian who admitted that preconceived notions, such as "the Danes hate us," were difficult to reject, but the conference's people-to-people approach helped. Another Arab youth, from Saudi Arabia, where Danish goods were initially boycotted, said that he was surprised in a positive way about the Danish young people, for "They were much more open and understanding about our culture than I had expected." But was he about theirs in the same way? He acknowledged that while dialogue and respect had been established at the conference, transferring the experience to his home country could prove difficult. He explained: "We'll be challenged when we come back to our countries, because some people have different attitudes. They use a different approach than dialogue, but we still need to work to spread the message that it is possible to live in this world together."[50] One wishes he were right.

The Danish Queen, Margrethe, more reflective than the British Royal House, stated that Islam poses a challenge both globally and locally, and the challenge should be taken seriously. In her published biography, based on interviews between the Queen and the book's author, journalist Annelise Bistrup, the Queen affirmed that

> There is something impressive about people, whose existence is immersed in religion from dawn to dusk, from the cradle to the grave..., but it is a challenge, which we need to take seriously. We have admittedly ignored it for too long. Because we are tolerant and a little lazy, I don't find it easy at all. Nor especially pleasant.[51]

Unlike other royals and politicians who make gratuitous declarations just to please their Muslim citizens or to placate their wrath, Queen Margrethe has studied Islam through her archaeological pursuits, and says that she does not feel entirely unprepared to enter the debate. "There is something fascinating about people who go to such lengths to surrender themselves to a religion. But there is also something

---

[50]Ibid

[51]Ibid, pp 41-2.

frightening about the all-encompassing side of Islam," she said, and then courageously added, "The challenge must be met, at the risk of getting some less flattering labels attached, for there are some things we should not meet with tolerance. When we are tolerant, we should be careful to note whether it stems from convenience or conviction." Queen Margrethe explained that her nation and the West stand at a crossroads, but it needs to be recognized that crossroads often only reveal themselves when they are crossed. She warned that "one doesn't always turn out to have taken the right road. But we have at least realized that we cannot let ourselves be shooed off by things that frighten us. We cannot compromise our notions of justice and legitimacy." Queen Margrethe pointed out that her interviews with her biographer Bistrup brought up forgotten memories that could be worthwhile for others, especially young people, to hear. She was most certainly referring to the seeming nonchalance with which the worriless young generation looked upon their multi-cultural states which were being subsumed by Islam.

Loyalty, Statecraft, Law, and Order

Part of the friction between the Muslim minorities in general, and the Muslim minority in Israel (20%) in particular, and their host societies, arises from the Muslim attitudes toward the state and the rule of law, and from the social and family ties and loyalties that they cultivate in their midst. On the most fundamental level, they experience a great difficulty in interacting with democratic state institutions that are remote and impersonal, sanctify the individual and the secular, and discount the religious and the affective links of the clans and the families. For them, custom and tradition, social conventions and a culture of shame, which are governed by personal relationships and the rule of the notables, take precedence over state law and cold un-negotiated rules of conduct imposed on them by the alien culture that surrounds them. Hence the very different Muslim notions of right and wrong, just and coercive, legitimate and unlawful, which make for the failed states their culture is accustomed to, and the ensuing clashes between them and their host societies.

While the democratic principle was posited by Giuselmo Ferrero as a prerequisite for legitimacy of rule, Muslim regimes cannot by definition subscribe to it, hence their difficulty to comprehend it and deal with it in the Democratic countries where they live or in their interaction with democratic countries. Indeed, Islamic regimes as well as Islamic movements, regard democracy western-style as inimical to the rules of the Islam. For them, *Shari'ah* Law is the best of systems. In classical Islam the acceptance of the ruler was performed through the *bai'a* (the oath of allegiance) in the public square, which was then ruthlessly translated into popular legitimacy, and any insurgence challenging it was deemed rebellion against the legitimacy of the ruler. But it was evident that the genuine legitimacy of the ruler (Caliph or Sultan) remained based on the capacity of the autocrat to enforce the *Shari'ah* Law and protect it. Today, Muslim rulers may use the terms of "democracy," "human rights," "elections" and such, but they profoundly misunderstand them. It is not that they understand and manipulate them, in line with Ferrero's typology of "fraudulent democracy" typical of fascist regimes, they only seem so to Western minds who cannot imagine that others fail to comprehend what is obvious to them. There is a link between legitimacy and succession. Mubarak or Qaddafi have "succeeded" themselves many times and they regard themselves as legitimate, though no rival would dare or be allowed to run against them. They cannot be opposed during an "election," genuinely believing that opposition and competition, the trademarks of Western democracy, are signs of division and controversy which are inimical to the rule of "unity." They sense that since they were overwhelmingly "chosen," unopposed, by 95 percent of the masses, that is their base of their legitimacy.

We speak in the West of the people as the sovereign and the source of legitimacy. Islam hails Allah as the only

sovereign of the universe and brands any attempt to impute sovereignty to humans as *shirk,* namely imparting divine qualities to anyone other than the Almighty. As this is
seen as blasphemy deserving of capital punishment, Muslim
radicals do not recognize most governments in the Islamic
world, and are particularly incensed by monarchs who dub
themselves "sovereign," for the only form of government
acceptable to them is the Caliphate where the Caliph was
the Vicar of the Prophet, not a sovereign in his own right.
In their view, Allah, the Sovereign, has already dispensed to
humanity the most perfect of legal codes—the Qur'an and
the *Shari'a,* and for any human to pretend that it can be ame-
liorated via parliamentary legislation, would also amount
to blasphemy. In the West consensus is the fruit of political bargaining based upon a give-and-take process between
political, ethnic, religious, linguistic, and cultural groups, or
lobbies of particular interests, which recognize the relativity
of the truth and the need to balance the various interests in
order to arrive at a social pact which governs the state and
social institutions, like the maintenance of law and order and
enforcement thereof. Muslims, however, especially the radicals among them, have enormous difficulties in compromising or striking deals of this sort because for them the Truth
is one and eternal, an either-or-affair, anchored in a demand
for everything now. Since most governments are regarded as
anti-Islamic, often violence is encouraged against them, be
they in Islamic countries proper, and much more so in Western countries and Israel, which do not recognize Islam yet as
part of their legitimate system.

This problematic Muslim view of Western democracies
as not totally legitimate due to their ignorance of the Divine Law decreed by Allah, is precisely what has prompted
many a Muslim leader in the West and in Israel to declare
that his purpose is to introduce *Shari'a* Law into the country's system. The capitulation of some governments, and judicial and clerical officials in this regard in some European
countries and in some Israeli circles, has caused Muslims

to further raise their voices against the existing western order and clamor for more Muslim legislation. Open statements by some of their spiritual leaders that they have come
to change the western world, not to submit to it, not only
make the existing order dispensable in their eyes, but they
endeavor by demonstrations, use of violence and acts of terror, to hasten its demise and substitute for it the *Pax Islamica*
of their dreams. Hence the frequent clashes between Muslim
communities in the world, Israel included, and the forces of
order, of which Jews are often the victims. The problem is
not only the illegitimacy in their eyes of non-Muslim government, but the tribal and family loyalties in Muslim society which make for their social atomization and for the shift
of their political loyalty from their country to their religion,
community, family, clan, tribe, people, persona of the tribal
or religious leader. That creates frictions with their host societies in their attempts to preserve their age-old customs and
ways of conduct, to the point that they threaten to make their
host countries ungovernable and arouse the non-Muslim local majorities against them. When those populations come
to realize that their democratic, free and open societies were
abused by the Muslim minorities, they might turn against
trhem, in self-defense and alter their status altogether.

The old Bedouin adage saying: "I am against my brother;
my brother and I are against our cousins; our family is
against the rest of the clan; I and my clan are against the rest
of world," which has been a societal constant of the Islamic
world, seems to have crossed the oceans and transplanted itself into Western society, Israel included. The states of which
Muslims have become citizens, do not provide the glue to
link their new citizenry to them, hence the constant unrest
among Muslim communities who have failed to become integral parts of their countries. So, instead of contributing to
the security, prosperity, creativity and welfare of their state,
they often become a security hazard and a societal burden
which is resented by the majority which shoulders the burden. The high percentage of crime among Muslim residents

in all western countries where they reside, way out of proportion to their rate in the population, especially the ideological crimes such as terrorism, undermining of the state institutions, reluctance to pay their taxes and dues, and focusing of sucking from the state their services without lifting a finger to its welfare, are more indicative of this turn of events than the petty crimes against property which can be attributed to economic disadvantage. It does not appear to them that acting in contravention to the public order, which is not theirs, and opposing, at times violently, their own country against its sworn enemies (Like the Hamas and the Hizbullah by Israeli Muslims), is in violation of any legal or moral rule. Their yardsticks of justice, order, right, fairness, and rightful conduct are the Muslim ones which are non-negotiable and absolute. For example, it would not occur to them that in any conflict involving Muslims and non-Muslims, the latter, including in their own country or residence, may also be right or entitled to defend themselves. If Britain battles against terrorism in Iraq and Afghanistan, or Israel in Lebanon or Gaza, they do not deserve the right of self-defense, thus counterattacks against them by their own Muslims, who are the natural allies of all other Muslims, are to be expected and justified.

Take, for instance, the troubling question of "honor killing" among Muslims in non-Muslim lands, or of forced marriage on under-age women, as an extension of the custom from Muslim lands. Muslims feel it is "their" women who are in question, therefore what right does the Western state have to interfere in their "private" affairs? These are some of the problems which will face Israel in the future, with regard to its Muslim minority, in view of the mounting arrogance and self-confidence of the Muslim minorities in the West, which learn one from the experience of the others. The problem is that while in other places in the West Muslims constitute between 2% (in the US) and 10% (in France) of the population, in Israel they already make up more than 20%.

Chapter 4

The International Disposition of the Muslim World.

The limited circle of the Arab world, which pits 300 million Arabs against Israel and determines the fortunes of war and peace in the Middle East, has been influenced, and increasingly so, by the growing impact of the wider Muslim circle, which encompasses some 1,5 billion Believers. While in the era of the conventional wars, Muslim countries supported the Arabs but were not directly involved in the Middle East conflict, the new reality of asymmetrical wars finds much more involvement of the Islamic world. Not only the Islamic bomb of Pakistan has been invoked as part of the Middle East equation, but also the Iranian nuclear and missile power, and occasional threats voiced against Israel in the Indian sub-continent or in South East Asia, and even a vocal alignment of Turkey with the Arabs and Hamas since the Islamic Party came to power there in 2002. One of the most blatant manifestations of this shift, which has widened the circle of the conflict at the same time that it rendered it amorphous, evasive and hard to pin down and deal with, has been the increasingly open and violent anti-semitic sentiment prevalent in the Islamic world. In view of the fact that anti-semitism has erupted publicly once again in Europe, *inter alia* under the impact of the immigrant Muslim population there[52], Muslims around the world do not feel inhibited any longer to advertise their own.

---

[52]See R. Israeli, *Muslim Anti-Semitism in Christian Europe*, Transaction, 2009.

Muslim International Relations

The mounting involvement in the Middle Eastern conflict of Muslim regimes, like Iran, and more so of Muslim
movements like al-Qa'ida, *Laskar-a-taiba,* Hizbullah and
Hamas, Islamic Jihad and others, which have elaborated an
anti-western ideology and a religious rationalization for the
upheaval they are causing, has added an international dimension to this already difficult dispute. For if previously
conventional wars required the direct, but limited and well-
defined, playing of regular armies, like the expeditionary
forces of Iraq in 1948 and 1973, or of Moroccan troops in
1973; the era of asymmetrical wars involves irregular forces,
informally recruited, and stealthily hauled to the frontlines,
or otherwise illicitly operating in any arena of their choice
worldwide, like al-Qa'ida against Israeli interests in Europe,
Africa or Asia; or the Hizbullah against Israeli embassies in
Latin America, or *Laskar-a-taiba* against Israeli presence in
India or in Kashmir. For this reason, the global Jihadi movement and its ramified activity, will be a growing concern to
Israel as it faces the world Islamic resentment against it. Let
us explore some facets of that danger and the discourse they
use to express it.

The Islamic world has been a world apart in terms of modern western thought: democracy is not a system they aspire
to, because it runs counter to the more of less authoritarian
regimes they are accustomed to; when they demand justice,
they mean Islamic justice which is not exactly ours; tolerance to them is not unconditional acceptance of the other
as is; terrorism is what others do to Islam, not the other way
round; pluralism is altogether unheard of; ending a conflict
can only be done via victory, not a compromise; sovereignty
belongs to Allah, not to the people; legislation is not the pre-
rogative of humans but of the Divine Will, of which they are
the latest and most updated representatives and interpreters;
western values amount to corruption and blasphemy; logic
and reason must follow the Muslim ways of thinking; they

expect and demand respect for Islam but easily dispense of respect to other faiths; they regard their own shouting and abuse as a show of force, and their foes' dignified quiet and restraint as evidence of weakness; everybody owes them everything, but they owe no one anything; they view their attacks on others as lawful and legitimate, but any act of self-defense by non-Muslims is nothing but aggression. These ideas have again gained the upper hand in the public square of most Islamic countries, because most existing regimes are illegitimate, and Islam seems as the only viable alternative that is able and willing to contend for predominance and power.

Almost since its inception, Islam has recognized the division of humanity into three categories: the Muslims, the People of the Book (initially Jews and Christians and then extended to include others) and the pagans who knew no God. The lands of the globe were similarly divided into two domains: *Dar-al-Islam* (the Abode of Islam), and *Dar-al-Harb*, (the Abode of war) While, for practical purposes these categories are no longer operative because they would otherwise throw international relations into chaos, in the circles of Muslim radicals, both those in power and those in opposition to the rulers in place, this terminology has been revived and widely used to analyze internal and external affairs in accordance with the requisites of the *Shari'a*, namely the Holy Law of Islam. But one has to realize that the religion of the radicals is one and the same as classical Islam, and its vocabulary and symbolism are identical. Therefore, when their statements or deeds are apologetically condemned by other Muslims as "non-Islamic", this is merely a blanket statement calculated to skirt the embarrassment caused by the excesses of their coreligionists. Since *Shari'a* submits to eternal and Divine laws, it cannot be abrogated or amended at the whim of anyone. It is either applied more or less strictly, as do the radicals, or it is, partly or wholly, ignored by many Muslims who have elected modernity over medieval outdated concepts and practices. The difference is then only in the degree of enforcement, for they are all aware and caring about the tenets of their faith, but may be lax about the implementation of some of them, even as they insist on their Muslim identity and commitment. The radicals just display their burning passion for full implementation, here and now and at almost any cost.[53]

Yussuf al-Qaradawi, a Muslim radical sheikh in exile from his native Egypt and now living in Qatar, regularly appears on *al-Jazeera* network to expound his ideas and deliver *fatwas* (new decrees which for his followers become law). He is also the President of the European Fatwa Council, namely the recognized authority of all European Muslims, to ponder on their problems, religious or otherwise, and deliver verdicts that are seen by many as authoritative and enforceable. In one of his pronouncements, he recommended to his followers to "continue to battle the Jews. They will try to defend themselves, but you will get them ultimately. For the Jews will hide behind trees and rocks, which will announce out loud: 'a Jew is hiding behind me, come and kill him'. This will be the prerequisite for the coming of the Day of Resurrection"[54.] This commandment is an oft-repeated tradition of the Prophet (a *hadith)*, recurring *ad nauseam* in Islamic writings and cited in full in the Charter of the Hamas. But hardly anyone wonders how it is that the followers of the Prophet, who feel insulted every step of the way for whatever is said of him or against him, and are even ready to indulge in violence in retribution to any insult of his honor, are not incensed by this *hadith's* appeal to wanton and indiscriminate murder of the followers of another faith, by those who claim to represent a "religion of peace and tolerance". Sheikh Qaradawi has made some stunning statements not only about politics but also about social issues that hardly qualify him or his followers as moderate. He said, for example, that [John] Kerry who ran against Bush in the 2004 elections, was supported by homosexuals and

---

[53]See for details, R. Israeli, *Islamikaze etc...*, especially Chap. 2, pp. 33-70.

[54]*Le Point*, 1727, 20 October, 2005, p. 37

nudists. But it was Bush who won, because he is Christian, right wing, tenacious and unyielding. In other words, the religious overcame the pervert. So we cannot blame all Americans and westerners.

> But unfortunately, because the westerners... want to flatter these people on account of the elections, disaster strikes. In order to succeed and win the elections, he flatters these people, rather than saying to them:" No you are sinning against yourselves, against society, and against humanity. This is forbidden. ... Lesbians and homosexuals should be punished the same punishment as any sexual pervert, the same as any fornicator. The schools of thought disagree about the punishment. Some say they should be punished like fornicators, and then we distinguish between married and unmarried men, and between married and unmarried women. Some say both should be punished the same way. Some say we should throw them from a high place, like God did to the people of Sodom. Some say we should burn them, and so on,. There is disagreement. The important thing is to treat this act as a crime... Lesbianism is not as bad as homosexuality, in practical terms.[55]

If these are the envisaged punishments to be meted out to Muslim sinners, how much more so for Unbelievers who were deemed as sinning towards Muslims! One of the most respected Deobandi scholars believes that aggressive military Jihad should be waged by Muslims "to establish the supremacy of Islam" worldwide. Justice Muhammed Taqi Usmani argues that Muslims should live peacefully in countries such as Britain, where they have the freedom to practice Islam, only until they gain enough power to engage in battle. His views explode the myth that the creed of offensive, expansionist Jihad represents a distortion of traditional Islamic thinking. Usmani sat for 20 years as a *shari'a* judge

---

[55]Interviews with Sheikh Qaradawi, :"Homosexuals Should be Punished like Fornicators, but their Harm is less when not done in Public", *Al-Jazseera*, 5 June, 2005. Taped on video by Memri 1170, 5 June, 2006.

in Pakistan's Supreme Court, and has been an adviser to several global financial institutions. Polite and soft spoken, he revealed to *The Times* a detailed knowledge of world events and his words, for the most part, were balanced and considered. He agreed that it was wrong to suggest that the entire non-Muslim world was intent on destroying Islam. Yet, this is a man who, in his published work, argues the case for Muslims to wage an expansionist war against non-Muslim lands. Usmani's justification for aggressive military Jihad as a means of establishing global Muslim supremacy is the climax of his book, *Islam and Modernism*. The work is a polemic against Islamic modernists who seek to convert the entire Qur'an into "a poetic and metaphorical book", because, says he, "they have been bewitched by western culture and ideology". The final chapter delivers a rebuke to those who believe that only defensive Jihad is permissible in Islam. He refutes the suggestion that Jihad is unlawful against a non-Muslim state that freely permits the preaching of Islam. For Usmani, the question is whether aggressive battle is by itself commendable or not. If it is, he contends, then "why should the Muslims stop simply because territorial expansion is considered there days as bad? And if it is not commendable, but deplorable, why did Islam not stop it in the past". He answers his own question thus: "Even in these days, aggressive Jihads were waged... because they were truly commendable to establish the grandeur of the religion of Allah". These words are not the product of a radical fanatic, they come from the pen of one of the most acclaimed modern scholars of Islam.[56]

There is no prospect of resisting and surviving this wave of renewed Muslim proclivity for confrontation and triumphalism unless one defines facts and events unequivocally and sets one's mind on facing them without recoiling. No other groups of people, no adherents of any other faith have so relentlessly vowed to destroy western culture in general, and

---

[56]Andrew Norfolk, "Our Followers must live in Peace until Strong enough to wage Jihad", The Times, 8 September, 2007.

Israel in particular, as modern Muslims have. The repeated pledges of Iran's Ahmadinejad, who has nothing to do with the Arab-Israeli conflict, to "wipe Israel off the map" for purely Islamic reasons, have perhaps blunted the sensitivity of world peace and human rights champions, who beyond the ritual statement that this is "unacceptable", have done nothing to oust the culprit from the international community of civilized nations or to discontinue their business with him. There are plenty of poor and frustrated people in the *favelas* of South America, the shack cities of Asia and the jungles of Africa. But in none of them is this unstoppable desire to kill westerners and Jews as evident and manifest as in the case of Muslims and their Islamikaze vanguards. Western countries have tried in vain to skirt the issue of Islamic terrorism in the hope that it might disappear. But it did not. Only a clear western definition of what constitutes terrorism, which has to be announced, not negotiated, can indicate the decision of civilized nations to stand fast against this aggressive mood which nurtures Jihad. In Muslim eyes, terrorism is what is done to them, like the US in Iraq, NATO in Afghanistan, Israel in Palestine and Lebanon, and India in Kashmir. What Muslims do is only self-defense, therefore they can never be accused of terrorism, meaning that any violent act committed by Muslims is justified by definition, because they are oppressed, humiliated and frustrated by the western rivals. While the west pursues the means-oriented criterion to define terrorism, namely that regardless of the goals or motives of terrorists, noble as they may be to them, innocent civilians cannot be harmed intentionally and indiscriminately, Muslim countries systematically reject this concept. For them, in the "struggle against tyranny and injustice", all means are acceptable and none of them is deemed illicit. For the citizens of western countries and Israel, who share the "unjust and tyrannical" regimes of their countries, cannot be deemed "innocent", and are in their thinking "permissible".

For many Muslims there is even a Qur'anic justification for terrorism (*irhab*) against Unbelievers, since the Holy text prescribes to Muslims to sow *irhab* in the hearts of the enemy. And since the enemy is identified as Israel or the west in general, that in itself provides a doctrinal rationalization of terrorism. Iran, Pakistan, Syria, the Palestinian Authority and others continue to give shelter to terrorists, but they are rather proud of doing that, and no longer embarrassed. For the Iranians, al-Qa'ida, the Hizbullah, the Hamas and such, encouraging terrorism is simply a practical manifestation of their doctrinal convictions and commitments. One should not be fooled by this double talk which reflects the Muslim state of mind. Even when they dispatch or *post-factum* approve of, acts of obvious terrorism which they call "martyrdom", i.e. praiseworthy and religiously sanctioned deeds (like Islamikaze), for the sake of Allah, that cannot be, by definition called "terrorism", which is a down-graded and damnable mode of action in the West. That is the reason why whenever a major terrorist attack by Muslims is perpetrated against the west or Israel, there is jubilation in the Muslim street, regardless of the numbers of innocent civilian victims. That is also the reason that UN attempts to come to a unified definition of terror in order to optimize the world battle against it has fallen on death ears, as long as all Muslim coun-tries insist that "resistance" against "occupiers" is not terrorism, and when they admit it is, then it is of the worthy martyrdom kind. Muslims reserve to themselves the right to define who is an occupier, be it Israel in Palestine, India in Kashmir, Russia in Chechnya, the US in Iraq, NATO in Afghanistan. In a Mus-lim conference in Stockholm, Qaradawi made his differentia-tions, specifying that Islamikaze attacks (what we erroneously call "suicide bombings, and consider the epitome of terrorism) are not only permitted in Islamic law, but condoned and rec-ommended. His main arguments were summed up in a major Arabic medium published in London[57]

In view of their understanding of the present state of af-fairs, Muslim militants have drawn several lessons and they

---

[57]*Al-Sharq al-Awsat*, 19 July, 2003. These passages are translated and summa-rized in R. Israeli, *Muslim Minorities, in the Modern States*, Transaction, N.J., 2009, pp. 101-103.

prepared a blueprint for the confrontation with the west, which in its gradually emerging details is proving quite popular with the masses of Muslims in general, who are in no mood of compromise and accommodation. The sense that Allah has been blessing their venture is so deeply rooted in their hearts that they fear no fatigue, and they do not recoil from implementing their plan even if, or precisely because, there seem to be obstacles and difficulties on the way to realization. For Allah had tested in the past many of his followers and he ultimately ensured their victory, as one of his many names (*al-Nasser* - the Victorious) connotes. Victory is sought and nothing less. The Muslims who wish to confront the West and Israel are equipped with the requisite faith, zeal and enthusiasm, as the acronym of *Hamas* (the Islamic Resistance Movement) indicates; they are boundlessly devoted to Allah, as their various Hizbullah (Party of God) groups profess; are determined to pursue their *da'wa* (Mission, Call) the world over, as many of their organizations mention; are intent to wage a merciless Jihad if their "peaceful" messages demanding surrender are not heeded by their enemies, as many of their associations ("Islamic Jihad") remind us; and lastly, many of of them are coordinated by the main base (*al-Qa'ida*),physical and spiritual, which used to train candidates for Islamikaze, finance their operations, plan their schemes and initiate the time and place of their spectacular strikes. Admittedly, after the temporary defeat of the Taliban in Afghanistan, al-Qa'ida is no longer what it was, and its activities have been largely decentralized, but the flame was not extinguished as evidenced by the spectacular comeback of the Mujahideen in the fields of Qandahar, Helmand and Jalalabad.

The main components of the Muslim blueprint can be summarized as follows:

1. The west must be defeated, or at least weakened, frightened and put on the defensive. For not only does the West corrupt the Muslim world with its debauchery, permissiveness,

alliance with certain Muslim countries and its value-less societies, but by its posing a luring alternative to young Muslims, with its immodest dress, co-ed education, pop music,
pornography, mixed partying and frolicking, alcohol, and
western movies, it threatens the next generation of Muslims.
Naturally, militant Muslims, with the acquiescent silent support of conservatives, dread the prospect of their societies
slipping from under their grip and supervision. Therefore
they enlist for their endeavor any Allah-fearing Muslim, who
though not necessarily of their affiliation, is concerned, like
them, about the rapid drift of the young towards modernity
and the West. This matter is particularly acute in the Palestinian territories, where their daily frictions with the Israelis
make them more prone to such a deviation from traditional
Muslim norms.

2. A first step towards the goal of defeating the west is to
cultivate the rift between pro-Arab, pro-Muslim Europe, on
the one hand, and "Zionist-controlled America" on the other.
Thus, while both belong to the evil west, it is imperative to
go easy on Europe for now, due to its assistance, both directly
to the Muslim world, and indirectly by diminishing America's power and somehow keeping it in check. This policy has
proven a success for the time being, inasmuch as the European Council has been openly favoring the Palestinians over
the Israelis despite American misgivings, while the Muslims
have succeeded in enlisting the Europeans to their side in the
Balkans (in Bosnia, Kosovo, Macedonia). The Muslims have
even managed to engage the US in implementing jointly
with NATO those European-Muslim designs. The change of
government in the US, with the seemingly more engaging
policy of Obama on the one hand, and the schism within the
Palestinian people between the western-supported PLO and
Muslim-supported Hamas, seem to dictate new adaptations
of this policy orientation.

3. Europe's turn will come after America is driven out
of its hegemonic status in the world and Israel is eliminated. Muslim radicals speak about their own *reconquista* in

Europe, first of the territories that used to be under Muslim rule (Andalusia, southern France, Sicily) and then the rest of the continent. A special awareness of this turn of events has been evident among North African immigrants into Europe who are conscious of the historical reversal that has been under way. Indications of such a scheme dawned on the Europeans on the morrow of September 11, after which several major Islamic terrorist strikes were foiled in Paris, Strasbourg and Brussels. Al-Qa'ida bases and undercover lodges exist in practically all European capitals and can be activated when time comes, as has been the case with the many terrorist attacks in Spain, England and Germany since. Part and parcel of preparing for the showdown in Europe has been both testing the ground for the eventual Muslim takeover, first of the vestiges of Spanish colonial rule (Ceuta and Melilla) and some islands in the Mediterranean, and increasing the numbers of Muslim migrants to Europe. The upward of 30 million Muslims in Europe of the 27 today, who constitute between 5 and 10% of the population in virtually all European countries, hasten to take up political rights individually, and then will begin to demand cultural and group rights. Only the reversal, of late, of the liberal multi-cultural policies in countries like Holland and England, may begin to check that trend.

4. And above all the US, which by its military and economic power not only dominates the west and leads it but also attempts to battle Islam into submission (at least until Obama's advent to power), protects Israel and serves its purposes, and produces and disseminates the decadent sub-culture which arouses the wrath of Islam. The US is deemed to be the first model of emulation for youth all over the world, including Muslims, and this circumstance is purported to be the reason for all the ills of the world. If America cannot be reduced to submission, then at least it can be battered, threatened, humiliated and weakened, to the extend that it would no longer be able to protect its citizens and its interests around the world. The rationale and purpose behind this

outlook is so that its many allies, primarily Europe, Israel and the illegitimate Muslim regimes it sustains, would no longer trust the UN and rely on it. America is also singled out by the militants for being the only power that can, and is willing, to block effectively the fulfillment of their schemes. Hence the hatred of America, first and foremost, which is decried by the slogans and the propaganda statements of the militants, and also by the massive acts of terror committed against it.

5. Pending the anticipated Muslim victory, much long term groundwork is required, which the Muslim radicals wholeheartedly support and initiate, and even push Muslim governments and Muslim individuals to fund. The list is long : recruiting new converts in the West, lending financial support to families of martyred Islamikaze, raising money, either through bogus charitable organizations in the West, to be used against it, or from donor states or individuals (Saudi Arabia and wealthy sheikhs in the Gulf), erecting mosques and Islamic centers and *madrasas* in world capitals and significant concentrations of Muslims worldwide, ostensibly for Muslim populations in the west, but diverting their use to conversion programs, indoctrination, and the diffusion of hatred and propaganda, and recruitment of Islamikaze for martyrdom operations. They also use the funds to strengthen already Muslim countries of the periphery, like Central Asia, Indonesia, and raising Muslim consciousness among the Muslim minorities of Nepal, Thailand, India, Israel, Europe and America. IT is the fruit of such endeavors which supports the Taliban in the *madrasas* of Pakistan, the Shi'ite fanatics in the religious schools of Qum in Iran, the Hizbullah in the Lebanese fields of opium, the Islamikaze terrorists in Afghanistan, and the mosques of Europe and America, from whence emerged the planners and executors of September 11.

6. Jews, and by inference Israel and Zionism, have to be eliminated, as Bin-Laden, Iran, Hamas and Hizbullah have vowed. They are accused of having invaded the lands of Is-

lam in Palestine, established the Zionist state, which in effect tore off a valuable piece of *dar-al-Islam* and turned it into *dar- al Harb,* which requires Jihad for retrieval. The Jews constitute a western salient in the midst of Islamic society which they intend to corrupt and undermine from within. The Jews stand accused of desecrating the holy places of Islam in Jerusalem with a view to insulting Muslims. And, most dangerous of all, they act as the American agent in the Middle East, hence their close links to Washington, to the extent that makes it hard to determine who is subservient to whom. For all these reasons, Jews are targets not only in their Israeli state, but worldwide, as the frequent attacks against them, throughout their world diasporas, have demonstrated.

Andre Malraux, the great French luminary of the first half of the 20th Century, saw before most others the coming of the aggressive wave of Islam in the contemporary world. It is worthwhile citing his immortal words:

> The violence of the Muslim rise is the great phenomenon of our era. Underestimated by most of our contemporaries, it can be compared to the beginnings of Communism under Lenin, and the full extent of its impact is still impossible to predict. At the beginning of the Marxist Revolution, the belief was prevalent that problems could be patched up by improvised solutions. But neither Christianity nor organizations of employers or employees could find the answers. Similarly, the world does not seem today able to face the problem of Islam, which seems to be even more difficult to confront. Maybe the limited French aspect thereof could be tackled if there were a real statesman around to deal with it. The impression is that various forms of Muslim dictatorship will prevail in the Arab world. When I say "Muslim" I do not think necessarily of religious, but of civil structures emanating from Mohammed's doctrine. Already now, the Moroccan Sultan, as well as President Bourguiba [of Tunisia], are acting as dictators of sorts. It may be that current problems could have been patched up if they had been under-

taken in time... But it is already too late. "*Les miserables*" have nothing to lose any more, they will prefer to preserve their misery within their Muslim communities, and their lot will probably remain unchanged. We regard them from a western angle, but they will probably prefer their own future to the welfare that we pretend we are able to bring them. Black Africa will not stay for long indifferent to this process, and all we can do is to become cognizant of the gravity of this phenomenon and try to postpone its breaking point[58]

Muslim Pathological Anti-Semitism and anti-Zionism

Perhaps since Nazi Germany no amount of vitriol was poured on the Jews as such, not only Israelis and Zionists, as has been the case in the past few years by Arabs and Muslims, beyond what emanates from Islamic sources. We have heard nauseating repetitions of anti-Semitic attacks in the high echelons of Arab politics, not only in intractable Iran and Syria and their underlings, but even in the Egyptian mainstream press, which shamelessly recounts its lies and fabrications as "history," and avidly "quotes" from the *Protocols of the Elders of Zion* that never were, and retells with a sadistic delight that can only match its joy at the carnage in the Twin Towers, the Blood Libels of which Jews have been accused. This, of course, reflects the vitriolic attitudes towards Israel and Zionism, because if the Jews are evil, then by nature their state and their movement of national liberation can only be equally evil. Not one voice is there to stand up to the calumniators and intercede for ceasing that orgy of hatred, even in Egypt decades after its "peace" with Israel. All one has to do is to rummage through the hundreds of hate sites that are fed by Muslims and Arabs across the world, to realize the width and depth of anti-Semitic sentiment in the Muslim world, which has so poisoned Muslim minds in recent decades, that it is doubtful whether "peace" treaties are able to overcome it. The present Arab Spring only aggravated the situation.

---

[58]Malraux, 3 June, 1956, cited in *Valeurs Actuelles*, Paris, December 2001.

There has also never been any society since the Nazis which so cultivated and boasted of its hatred towards the Jews, as Muslim society today. Its preachers denigrate and humiliate them, incite against them, justify massacres against them, and associate them with America and the evil West. Reasons for this contemporary outburst of hatred, which has been manifest also throughout the democratic West where Jewish and Muslim communities live side by side, emanate perhaps from the reality in which Jews represent the successful middle-class that has made the West prosperous. For the Muslims it is painful to admit that Jews succeeded where they have failed, and the jealousy in this regard cannot be contained or suppressed. The same jealousy at Israel's success, as a neighboring society and a state, compared with their continued state of backwardness, feeds their intense hatred and generates stereotypes and pipedreams of destroying it. They compensate themselves by their prophecies about the "cowardly" Jews who in the end of days will run away and hide from the Muslims who will seek their destruction. There is no need, as some counsel, for Israel (and the West for that matter) to go into any soul-searching and to dig up the "reasons" (there must be reasons, right?) for this hatred, anymore than there was one when the Jews were made the scapegoats of the Nazis, and were murdered for what they were, with the burden of the "guilt" accruing to them. If anything needs to be investigated, it is the sick minds of the anti-Semites, today and of old. But for a book which purports to deal with security and strategic dilemmas, this does not seem to be the moment, beyond the enumeration of some traits of character of the Muslims, which make them so prone to accuse others in general.

If the Muslims and Arabs are indeed so fond of Hitler and of citing him, and they miss no opportunity to analyze "scientifically" the "reasons" for his victimization of the Jews, and they expectedly find the Jews themselves guilty, then words like "reason" and "cause" have been depleted of their meanings, and one is dragged to the realm of the incomprehensible and the irrational. But then, side by side with that, the Holocaust that the Jews were accused of having brought upon themselves, is vehemently, and again "scientifically," denied, and the Jews are relegated to the role of the Nazis themselves in their dealings with the Palestinians. Such a web of lies, presumptions, pretenses, denials and contradictions, only the modern Arab and Muslim mind could create. In any case, the delegitimation of the Jews, of Israel their state, and Zionism—their movement of national liberation, is so thorough, total, and irreversible, as to turn them into the target of the coming Islamikaze massacres, a fate which they deserve a-priori. By turning their hatred of Jews into a pathological phenomenon, as inseparable from their own being, they immunize themselves against any human compassion. Otherwise, it is hard to understand how crowds would jump from joy in Palestinian and Egyptian streets, at the sight of Jewish children blown to pieces, or entire families wiped out in one stroke of madness. They have turned so obtuse and cruel when Jewish victims are concerned, that it is necessary to remind them, from time to time, that they are evil to pursue civilians and murder them in streets, restaurants, and buses; even more evil are those who rejoice with them, and they must be excluded from the human race. If they call their massacres "Jihad", and their murderers "martyrs", that does not mitigate their crime; on the contrary, it discredits the faith that motivates them and the God in whose name they act. But the Muslim radicals' judgment is blunted by hatred, to the point that they can no longer differentiate between good an evil, human or inhuman.

Radical Muslims profess the evil of indiscriminate killing, which is dictated by their blind hatred, even if they should themselves be consummated by its fire in the process. They have no use for facts (for example the Holocaust), nor respect to values (the mass-murders they commit without a hitch), nor concern for the victims. Because only they, the fighters of Jihad, who are awaited in Paradise, count, and anyone in their way should be eliminated. They turn their own plight onto the Jews and accuse them of their own backwardness, oppression, and poverty; and they impute to Zionism the "oppression of freedom" of which they themselves suffer. Only a twisted mind beyond repair can accuse the Jews of the Twin Tower massacre, which they begin to believe themselves, and spread that lie as a fact, around the world. On Thursday night, the 6th of March, 2008, a lone Muslim gunman from East Jerusalem, who was employed by Israel and enjoyed the services offered by its city government, surreptitiously made his way into a *yeshiva* (Jewish religious school) in the heart of the Jewish neighborhood, and opened gun fire on unsuspecting teenage students who were rehearsing the end of the month portion of the *Torah* and *Talmud* that they were routinely studying and debating. Eight of them lost their lives, many others were wounded more or less seriously, until a passing-by reserve soldier, who had incidentally graduated from the same institution a few years earlier, was alerted by the shooting, rushed to the reading hall of the library where the carnage was unfolding and put an end to the massacre. That rampage was not the initiative of a lunatic and lone hatred-filled man, or the idea of a hallucinating misguided fanatic, exactly as the perpetrators of September 11 (2001) in New York and July 7 (2005) in London, even if locally grown, were the satanic messengers of worldwide Muslim organizations bent on murder and destruction.

The next day, the well-to-do family of the killed murderer erected a huge tent at the entrance to their house, to accommodate the Muslim well-wishers who began streaming by the hundreds to greet the bereaved family, not to present condolences, for his feat of hitting their enemy at its heart, thereby attaining the hallowed status of *shahid* (martyr). To boot, the mourners hoisted the flags of Hizbullah and Hamas on the tent, all under the open eye of the Israeli forces of order and the liberal attitude of "non-interference with the lives" of the Arab Muslims in Israel's capital city. Soon the Hamas took "credit" for that senseless massacre, driving any sensible human being to wonder why a young man of twenty-one, about to wed a wife within three months, would take that harrowing step and destroy his own life and his future. It could not be economic want, personal despair, momentary madness or a family rift. It was simply hatred, inspired by the relentless Muslim "education" to despise the "unbelievers," demonize them, and dehumanize them to the point of making their lives cheap and unworthy of respect. It was more important to harm them than to bring relief to himself. But it must be more than that, for that horrific act, like the many other acts of terror and killings that we witness in the Muslim world, or emanate from it, day in day out, does not explain in full the intensity, the unbearable ease and the persistence of these unending and revolting manifestations of contempt and abuse of human life. Two weeks later, another Arab from East Jerusalem, who was employed by an Israeli contractor in the west part of the city, seized a bulldozer on his site and went into a rampage in the city shoving people and cars, including a bus full of horrified passengers, until he was gunned down by passers-by and police. Within two more weeks, that same horrible act was repeated in another street of Jerusalem, by another young Arab of East Jerusalem, also using the same tool of shoving people and cars with the bulldozer he was supposed to operate on his construction site.

He too was gunned down by armed citizens and police. This begs the question: why should such a succession of murders of innocent civilians be pursued by young men who were employed and living quite comfortably in the outskirts of the city and were holding Israeli identity cards, which they had sought for their own wellbeing in the first place? Why would they take the risk of depriving their fellow Arabs from such jobs that no Israeli would trust them to hold in the future? What other explanation is there of this successive orgy of murders than hatred of Jews? Maybe the answer lies in the theory voiced by French philosopher Jean-Claude Milner that today's anti-Semitism does not originate from old people, but from youth, and thus it is not likely to disappear but rather to become stronger, therefore it is the anti-Semitism of the future.[59] Judging from the widespread indoctrination in the media and textbooks for the young of the Arab world, such indoctrination is more likely to be perpetuated there in the future than among the youth of Europe that Milner was talking about. More often than not we are now talking about he same youth who are indoctrinated by the same people who draw from the same sources. In these outbursts of anti-Semitism by Muslim youth there is also an element of contempt and abuse of other faiths, as when in the first case cited above that same Muslim murderer indiscriminately shot and ripped to pieces *Torah* and *Talmud* books, which the students were consulting, and which they left stained with their blood when they fell to the bullets of the assassin. And save for a few human and courageous voices of reason in Kuwait, the mood in the Arab/ Muslim world was not one of consternation, sorrow, shame or embarrassment, but when it was manifested at all, as in Gaza and among other Muslim circles, it was one of jubilation at the sight of the "feat" that their great "hero" had "achieved" in that religious school at the heart of the enemy.

It was as if a Jew, or a Christian, burst into a *madrasa* at the heart of the Muslim world and massacred students bent on their study. Can anyone in a civilized country imagine any sign of jubilation at that carnage? The rest of the Muslim world was busy with its own domestic massacres where people in countless thousands are eliminated on a daily basis in Afghanistan, Pakistan, Sudan, Iraq, and many other unreported places where human lives do not count. Expectedly, when the killings, intentional or incidental, are committed by non-Muslims, as in Iraq or Israel, they are invariably dubbed

---

[59]Claude Meyer, "Interview with Jean-Claude Milner", the author of *The Criminal Inclinations of Democratic Europe, in Actialites Juives Hebdo*, No 823, No 823, 11 December, 2003. Cited by Manfred Gerstenfeld, "Antisemitism: Integral to European Culture", in *Post Holocaust and Antisemitism*, No 19, 1 April, 2004, p. 4, published by the Jerusalem Center of Public Affairs.

as "aggression" or "murder" against Muslims, which in every case reaches the scope of a "massacre" or a "holocaust." But the many more Muslims who are slaughtered by other Muslims and whose deaths cannot be directly blamed on the West, are simply disregarded and discounted and no grief seems to accompany them or any account taken of them. So, the real massacres by car-bombs and by Islamikaze assassins, of Afghani Muslims by other Muslims, Iraqi Sunnites against Shi'ites, Iranian Shi'ites against Sunnites, or Pakistani Taliban against their own kin, or Hamas adepts in Gaza against their Palestinian brethren from the PLO, go unnoticed and unreported. What imports for Muslim propaganda is not how many Muslims are killed, but who kills them, regardless of the reason or the justification for it.

Anti-Semitism is an irrational phenomenon, which has defied definition, let alone explanation or justification in the past two millennia. Yet, the entire field of study of anti-Semitism has attempted for generations to analyze it by rational tools. For example, if we say that murdering Jews is the result of anti-Semitic contempt and hatred, then how to explain the massive physical elimination of other Muslims by their coreligionists: black Muslims by Sudanese-supported Muslim *Janjaweed* in Darfur, or the widespread cases of mass killings in the Arab and Muslim world, like Libya, Iraq, Syria, Lebanon, the Palestinian Authority, the Yemen, Algeria, Pakistan, Afghanistan, and all the rest? The inescapable conclusion is that the trigger-happy Muslims who are propped by Jihad, external or internal, and their innate disregard for human life, renders execution, capital punishment, beheading, hanging, mass murder, mutilation, and torture an acceptable norm of conduct. Implementing *Shari'a* rules in domestic penal law is in itself the best indication of the low value of human life in their eyes. When this worldview is practiced against Jews, it is rationalized as anti-Semitism; against other westerners, as "vengeance," "self-defense," reaction to western "arrogance," "humiliation," or "desecration" of Muslim values; and against others -by any amount of other trumped up justifications. Underlying all those instances is the burning desire by Muslims to impose by force their ideals and rules of conduct, both on their own nationals when they are viewed as apostates, thus deserving death, and certainly on their rivals and enemies, who are often considered as enemies of Islam and Allah, and therefore are equally deserving of annihilation. No debate, negotiation, compromise, or argument is possible with this "will of Allah," and therefore no perceived offense or deviation from these rules is tolerable or forgivable.

It is often claimed that this strict interpretation of Islam with its abuses, including anti-Semitism, is only the lot of "fanatic," "radical," "fundamentalist" Muslims, usually quantified as some 15 percent of the 1.5 billion world Muslims, as if that were a different faith embracing different principles than those followed by the rank-and-file Muslims. In fact, we are talking about the same one creed, which upholds *Shari'a* law to various degrees, but those who do not follow it to the letter, as in any other religion, are not adepts of an alternative "moderate Islam," the one that is sometimes dubbed "religion of peace," to distinguish from the faith of aggressive "extremists." The truth of the matter is that no such separate Islam exists, though there are certainly many truly moderate Muslims, who have broken away from the bloody road of Islamic *Shari'a,* especially when they conveniently moved to the West, and could from a safe distance criticize the killings in their original countries of those dubbed there "apostates," or "traitors," or attack the phenomenon of the Islamikaze bombers against Westerners and Israelis, or the culture of death that is cultivated in many Islamic lands, or indeed the unbridled anti-Semitic calumnies that are rife in their own culture. But they have yet to produce an alternative doctrine and worldview that could rival official Islam and posit a creed and a set of rules which can attract Muslims to relinquish the *Shari'a* and embrace another way. If they did, they would no longer be Muslims in the eyes of established Islam. Moderate Muslims often accuse the radicals, who are in fact the common Muslims who behave in accordance with the accepted rules championed by the *Shari'a,* of having "hijacked" Islam or "distorted" its "real" meaning, or misinterpreted it, and they in turn are condemned for having abandoned the path of Allah and having been corrupted by western ideologies. But it is the standards of the former that prevail in the Islamic world.

One can simply watch the mass demonstrations in the streets of Gaza, Quetta, Casablanca, Durban and Jakarta, or in the Muslim neighborhoods in Paris, London, Marseille, Amsterdam, Sydney, and Toronto and realize how much alive, universal and popular are the Muslim slogans and rampages which are performed daily against Jews by Muslim masses of men, women, children of all walks of life, and including their lay leaders and clerics, of all ages. Are they all "radicals"? No, they are simply Muslims, and the common denominator which links them together in their hatred of the West and the Jews is Islam, standard Islam, under the justification of the *Shari'a,* which is promoted by their Imams. While some moderate and courageous Muslim individuals will fortunately always be there to save the honor of Islam when they raise their lone voices against the abuses perpetrated in the name of their faith, the mainstream in the world of Islam, including westernized and modern professionals and intellectuals, will always be there to glorify in mirth the killings of westerners and Jews, to write or broadcast in exhilaration in favor of the Islamikaze, and distribute in jubilation sweets in the streets to "celebrate" the death of Americans or Israelis. The champions of the spurious distinction between the so-called "Islamist" minority, and the "peaceful" Muslim majority, who become entrapped in their reluctance for a carpet condemnation of Islam lest they be accused of Islamophobia or racism (as if Islam were a race), if they are non-Muslim; and of treason if they are, are also enslaved by another distinction of their own making, which has equally no leg to stand on. That is "Judeophobia," a parallel to Islamophobia, to distinguish from anti-Semitism, which is universally condemned in those circles, as it is no longer in vogue, at least not in public. They explain to us,

that Islam has never been anti-Semitic, proof of their ignorance of Islamic sources, while the current dislike of Jews
is no more than Judeophobia, which has no historical roots
and has been a modern, circumstantial, and fleeting phenomenon which does not warrant uncalled for anxiety. If
anti-Semitism is reduced to Judeophobia, it would merely
become a junior counterpart of Islamophobia, and a lesser
evil than anti-Semitism, and therefore less objectionable and
more "acceptable," on par with "Islamophobia," as a modern
phenomenon in Western society. Generally speaking, they
would simplistically argue: "how can Muslims, and especially Arabs, themselves Semites, be anti-Semitic?"

It is exactly this war of words, which has been engineered
to obfuscate substance and increase the currency of Muslim
terminology, while at the same time depriving the Jews and
their supporters from their traditional arsenal in the battle
against anti-Semitism, which we will have to tackle and clar-
ify here. Can anyone explain in what way the Qur'anic condemnation of Jews as "descendants of pigs and monkeys,"
which is routinely and universally preached to Muslims
(not necessarily radicals) by their clerics in both the Islamic
world and Europe, is "Judeophobic" and not "anti-Semitic"?
Is this hallowed Qur'anic reference, eternal as the Word of
Allah, a circumstantial and fleeting pronouncement? To say
so would be a blasphemy. It is used by Muslim clerics, as
a matter of course, in such "moderate" and "pro-Western"
countries as Jordan, Egypt and Saudi Arabia, as a continuation of the traditional way of demonizing and dehumanizing
the Jews in order to facilitate their annihilation. What more
would it take to call this a blatant anti-Semitism? Words were
created to transmit conventionally agreed upon meanings. If
each actor chose to lend to his words a different significance
or accuse the others of "distorting" their meaning, then we
would no longer be able to call a spade a spade or commu-
nicate with others. Anti-Semitism is the millennial irrational
hatred of the Jews, and it has been called so since the onset
of modern research on this sinister issue in the nineteenth

century. No amount of masking, manipulations with words and creation of parallels to dilute that terminology, can succeed, exactly as no coupling of the unique term "Holocaust" with Armenians or Darfurians (incidentally both perpetrated by Muslims), can blunt the poignancy of the Jewish Holocaust or rob it of its uniqueness. No wonder, then, that the most frequent manifestations of anti-Semitism these days, both among Muslims everywhere and their anti-Semitic allies in Europe, has been Holocaust denial, meaning that that devalued term in the eyes of the deniers has acquired a generic usage for all sorts of massacres, and the hated Jews cannot even claim to have acceded to the "honor" of having been the unique victims thereof.

Anti-Semitism in the core Islamic world, which exports its teachings to the Muslim peripheries and diasporas, consists of three layers whose combination determines the conduct of Muslims at any given time in any given place. The first is the immense anti-Jewish literature, which is enshrined in Qur'anic verses, in the *hadith* stories, in accounts of the *sirah* (the biography of the Prophet) and in treatises of jurisprudence, which have the force of law. The second is the massive Christian anti-Semitic literature, which was adopted by Muslims in later centuries as a result of the interaction between the two civilizations. The third is the wealth of reports and commentaries, which accompany, day after day, the fortunes of the Arab-Israeli dispute, and tends to intensify or quiet down in accordance with the swing of the war-and-peace pendulum which frequently reverses it both ways. All three layers have become indistinguishable and have merged into one major cataract of hatred and calumny, which submerges all the compartments of Judaism, Zionism, and Israel without distinction.

The Muslim Component

Numerous in volume and overwhelming in content are the Qur'anic passages, which serve as the basis of Muslim

elemental anti-Semitism, and which have become the building stones of the massive propaganda that shapes the minds
of young Muslims everywhere. What is striking is that at the
same time that the foundational texts of Islam affirm their
basic contempt and hatred towards Jews (and Christians),
they now find it expedient to deny this fact, and this denial
has served many non-Muslim apologists of Islam in their attempt to hide, obscure, or otherwise dwarf this innate trait of
Islamic history. This at a time when the Qur'an and *hadiths*
(traditions of Muhammad) have numerous passages which
proclaim enmity towards the Jews who are declared to be de-
ceivers, conspirers, and killers of Muhammad (by poisoning
him). As Mark Durie has written, Islam's foundational texts
express hostility to four religious groupings: Jews, Christians, pagans, and Muslim renegades. *Jihad* is mandated
against all four of these groups, and whereas the rules of
war are more merciless against the pagans and Muslim renegades—for only Jews and Christians are being allowed to
keep their faith after Islamic conquest—or the two "Peoples
of the Book" it is the Jews who attract he most intense expressions of hatred. There is less anti-Christian sentiment in
the Qur'an and *hadith*s than there is anti-Jewish sentiment,
and in Muhammad's biography his dealings with the Jews of
Arabia—leading to a genocide of Jewish tribes in Medina,
and the bloody conquest of the Jewish oasis of Khaybar—
loom much larger and are much more negative than his dealings with Christians.[60] Take for example the Islamic daily
prayers which include repeated recitations of *al-Fatihah*, the
opening chapter of the Qur'an. In these few verses, every
Muslim prays that members of his faith be guided on the
straight path of Allah, not like the Christians ("those who
have gone astray") or the Jews ("those who incur Allah's
wrath"). This simple contrast, that whereas Christians have

---

[60]Mark Durie, "On Islamic Antisemitism," *ICJS Research*, Melbourne, June 23,
2008.

lost their way, Jews have fallen under the anger of Allah, neatly summarizes Islam's attitude to the Jews.

The standard commentators, *al-Jalalayn* (the Two Jalals), as well as Ibn al-Kathir, whose *tafsir* (commentary) is popular among English-speaking Muslims, explain in almost the same terms the distinction in their discussion of *al-Fatihah*:

> Before these two paths are the paths of the Christians and Jews, a fact that the Believer should beware of so that he avoids them. This signifies that while the Jews abandoned practicing the religion, the Christians lost the true knowledge. This is why "anger" descended upon the Jews, while being described as "led astray" is more appropriate of the Christians. Those who know, but avoid implementing the truth, deserve the anger, unlike those who are ignorant. The Christians want to seek the true knowledge, but are unable to find it because they did not seek it from its proper resources. This is why they were led astray. We should also mention that both the Christians and the Jews have earned the anger and are led astray, but the anger is one of the attributes more particular of the Jews. Allah said about the Jews, "Those (Jews) who incurred the curse of Allah and His wrath" ([Sura] 5:60). The attribute that the Christians deserve most is that of being led astray, just as Allah said about them, "Who went astray before and who misled many, and strayed (themselves) from the right path ([Sura] 5:77)." Here Ibn al-Kathir is explaining that, whereas Christians are merely ignorant, Jews know the truth but deliberately reject it, thus making themselves objects of Allah's wrath.[61]

Durie also reminds us that this libel which is repeated in every observant Muslim's obligatory prayers, several times a day, shows that Islam's rejection of the Jews is not peripheral or negligible. Many years ago, Mark Durie, an active priest in Melbourne, Australia, was personally surprised to discover hatred of Jews among the Muslims of Indonesia, a country which has had virtually nothing to do with Jews in its history.

[61]Ibid

When Amrozi, the mastermind of the mass murder in Bali, cried out threats against Jews at his sentencing in a Balinese courtroom, this was not because he had ever met a single Jew. His hatred was purely theological. So, in spite of the reality of denial, which is shared by some Jews who could not free themselves of their *dhimmitude*, Islam's anti-Semitic legacy is persistent and tenacious. Durie also attests that his friend, Dr. Daniel Shayesteh who was one of the Iranian founders of Hizbullah, became a Christian after he fled from the Ayatollah's murderous regime. Shayesteh explains in his testimony the hatred of Jews, which he absorbed as part of his Muslim upbringing in Iran, and the intention of the Iranian revolutionaries to destroy Israel. Indeed, the visceral hatred which shaped Hizbullah's dreams of conquest and destruction has not died out, and continues to plague the world.[62]

Take, for example, the infamous passage from the Book, which is cited in sermons in the mosques throughout the Muslim world, and which depicts Jews as "descendants of pigs and monkeys." We understand today that Muhammad had pronounced those derogatory words of the Jews when they rose against his authority in Medina at the outset of his political career there. But today, when they are repeated *ad nauseam* throughout the Muslim world on Friday sermons, out of any context, they serve no other purpose than disparaging the Jews and insulting them. What is that if not anti-Semitism, irrational as it may be? That derogatory reference, which is seconded by many others,[63] has had a profound and lasting impact on Muslim thinking, behavior, social norms, and the education of their children, and not necessarily in areas of conflict with Israel or adjacent to it, sometimes even in parts of the world that have never seen a Jew. Andrew Bostom begins his copious volume on Islamic anti-Semitism by a well-tailored survey of the theological, historical, and juridical origins of Islamic anti-Semitism, including the

---

[62]Ibid.

[63]See e.g. Suras 2:61, 4:44-46, 4:160-61, 9:30-31, 5:64, 5:82, and more.

Holy Qur'an, the *Hadith* and the *Sirah* (the hagiography of the Prophet); he proceeds to an insightful description of the *dhimmis* in the main lands of Islam, to test the theory of the cited sources against the practice of Muslim rulers, in the entire area spanning the Middle East, North Africa, the Iberian Peninsula (Andalusia), and the Ottoman Empire. The picture one gets from these documents reverses in a dramatic way many of the ill-conceived and misjudged information, which had attempted in the past to ascribe to the lands of Islam a much more benign and idyllic image of their (mis)treatment of the Jews. *Inter alia*, the coalition between the Palestinian Mufti of Jerusalem and the Nazis during WWII is conjured up by the author to summarize this introduction. Then, the author delves in considerable detail into the main sources of the body of Islamic jurisprudence—the Qur'an and the *Hadith*, complemented by the *Sirah* where an abundance of references, usually uncomplimentary but rather derogatory, are made to Jews, collectively known as *Israi'liyyat* (Israelites' stories). This is a trove of anti-Jewish stereotypes which have become the *shari'a*-based uncontested "Truth" about the People of the Book. Those accounts are invariably cited in sermons during Friday prayers, thus assuring their universal diffusion among Muslim constituents and the constant poisoning of the souls of young and adult Muslims alike, something that makes their fundamentally negative attitudes to Jews and Israel unchangeable. This extremely important collection from the holy sources is supplemented by the thinking and judgment of the most authoritative Muslim jurists whose every word has been awaited and avidly digested by Muslim constituencies the world over. The great medieval masters such as Tabari and Jahiz, are reinforced by more recent ones such as the Egyptian Tantawi and Egyptian-in exile Qaradawi, who represent the two poles of established Islam and popular Islam in our contemporary Sunni world, though they agree among themselves more often than not.

Finally, an impressive selection of observations made by prominent Western scholars (Bernard Lewis excepted), and eye-witness reports made by travelers, consular representatives, journalists, and writers about the condition of the Jews in Arab lands, is conjured up to lend their backing to the basic, and well-documented thesis of the author, that the anti-Semitic record of the Islamic world rather leaves much to be desired. All in all, one can hardly exaggerate the vast importance of this volume, which will henceforth become indispensable for any student of Islam, of Judeo-Islamic relations, of anti-Semitism in particular and of hate-literature in general. It also provides the indispensable background to comprehend the underpinnings of the "New Muslim Anti-Semitism," whose new avenues of hatred have come to be expressed most virulently by Ahmed Ahmadinejad, the President of Iran, who again raises the specter of annihilating the Jews and their state. The paradox implied in the saying that the media achieve immediacy, especially the widespread use (and abuse) of Internet sites to diffuse the venom of radical Islam globally, has extended its applicability to the growing Muslim populations in Europe who have become among the chief proponents of anti- Semitism in the West today. The old and stale anti-Jewish stereotypes that appear in classic European anti-Semitism, and have been copiously replicated in Arab and Muslim anti-Semitic writings, have of late effected some new twists, concurrent with the enhanced anti-Semitic mood in the West. Their main sources of inspiration have not changed dramatically, and they sustain their leaning on Muslim scriptures (like dubbing the Jews the "descendants of apes and swines", etc.), their borrowings from the Christian themes of Blood Libel, the *Protocols of the Elders of Zion*, the world Jewish conspiracy and the idea of "poisoning" in various forms caused by Jews; and their depending on the fortunes of the Arab-Israeli conflict, in the process parading anti-Semitism as anti-Zionism or anti-Israelism.

The new twist consists in operationalizing the old stereotypes and the anti-Semitic vocabulary of old into concrete acts to enhance the monstrous image attached to the Jews, and take action to check the "wild" and "uncontrollable" conduct of the Zionists and the Israelis, to the point of declaring the desirability of their liquidation and preparing the tools of mass-destruction to achieve that goal. The areas where this new operationalization of anti-Semitism works are varied and widespread. Here we can only briefly address several of them, before we reach some tentative conclusions. They are: firstly, using Christians, both in the Middle East and in Europe, many of whom have succumbed to the *dhimmi* state of mind, to denigrate Jews and Zionism; secondly, to expand the range of Jew-haters and hate-mongers from obscurantist clerics to vast strata of mainstream intellectuals and professionals; thirdly, to encourage anti-Semitism as a legitimate tool to combat Israel; fourthly, to prominently add to the old Christian anti-Semitic themes also a pathological Holocaust denial; fifthly, to "perfect" the theme of "poisoning" to new heights, in line with the world of hallucinations where many Muslims dwell; and finally, to vilify the Jews to such an extent as to fill all crevices of the Muslim soul with a paranoiac contempt and disgust of the Zionists and Israelis, so that the overt Jewish appellation is somehow prudently circumvented.

Christians as a Tool

In an article published in the establishment *al Ahram* in Cairo, an "enlightened" Coptic scholar, Dr. Babawi, lambasted the American Congress for not stopping "Israel's artillery attacks on the Nativity and the Aqsa Mosque," and he urged American Muslims and Copts to demonstrate against "crazy Sharon, who began behaving like a madman after he was hit in his sensitive place by a bullet during the 1948 War, which left him with only one testicle, something that has affected him psychologically, and he has become a crazy psychopath, using power to hide his weakness...."[64]

This broadside, which in Arab tradition demeans the man by pointing to his sexual weakness, sought to twist the

---

[64]Reference is made to the attempts by Israeli troops to rescue the Church of Nativity from the takeover by armed PLO men. Arab culture is so sensitive about "manhood", that the writer found it best to dishonor Prime Minister Sharon by denying him his masculinity.

Nativity event, where Palestinians invaded the Holy Church at gun point, by imputing the moral wrong to Israel who tried to dislodge them from there. But no one could have missed the point: a Copt in Egypt, a member of a persecuted and dispossessed minority in an Islamic country, must be more Arab than his Muslim compatriots, to evince his loyalty, and there was evidently no better ground for that exercise than an anti-Jewish attack. The Bishop of the Assyrian Church in Lebanon followed suit by asserting that though the heads of the Church today are not Jewish, they are "led by Jews, whose faith is inimical to God, to the people and to Christianity." He cites Jesus as having said to the Jews: "You are the sons of Satan, and you practice the will of Satan your father," to which they supposedly answered: "No, we are not the sons of Satan, we are the sons of Abraham." But he insisted: "Had you been the sons of Abraham, you would be acting in accordance with the precepts of Abraham.... You are the sons of Satan."[65] This wholesale discredit of the Jews, to gain favor with the thugs of Hizbullah, defies logic insofar as the dwindling Christian minorities in the Islamic world, who should have made common cause with the Jews, were evidently exploited and intimidated by Muslims and forced to "prove" the universal disgust that they sense towards Jews.

Many of the anti-Jewish stereotypes among the Muslims are imported from Western Christianity while others are Muslim-made, but both parties liberally borrow from each other, through the intermediary of the Eastern Christians in the Muslim world, who master both cultures and traditions, including as regards anti-Semitism, and who have not been reformed by the far-reaching concessions made to Judaism by the Catholic Church. Furthermore, during the al-Aqsa *Intifadah*, which has pushed the Islamikaze martyrs (*shuhada*) to the forefront of the Palestinian experience, some Christians found them comparable to Christ's martyrdom even as they invaded the Nativity at the height of their violence:

---

[65]*Al Ahram*, April 25, 2002

We kneel before the Palestinian people in the Nativity. He starves and thirsts, but he is steadfast.... The one who said "I am hungry" when he was on the Cross was our Lord Jesus himself.... Our Palestinian people in Bethlehem died like a crucified martyr on the rock, guarded by Israeli soldiers armed from head to foot, who have no compassion, love, life or tolerance.... The Jew has a principle from which we suffer and which he tries to impose on people, and that is the principle of Gentiles. To him, the Gentile is a slave. They give the Palestinians working in Israel only a piece of bread, and tell them: "this piece of bread that you eat is taken from our children, and we give it to you so you will live as free men in your land, but as a proletariat and a slave in Israel, to serve us...". *The Protocols of the Elders of Zion* are based on this principle, and anyone who reads the *Protocols* feels that we are in this period with the Jews.[66]

Expanding the Scope of Hatred

When one peruses through Arab and Muslim publications and media one cannot help notice that the scope of anti-Semitism has been expanding beyond obscurantist clerics or fanatically nationalistic elements in those societies, and has come to embrace also supposedly liberal, enlightened and professional mainstream milieus. In that discourse, the interchangeability between Jews, Zionists, and Israelis is unmistakable when all three are alternately threatened of outright extermination. An Egyptian, Dr. Adel Sadeq, a senior psychiatrist by profession, who often bashed President Bush and the West for their ignorance of the Arab psyche, had no qualms about fighting Israel to the finish, more than two decades after his country signed peace with it. He wrote:

What is happening now indicates that Israel will not exist for ever. We as Arabs must know that this war will not end..., and anyone who deludes himself that there will be peace must understand that Israel did not come to this region to love the Ar-

---

[66] *Al Manar Television*, (Lebanon-Hizbullah), April 24, 2002.

abs or to normalize relations with them.... Either the Israelis or the Palestinians, there is no third option.... There are no Israeli civilians, they are all plunderers, for history teaches this. I am completely convinced that the psychological effect [of the Islamikaze] on the Israeli usurper will be his realizing that his existence is temporary....Remove the *Apache* [combat helicopters] from the equation, leave them one on one with the Palestinian people with the only weapon being dynamite, then you will see all Israelis leave, because there is not even one Israeli among them willing to don a belt of explosives.... We will throw Israel into the sea, there is no middle ground. Coexistence is total nonsense.... The real means of dealing with Israel directly is those who blow themselves up. According to what I see in the battle arena, there is no other way but the pure, noble Palestinian bodies. This is the only Arab weapon there is, and anyone who says otherwise is a conspirator.[67]

If statements of this sort are made by mainstream opinion makers, often graduates of Western universities and bearers of Ph.D. titles, especially in such "moderate" countries as Egypt and Saudi Arabia, how much more so in the Muslim fundamentalist circles where license is given to the most abominable Judeo-phobic rhetoric. At the heart of the Egyptian establishment and consensus, for example, is the weekly *October*, founded and edited by one of the most virulent anti-Semites in the Arab world—Anis Mansur[68]—who was a close associate of President Anwar Sadat. This is what a retired general, Hassan Sweilem, had to say in that journal, taken straight from the *Protocols of the Elders of Zion* and the Hamas platform:

Along history, since Emperor Justinian and down to Hitler, Europe's rulers had been trying to rid themselves of the acts of

---

[67]*Iqra'Television* (Saudi Arabia and Egypt) April 24, 2002. See *Memri* 373, April 30, 2002.

[68]For some of his most harrowing condemnations of the Jews, see R. Israeli, *Peace is in the Eye of the Beholder*, Mouton Publishers, Berlin and New York, 1985, especially the concluding chapter.

violence, barbarism, corruption, conflict mongering and other deeds that Jews were, and still are, in the custom of doing in European societies..., like, for example, their domination of monetary systems, treasuries, banks and commercial monopolies, which has caused widespread bankruptcy and economic destruction. They also diffuse drugs, prostitution, trade of women as sexual slaves, and alcohol. They have also monopolized the gold and precious stone trade, paid bribes to rulers and extorted them throughout history.... The Jews stood behind wars and internal strife, and that caused European rulers to expel them and kill them. For example, the Crusader armies, passing through the Rhine basin on their way east, massacred them and burned their houses as an act of repentance to their God. When the Crusaders entered Jerusalem, they collected the Jews in a synagogue and burned them live. Their kin in Russia suffered a similar fate....They were expelled from France, England, Germany, Hungary, Belgium, Slovakia, Austria, Holland, and finally from Spain, after they underwent the Inquisition trials for their conspiracy to penetrate Christian society like a Trojan horse.... The Jewish conspiracy to take over Europe generated civil revolutions, wars and internal strife....The Cromwell Revolution failed in 1649 England, following the Jewish Conspiracy to drag England into several wars in Europe.... Then the French Revolution broke out, which the Jews had planned, based on the first conference of their rabbis and interest-loaners that had been convened by the first Rothschild in 1773 in order to take over all the world resources.... That conference adopted 24 protocols, including the uprooting of the belief in God from the hearts of the Gentiles, distracting people by distributing among them literature of heresy and impurity, destruction of the family and eradication of all morality...[69]

This goes on *ad nauseam,* evincing the primitive, delusive, and bigoted minds of the writers and of those who facilitated those heaps of utter nonsense to gain "respectability"

---

[69]October, June 17, 2001.

by being published in a truly respectable medium. The Jews were "credited" in that *October* article with putting Napoleon on the throne and then of causing his demise, of the 1775 war between Britain and the nascent USA, of establishing the Bank of America in 1881 with a view of controlling the wealth of the fledgling U.S., and then of kindling the fire of the American Civil War. He told how the *Protocols* were written in 1770 by a German rabbi, financed by Rothschild, again in order "to destroy all governments and religions, spread anarchy and revolution, trigger wars, take over the wealth of nations, spread corruption among the youth, and control rulers by implanting in their governments Jewish ministers and advisers." This mainstream sick mind goes on: the Jews ordered the start of World War I, and got the U.S. to get involved by spreading the rumor that an American ship had been sunk by the Germans. During that war, they prepared the grounds for both Communism and Nazism, as a follow-up to the work done by the Jews Marx and Engels half a century earlier when they circulated the Communist Manifesto in London. Eventually, Communism and Nazism took over power and came to confront each other, "exactly as the Jews had planned." The second world war erupted due to the limitations imposed by the Allies on the Germans in Versailles, by order of the Jews, thus pushing the Germans to revolution and to the rise of Hitler. The Jews also brought about the fall of the Ottoman Empire and they were to reap the fruit thereof by concentrating all wealth in their hands.[70]

Anti-Semitism as a Tool to Combat Israel

This repulsive verbiage, which also includes the claim that the Jews caused the Great Depression in order to pave the way to WW II, is not innocently geared to disclose great new historical findings to the world, for educational or didactic purposes, but primarily to discredit the Jews and point to

---

[70]Ibid

the "dangers" they pose to the world, thereby implying that
the Jewish state is as dangerous to world peace and therefore illegitimate. These calumnies, part of which had been
concocted for centuries in Europe and were imported to the
Middle East and then re-exported to the West, are not believed by Muslims to be a tool of propaganda, because they
are so much replicated and repeated that their forgers end
up believing them as conventional wisdom and documented
history; and because there is almost no decent intellectual,
researcher, or scientist in the Muslim world who would dare
to contradict them or question their validity, rationale, verac-
ity, and the authenticity of their detail, lest he be considered a
"traitor" to the Arab/Islamic cause. And so, forged citations,
made-up "facts," fake sources, trumped up accusations, and
all manner of other hoaxes, for which one can be prosecuted
in civilized countries and serve prison terms, become widespread currency in Islamic countries, for the most part with
impunity (either on the part of peer scholars or by the state).
The innocent and misguided masses, who have neither interest in the facts, nor any way to learn them beyond the propaganda they are exposed to, take that nonsense as gospel and
as a legitimate way to battle Israel and the Jews.

Islamikaze bombings by Palestinians against Israel, have
often been rationalized in terms of anti-Zionism and encouraged against the background of the pathologically vilified
Jews, who have "earned" the onslaughts against them due
to their schemes and the dangers they pose to the world. An
Egyptian columnist, for example, preceded and followed
by many others, specifically urged the Islamikaze to step
up their operations against the Jews, and called upon more
Muslim volunteers to join the murderers. His imagination is
gruesome in its detail and inhumanity:

> ... with every blow struck by al-Aqsa *Intifadah*, my conviction
> grows stronger that I, and those like-minded, have been right
> all along, and I am still right in my belief that the despised rac-
> ist Jewish entity will be annihilated. Contrary to others, how-

ever, I am not ashamed to speak about driving them into the sea, to hell or to the trash heap where they belong... I maintain, and Allah is my witness, that the annihilation and defeat of the Israelis, after which there will be no resurrection, does not require all those things. All that is required is to concentrate on acts of martyrdom, or what is known as the "strategy of the balance of fear".... Let us do some mathematical calculations: 250 Palestinians have signed up for martyrdom operations, and it is not impossible to raise their number to 1000 throughout the Arab world...i.e, one *fida'i* out of every 250,000 Arabs. The average harvest of each act of martyrdom is 10 dead and 50 wounded. Thus, 1000 acts of martyrdom would leave the Zionists with at least 10,000 dead and 50,000 wounded. This is double the Israeli casualties in all their wars with the Arabs since 1948 [sic].[71] They cannot bear this. There is also the added advantage, not noted by many, of the negative Jewish emigration, which as a result of 1,000 martyrdom operations, will come to at least one million Jews, followed by the return of every Jew to the place whence he came... I am signing myself up as the first martyr from Egypt and declare that I am ready to commit an act of martyrdom at any moment. I will place myself under the command of Hassan Nasrallah, the Hamas, Islamic Jihad and any other Jihad movement....

Never in my life have I asked Allah for money, honor or power. All I have asked, all I ask, all I will ask, is that Allah allow me to become a *shahid* and grant me the honor of reaping as great a harvest as possible of Israeli lives...[72]

This rabid anti-Semitism, which unabashedly proclaims its genocidal aims in a mainstream journal, without encountering the least resistance or objection from fellow-writers, the authorities, the media, the public, human rights groups anywhere, and in a country which had signed a peace treaty with Israel more than two decades earlier, naturally did not

---

[71]In fact the amount of Israeli casualties has long surpassed the 20,000 mark, that is, four-fold the author's estimate.

[72]*Al-Usbu'* (Egypt) May 28, 2001. *Memri* 224, June 4, 2001.

remain isolated in other Islamic media. In Iran, the hub of Islamic violence and support for terrorism against Israel, reports came out about funds raised to support Palestinian "suicide operations" against Israel, and about promises from Tehran to Islamic Jihadists that their financial sustenance would no longer be channeled through Hizbullah but disbursed directly to them.[73] Israel is perceived by them as a danger to the entire region, not only to the Palestinians, and Imam Khumeini was cited as determining that "the goal of this virus [Israel], that was planted in the heart of the Muslim world, is not only to annihilate the Arab nation, therefore the solution is to annihilate this virus, for there is no other treatment.... The Islamic states and the Muslims should initiate the annihilation of this den of corruption in every possible way. It is permitted to use charity money for that purpose...."[74] Similar calls to "annihilate the Jews" have become routine in Muslim mosques as well as in the writings of Saudi and other Muslim writers.[75]

Holocaust Denial

Even though Holocaust denial is not new in Muslim countries, and sponsoring lecture tours by infamous "revisionist historians" (Faurisson, Garaudy and Irving) has been going on par with prohibiting the projection of *Schindler's List* within their boundaries, it seems that since the eruption of the al-Aqsa *Intifadah* (September 2000), this has become one of their favorite pastimes. They do it not out of concern for "historical truth," but simply to sustain their long-standing accusations against the Jews and turn the blame of terrorism against Jews by blasting them for "using organized terrorism to cultivate that legend [of the Holocaust] and

---

[73] *Al-Sharq Al-Awsat*, (London), June 8, 2002.

[74] *Al-Manar Television* (Hizbullah, Lebanon), June 2, 2002.

[75] *Al-Mustaqbal* (Lebanon) March 19, 2002; Al-'Ukadh (Saudi Arabia), November 22, 2001; *Al-Riyadh* (Saudi Arabia) November 22, 2001.

turn it into a fact which ties down the hands of historians."[76] The Jews are also condemned for "forging history," an accusation of long date since the inception of Islam, aided by the "constant refutation by scientific articles which "have proven that never were there gas chambers, or that the numbers of the dead were significantly lower."[77] Some Muslim media even claimed that, far from being hurt by World War II, Jews on the contrary profited from it, for had Japan and Germany won the war, the Jews "could not have continued to blackmail the Gentiles with their lies."[78] Abu Mazen, the "moderate" successor of Arafat in the Palestinian leadership also joined this cacophony of Holocaust denial in his infamous doctoral thesis, written in Communist Moscow and published as a book in 1984.[79]

From denying the Holocaust, or diminishing its horrors, to accusing the Jewish victims of Nazism as having conspired with it against their own people, as Abu Mazen did, the road is short to defending Hitler against the "offences" caused him by the Jews and their supporters. Following Western and Israeli protests to the Egyptian government regarding the unbridled sympathy for Hitler that is current in the Egyptian and Arab press in general,[80] the government daily *Al-Akhbar* relented for a while but could not contain its irresistible fascination with Hitler for long, and soon reverted to it with vengeance. This time a cleric from al-Azhar, Mahmud Khadr, entitled his contribution "in Defense of Hitler," and

---

[76]*Al-Wafd* (Egypt), February 13, 2000; al-Ahram, April 19, 2000; and the *Egyptian Gazette*, April 20, 2000.

[77]*Al-Ahram*, December 30, 1999.

[78]*Al-Hayat*, January 31, 2000; *Al-Akhbar*, January 26, 2000, *al-Ahram*, April 18 and May 17, 2000; *The Egyptian Gazette*, April 17, 2000, and more and more.

[79]*The Secret Ties between the Nazis and the Zionist Movement Leadership* (Arabic), Dar Ibn Rushd, Amman, 1984.

[80]See R. Israeli, *Peace is in the Eye of the Beholder*, Mouton, Berlin, 1987, especially pp. 33-4, 231, 326 and more.

used the occasion to bash not only Israel and the Jews but also the hated West:

> ...Hitler and many of his ministers took their own lives so that they would not have to see the faces of the old ape, Churchill, and the big bear, Stalin, who would sentence them to death with no one to defend them.... Each one of them has a right to his defense..., but Hitler's executioners took his right away and attributed to him crimes, whether he committed them or not. I do not know what would have happened to Roosevelt, Churchill and de Gaulle, had Hitler won. Perhaps the crimes for which they deserve the death sentence would have been much worse than all that Hitler had done.... But all of Hitler's crimes and infractions were forgotten, except for the crime that was exaggerated and blown completely out of proportion, thanks to the insistence of world Zionism to continue to stoke the fire. The reason for this was the emotional need of the sons of Jacob to extort Germany and to eat away at its resources. It is amazing that Westerners, who are entitled to their own thinking, to confirming or denying anything, including the existence of the Prophets of Allah, cannot address the Jewish question, or more precisely the false Holocaust, whose numbers and scope they have exaggerated, until it has reached the level of the merciless destruction of six million Jews, only because Hitler saw them as an inferior race unworthy of living next to the Germanic race, which must rule the world.... Anyone who knocks on this door is accused of the most horrible things, and is tried in all Western courts for anti-Semitism..., for two reasons: one is due to Zionist control of thinking in the world and the degree of oppression of thought by the Zionist propaganda apparatus in those nations. No one can oppose this oppression for fear of going to prison or having his livelihood or reputation threatened.... The second is the fear that the lies of Zionism would be exposed if the subject of the Holocaust is investigated factually and the logical conclusions are drawn.... The first dubious fact is the number of six million Jews who were burnt in the gas chambers. Did they have children or families who demanded

compensation, or did Zionism see itself as their heir? If we assume that everyone had an average of five family members, this would bring the number of the Jews affected to 30 million. It is certain that many Jews escaped before the ship sunk, that many of them survived, despite the so-called extermination and burning. This would mean that the number of Jews in Germany amounted to 60 million, although the total number of Germans has never reached this many.... Even if we cross off one zero from the six million and we are left with a tenth of this number, it would still seem exaggerated and would have to be investigated...[81].

It is difficult to imagine that the writer did not know the numbers of Germany's population during the war, or that most of the exterminated Jews were not German but Polish, Baltic, or Soviet, or that since entire Jewish families, often over three generations, were decimated, no heir was left behind to claim damages. All these harrowing manipulations of numbers, of which Abu Mazen was also guilty, and which have no leg to stand on, are pages taken from the books of *Sho'ah* deniers and have no other purpose than to diminish its dimensions and accuse the Jews of its inflation. A follow up of that line of thought has been to show that Hitler had no reason to exterminate so many Jews, therefore, in fact, he did not. But deniers of the *Sho'ah*, including Arabs and Muslims, are caught in the contradiction of both diminishing its numbers, in order to relegate the horror to a "footnote in history" as Jean-Marie Le Pen would have it, but at the same time explaining and blowing up the "threat that Jews posed to the Germans," hence the "imperative" to eliminate them.

Poisoning as the Ultimate Jewish Conspiracy

The repetitive use of the *Protocols* and the Blood Libel in the Arab media, especially the manufacturing of new popular tele-novellas and other "documentary" series on television

---

[81] *Al-Akhbar*, May 27, 2001. See *Memri* 231, June 20, 2001

during the peak—watching month of Ramadan, create the ambience in which any calumny against the Jews is readily believed and repeated in other media as well, not least in countries such as Jordan and Egypt, which have supposedly made peace with Israel. In this atmosphere the most abominable lies spread about the Jews are picked up and diffused, and the masses are only too eager to absorb them, and further spread them around as "facts," without investigation or critique. The most virulent kind of hoax of this sort, which easily catches up and propagates, are the stories of poisoning that are attributed to the Jews, and certainly originate from the well-poisoning calumnies inherent in European anti-Semitism. One could hear Yasser Arafat often attributing to Israel the distribution of poisoned sweets among Palestinian children in order to maim them, or the use of depleted uranium in bullets that quelled the *Intifadah* in order to sexually incapacitate Palestinian fighters and thus contribute to diminishing their numbers. At the height of this campaign, the Palestinian representative in the Human Rights Commission in Geneva, a Doctor Abdallah Ramlawi, accused Israel of injecting the HIV virus into 300 Palestinian children in order to impair their reproduction organs. When Israel sent its experts to Egypt to develop high tech agriculture in the Nile Delta area, with astounding results, reports abounded in the press that the Jews had no other purpose in coming to Egypt, which did not need them and could itself teach them what agriculture was all about, than poisoning the soil of Egypt and destroying its age-old and advanced farming. Papers also recycled *ad-nauseam* the allegation that Israel distributed, through the Arab world an aphrodisiac, chewing gum geared to raise the sexual desire of Muslim women in order to lead them astray. But perhaps the greatest hoax in this regard, which was constructed by Palestinians, and then built up by other Arabs, Muslims, the UN, the European press, and even the Red Cross, and became *cause celebre* during the months of March-April 1983, was the story of "poisoning school girls" in the Jenin district, which was then under Israeli rule. Against all available evidence, and in spite of the fact that a number of official investigations were launched by Israel and international bodies, which produced no incriminating findings, the story reverberated across the world, until proven false.[82]

But even then, no one outside Israel found it necessary to castigate the manufacturers of the hoax. The end result was that the Palestinians, and other Arabs and Muslims for that matter, discovered that splashing mud on Israel could go on with impunity, and they pursued their practice wholeheartedly. It is interesting to note that the depleted uranium story and the AIDS injection hoax followed the girls-poisoning episode. After the September 11 (2001) horror and the onset of the Anthrax panic in the U.S., the scientific Egyptian journal *al-'ilm*, turned the tables on the U.S. and Israel, accusing them of the most hideous war crimes, including the use of non-conventional weapons of mass destruction. With regard to Israel and the Jews, this is what this "scientific" publication had to say:

> ...In the summer of 1949 cholera spread throughout Egypt, following the establishment of Israel in 1948. Egyptian documents indicate that the disease originated from Israel.... The US used germs in Vietnam and against North Korea and China.... Biological weapons research is being conducted by Israeli universities. Prior to the October War (1973) they injected birds with germs and released then above Jordan, Palestine and the Suez Canal.... The US and Israel keep biological weapons at American bases; if they were to be used, they would destroy half the population of the area under attack. Some of this weaponry makes women miscarry.... Also, Jewish tourists infected with AIDS are traveling around Asian and African countries with the aim of spreading the disease.... It is no coincidence that the US is the only member of the UN that has not signed

---

[82]See R. Israeli, *Poison: Manifestations of a Blood Libel*, Lexington Books, NY and Oxford, 2002.

the agreement on punishment for the collective annihilation of people... Israel continues to use germ warfare to destroy the Palestinian people on its occupied land, thus challenging the international community...[83]

These materials are so repetitive, steady, omnipresent, prevalent, and diffused in all strata of Arab and Islamic society that they are regarded as a matter of course. Children are "educated" in their "light," the educated adults read or write about them in the press, clerics preach them in mosques, politicians occasionally refer to them in their public addresses, and the media, written and electronic, abound with them. To the point that they have become part of the infrastructure of education and socialization in those countries. The hierarchies in those societies, including those who have signed peace with Israel, do nothing to criticize the writers, much less to call them to task or to prosecute them. Quite the contrary, the authorities turn a blind eye, some of them blinking in approval, which in turn is interpreted as official backing for these atrocious pronouncements. In turn, these writings, especially those emanating from Egypt, which is considered the cultural hub of the Arab world, are widely read, cited, and appreciated and create a mood of expectation from more writers to produce such vitriolic pieces. One has to admit, nevertheless, that the leniency with which Israel deals with these matters, not insisting on their total elimination as prerequisite to any diplomatic exchange, in itself unwillingly contributes to their persistence. It is not enough to demand that an end be put to incitement against Jews in Muslim countries, but that a mechanism for monitoring those abominations and acting upon its findings must be devised, if we can hope that the vitriol might decrease one day to allow for a reconciliation of the hearts to occur between Israel and its neighbors. We remember that when

---

[83] *Al-'Ilm* (Science) Egypt, November, 2001, *Memri* 322, December 28, 200

Jorg Haider's party joined the Austrian coalition, the Israeli government reacted so swiftly that the Ambassador of Israel in Vienna was recalled, even though Haider recanted on his pro-Nazi statements. In the case of the Arab leaders, clerics, intellectuals, and columnists, the anti-Jewish vitriol is much stronger, more threatening, widespread and persistent, but official Israel dares not say or do anything against it. The Holocaust denier, Abu Mazen, has become Israel's "moderate, peace-loving" partner while the Arab media, even in the countries that signed peace with Israel, pursue their anti-Semitic campaigns unabated, while their rulers who could control them if they wished to, look the other way. How then can they or the rest of the world take Israel's protests seriously?

Part Two

The Imperative of Revival

Chapter 5

Israel's Socio-political Upheavals

The constant external dangers that surround Israel and reduce her to a long and unrelenting siege on the part of the Arab and Muslim worlds, even on the part of the countries which have concluded a formal peace with it, force it to rethink its basic assumptions, to tighten its social organization, to put an end to the appeasement policy of its unruly neighbors, to-re-evaluate the risks and dangers posed by the tough neighborhood where it lives, and to revise its political system so as to make it more responsive to the new emerging conditions. What Israel has done economically, which catapulted it to the category of one of the most developed and advanced nations, through its technological prowess and its know-how and inventiveness in agriculture, industry, high-tech and the military, must be applied to the fields of education, social and political organization, the cultivation of quality-living, and the harmonization of the various ethnic groups of Israeli society. This daunting project rests on the assumption that several dichotomic situations have paralyzed Israeli society for too long, and that only a vigorous shudder can shake the country out of its slumber. These dichotomies merit to be enumerated : between the old-timers and the new immigrants; between the cities and the development townships; between center and periphery; between secular and ultra-religious; between Jews and Arabs; between Israel Proper and the Administered Palestinian territories; between the wealthy and the poor; and between "oriental"-Sephardic and "western"-Ashkenazi Jews, though this latter has been diminishing in scope and in depth over the years. There are many overlapping categories where an Israeli can find one-self at one and the same time, but generally speaking, the Jewish population is divided between the Ashkenazi-well to do- urban- old-timers-secular- dwellers of Israel proper and the Sephardic- poorer- religious- new comers- periphery and territories dwellers. But this is punctuated by so many exceptions, that it can hardly constitute a rule. A detailed discussion will fine-tune the particulars.

The Palestinian-Arab issue, which is the most divisive and the most bitterly contested among the Israelis, will be tackled first. This controversy rests on the different percep-tions which prevail in the country with regard to both the Palestinian Arabs who are part of Israel's citizenry (20%) and consider themselves Palestinian for all intents and pur-poses, and the Palestinians who have been overseen by Israel since their Jordanian-controlled territories were taken over by Israel in 1967. Combined, they constitute about 5 million Palestinians, enough to challenge the nature of the Jewish state should the territories be integrated in Israel. However, while about 1,5 million of those Palestinians are concen-trated in three large clusters within Israel (the Galilee in the north, the Triangle just East of Tel-Aviv, and the Bedouins in the Negev), the remaining 3,5 million are unequally split between Judea and Samaria (the West Bank) and the Gaza Strip. True, since the Oslo Accords in 1993, the Palestin-ian Authority (PA) was to take up civil responsibility for its population, while Israel reserved to itself the overall security controls of the territories and their borders, but in view of the 2000 *Intifada*, when Israel had to re-enter the cities of the West Bank, and more so since the Hamas ousted the PA from Gaza and monopolized government there, those ten-tative arrangements have lost their juridical base and once again blurred the situation. There is a PA, but it does not control the entire West Bank, and certainly not Gaza; there are Palestinian institutions but they are not recognized by all factions of the Palestinian people; there are two parallel gov-ernments: one PA and the other Hamas; and disagreement is rife upon whether, when and how new presidential and legislative elections should be held to succeed the existing incumbents whose terms have expired.

The Israeli public is divided down the middle between two major trends: the liberal left, which is, paradoxically, also pessimistic, and predicts doomsday and demographic inundation of Israel if it does not separate from the Palestinians forthwith, even at the cost of abandoning almost all the territories with their hundreds of Israeli settlements and their 300,000 "settlers", whom they deem "illegal", because they live on "occupied" territory. They also dread the scenario which predicts that due to the quicker Arab growth rate and the growing Arab and Muslim might, Israel might not be able to defend itself in the future, therefore better settle now for peace, even in disadvantageous conditions, than wait and be compelled to do so in the future under worse conditions. They believe that boundaries of peace are better defensible that geo-strategic borders that require military defenses. However, they do not provide answers to nagging questions of the wider Muslim negationists, like Iran, the Hamas and Hizbullah, who will continue to reject any peace settlement and act to destroy it, even assuming that the Arab signatories honor its terms. The other major issue which would remain unanswered would be the Palestinian Arabs within Israel, who are considered as equal citizens of Israel and would under no circumstance be included in the deal. To date, despite the massive waves of Jewish immigrants in the 1950s, 1960s and 1990s, the rate of Palestinian Arabs in Israel has increased from 11% in 1948 to 20% in 2008. Now that the sources of Jewish immigration have dried up, the rate of growth of the Arabs in Israel will be boosted, and the demographic scenario which justified, in the first place, separation from the Palestinians, will become valid again. The equilibrium between this liberal left and their rivals has been somewhat disturbed since the 2000 *Intifada,* as many Israelis woke up from their hopes, delusions and dreams and swelled the ranks of the opposite convictions.

The prevailing mood among the Israeli electorate in the 2009 elections, was more tuned to the Zionist right, which does not regard Israel's presence in the territories as "occupation", since it did not invade and occupy for the sake of expansion, but responded to the all out attack on Israel's then-vulnerable borders in 1967, which necessitated a take-over until a settlement is reached. In the meantime, Jordan, which lost the West Bank to Israel in 1967, decided in 1988 to renounce it totally, leaving Israel no one to contend with, save the Palestinians, who emerged as a new entity and demanded their right to inherit Jordanian claims. In addition to these pragmatic considerations, the doctrinaire among the settlers also invoke biblical history and religion to stake their claim on the land. They further claim that at a time when no one denies the right of 1,5 million Palestinians to live in Israel, it makes little sense that the right of 300,000 Israelis to dwell in a land claimed by the Palestinians should be denied. The settlers may be religious or not, but they regularly support right-wing politics, do not recoil from living in the neighborhood of the Palestinians, and find comfort in the early history of Zionism when isolated Jewish villages ensured Jewish presence in hostile territory and served as the nucleus for the future state of Israel. Many of them wish Israel to annex the territories and apply its law on them, but all Israeli governments have avoided that *demarche* so far.

Connected with the Palestinians in the territories is the status of the Arabs of Israel. Until 1967 they were a docile minority, on its way to integration within Israeli society, as they realized that the 1948 war had altered their fortunes for ever and they no longer belonged to the Arab majority of Palestine, which had rejected in 1947 the Partition Plan, and in their bid to take it all and dispossess the Jews from their part, they lost it altogether. But following the 1967 War, as the West Bank and Gaza came under Israeli control and the Israeli Arabs (as they were dubbed then) regained contact with their kin in the West Bank and Gaza, the old ties were revived and the communal feeling of one and the same people was reconstructed. The mounting national sentiment among the Palestinians in those years wove additional links to their Israeli brethren and turned the question of the Arab minority in Israel from a religious, ethnic, cultural and linguistic issue into a national one. Since then, the leaders of the Arabs in Israel have openly embraced a national course, demanding in effect to be recognized as a national minority, with group rights in the country, while the Israeli state, which has been reluctant to shed its Jewish character, was only disposed to accept them as individuals. Since then, majority and minority have been on the collision course, with the minority totally identifying with the Palestinian cause, which often runs against the interest of their country, and the majority urging them to respect Israeli law and to avoid trespassing the thin boundary between dissent and treason. What is more, while the Arabs in Israel have been vociferous about their rights as citizens of the country and about social payments due to them, they have been negative about contributing any service to the country, military or otherwise. In other words, in the midst of claiming and demanding to the full what the country gives to all its citizens, they stood steadfastly against any attempt to bring them into the fold and participate in any activity that might benefit Israel. They wanted rights without duties, i.e. to create some new kind of modern nobility, which deserves everything and owes nothing.

The division among Israelis between right and left, as regards the Palestinians and the territories, applies almost exactly the same way towards the Israeli Arabs. Because of this stalemate, all Israeli governments have elected to declare the Israeli Arabs "equal and loyal citizens of Israel", at times even operating affirmative action towards them in education and jobs so as to blunt their dissent, or to win their votes in elections, but never was any government courageous or perspicacious enough to hold the bull by its horns and face the brewing problem at its root. It was convenient for both successive Israeli governments and the divided public opinion, to continue to delude themselves that Israeli Arabs could persist in their contradictory role as "loyal" Israelis, at the same time that they totally aligned themselves with the sworn enemies of Israel—the Palestinians. Even the open statements by all 11 Arab members of the Israeli Knesset, to the effect that they supported the Palestinian "Right of Return", which meant, in effect, the end of the state of Israel, was not resounding enough of a wake-up call to shake the government and the public out of their irresponsible slumber. Nor was anyone disturbed when Ahmed Tibi, later a member of the Knesset, became a hired hand by Yasser Arafat, to counsel him on Israeli affairs. It is as if during world war II, German-originating Americans from Chicago and Japanese-originating Americans from California had declared from the podium of the federal and the state legislations where they were members, that they supported the cause of the enemies of their country, or that some of them were nominated advisers on American affairs to their home countries. It is not difficult to imagine the dismay of the American public, and the fury of the legal institutions in pursuing them to justice. In Israel, nothing of the kind happened. Quite the contrary, when Israeli Arabs joined the *Intifada* against the Israeli authorities, and hoisted the flags of the Hamas and Hizbullah in their violent rebellion, in support of the Palestinians who were fighting Israel, the weak and spineless Israeli government appointed a commission of inquiry (known as the Orr Commission), to investigate why 13 Arabs were killed during the rebellion they had triggered, instead of inquiring why and who instigated the unrest and the disturbance to public order.

But now, in view of the growing impertinence of the Arabs in Israel, and their publicized demands for autonomy from state institutions and the establishment of their own, while they feed from the hands of the Israeli government, the Israeli public has begun to awaken. Contributed to that development the much discussed 2003 arrest of Sheikh Ra'id Salah, the blunt and fearless leader of the Islamic Movement in Israel, who was indicted, together with his partners, for using his "charity" foundation *al-Aqsa*, to finance the Hamas, which were outlawed as a terrorist organization. His trial, which received much attention and had regional resonance, saw justice obstructed by a plea bargain, the like of which the state prosecution concludes with petty criminals, but this time bailed that dangerous ideological enemy of Israel out of a severe chastisement and long-term incarceration. The deep disarray it caused in the public in Israel, and some subsequent revelations of several cells of terrorism and spying which were disclosed among Israeli Arabs, finally convinced the unsuspicious and naïve Israelis that their good intentions towards their Arab minority, are not necessarily rewarded by a similarly well-meant conduct on the part of their Arab compatriots. Gradually, it dawned on people, that the Arabs of Israel can no longer be separated from the rest of the Palestinians, and have to be treated more as potential enemies than as equal citizens. This is a crucial change in Israel's strategic considerations, for if 20% of the population might be considered potentially hostile, then the forces that will have to be allocated for domestic defense, in times of emergency, would have to be deducted from the overall military capacity of the country.

While the solution of the Israeli Arabs, who consider themselves Palestinians, must be found, in the long run, as part and parcel of the general Palestinian problem, their immediate future is also in need of an interim break in the build up of tensions, which bring it close to explosion. For example, if for them the Jewish state symbols are unacceptable, and the story of Israel's independence is for them the narrative of the *nakba* (disaster), which had descended on them when they lost their war of annihilation against Israel in 1948, then there is little to celebrate in common. In addition, they stick to their separate educational system which is funded by the state, but educates Arab youth to a different set of values than their Jewish compatriots. In politics, they elect their separatist Arab parties and do not vote, with some exceptions, for the existing ideological parties, which could satisfy their tastes from the extreme right to extreme left. The result is that they do not participate in the political process and remain on the sidelines. However, if the Israeli government annulled the separate school system and conditioned its state funding on a universal curriculum, which would be taught in regional schools where all Jewish, Arab, religious and other children are taught the same values, then not only would there be a chance for all children to share the same values at adulthood, but the standards of Arab pupils would be elevated to the general level. Those who refuse to participate in the national schooling system, would have to study at their whim, but also at their expense.

Education is only the first step towards normalization of the citizenship of the Arabs in Israel. It stands to reason that all graduates of state schools would expect to serve in the armed forces, or fulfill some other sort of national service, as a way of full integration into the system and into Israeli society. If they embark on this course, they can expect to be recruited into the most sensitive security jobs and benefit of the high standards of living, of technology and social services in the country, and also be loyal and productive citizens. Those who prefer to work in their villages, avoid contact with Israel except when they line up for social welfare benefits, study in their own independent educational system, at their expense, and abstain from national service, would have to be differentiated from the others. Citizenship must become the positive and negative incentive to choose one course or the other. The full-fledged participants in state life, will also get its citizenship as of right, like individuals of the Jewish majority who will become entitled to citizenship after they have fulfilled their duties to the state. Those who do not, would be entitled to remain as permanent residents, but without the right to vote and without social benefits, and would come last in admissions to the universities. No country is obliged to raise in its midst its enemies and hand to them the implements to defeat her. The choice is theirs.

Basically, since neither approach of the two parties in Israel has produced any solution to the Palestinian issue, though they alternated in power since 1967 and particularly since Oslo (1993), some other avenue has to be explored, which would also include the problem of Israeli Arabs which has become an inseparable part thereof. Moreover, since King Hussein of Jordan understood the meaning of Oslo for his kingdom, and rushed to settle with Israel before the Palestinians did, the Palestinian problem became even more intractable, hence the need for a novel and imaginative scheme of action. By seeking, and obtaining, Israel's recognition of his Hashemite Kingdom, in what is essentially the Eastern part of Palestine, where the majority of the population is Palestinian, he shed responsibility for the Palestinian plight from his shoulders, he being the Chief of Hashemite Kingdom, not of the Palestinians, and elegantly and squarely handed it to Israel. But Jordan being the home of half the Palestinian people, no solution can be envisaged without it and outside of it, and so when Israel entrapped itself in the problem it cannot resolve on its own, Jordan got legitimacy in standing by and watching in the sidelines as if it had nothing to do with the Palestinians. Looking at it from the Palestinian point of view, Jordan is already theirs by virtue of the majority they constitute there. But if they claimed it officially, they would forfeit their right to demand another Palestinian entity in the West Bank and Gaza. So, they cashed this first achievement, while at the same time pretending that as "stateless" refugees, they are entitled to stake the claim to the West Bank and Gaza. When that too is fulfilled, then Greater Palestine can come about.

Israel and the West had along the years predicated the solution of the Palestinian issue on the division of Palestine into three different parts : Israel, Jordan and the territories; and the Palestinian people into five separate entities : those in Israel are Israelis, those in Jordan are Jordanian, those in the territories are Palestinian, those in Syria and Lebanon are refugees, and those in the west are "diaspora" Palestinians.

According to this analysis, only the Palestinians in the territories and their kin in the refugee camps required a solution, while the others ought to be taken care of by their countries of residence. But the problem is that those in Israel as well as those in Jordan, consider themselves Palestinian, as do those in the refugee camps and the diasporas. This means that even if an agreed solution had been worked out in the territories and the Palestinians acquired statehood as one of the two-state solution, this will not last. Demographically, the territories only consist of one third of the Palestinian population, and the remaining two thirds will continue to knock on Israeli doors and blame the Jews for their plight, especially for the refugee problem which will not disappear. That is exactly the reason why the Palestinians refuse to relinquish the "Right of Return" and to sign the finality of the conflict. This is also the reason why any lasting solution will have to encompass all parts of Palestine and all components of the Palestinian people, Israel included, for only then could the majority of the Palestinians come under one scheme and find one general way out. Since the takeover of Gaza by the Hamas, another complication has been added, that instead of one Palestinian entity in the territories, they might end up in control of two.

One possible solution which might constitute a way out, is to shuffle the cards and begin from the outset. Namely, only if historical Palestine (Israel, Jordan, the West Bank and Gaza) are taken as one unit, and the Palestinian people (in Israel, Jordan, the West Bank, Gaza, Syria, Lebanon and the Diaspora) as one whole, is there a chance to produce a permanent solution to the problem[84]. The premise is that Palestine, the Land of Israel in Israeli parlance, belongs to its two owners: Palestinian Arabs and Israeli Jews, and therefore it has to be partitioned between them, after both acknowledge mutual recognition of the two peoples' right for

---

[84]See R. Israeli, *Palestinians Between Israel and Jordan: Squaring the Triangle,* Praeger, NY, 1991.

self-determination, and accept the legitimacy of each other's movement of national liberation—the PLO and Zionism, as specified in Chapter One above. The exact division of the entire territory will be agreed through negotiation, and will end up in two separate states living side by side in peace. Jordan, which is nothing more than eastern Palestine, will be subsumed under the large Palestinian state, which can combine the existing Hashemite Dynasty with the majority-Palestinian population into the Hashemite Kingdom of Palestine, should the majority wish to keep monarchical rule, or convert it into a constitutional monarchy. After all, the Hashemites are not a country or a people, only a ruling dynasty, while the problem to be resolved is the Palestinian one, to which personal issues of rule must be subordinated. After boundaries are agreed upon, based on the re-division of all historical Palestine between its two entitled owners, the interwoven pattern of settlement, whereby Jews and Arabs are enmeshed within each other—many Arabs in Israel and many Israelis in Palestine- the alien inhabitants remaining on each side would be given a choice between liquidating their property and moving to their home-country (Israel and Palestine), or swear allegiance to their country of residence and gain full rights and undertake all the duties pertaining thereto, or remain as alien residents in their towns and villages but owe their political loyalty to their home country, like Canadians in the US or French in Belgium. Over time, in a condition of peace and of free passage across the borders, an exchange of population will slowly take place which will homogenize the populations on either side of the divide.

Such a scheme, while not responding entirely to the ambitions of either party, can nonetheless satisfy their main ambitions. The Israelis will hold secure and defensible borders where most Arab population will have either moved out (voluntarily), or reconciled to the idea of remaining as a protected minority within a Jewish and Zionist state, with all accruing equal rights and duties, or will elect to cling to its villages and rights of residency, while their Palestinian

citizenship will allow them to vote and participate in the political process of their country. The Palestinians, who will
control a large state, where all their scattered refugees and
diasporas can be resettled, will be in charge of the majority
of their people, in a large part of the land of historical Palestine, where their political, national and societal ambitions
can be finally fulfilled. The list of problems to negotiate and
settle is enormous, but probably much shorter and easier to
resolve than the present stalemate and interminable human
sacrifices that the non-solution entails. Great statesmanship
is not that which distinguishes good from bad, that would be
too easy. Eminent statesmen are those who seize upon the
bad before it grows worse. The present impasse was generated by the failure of leaders to accept the bad (e.g. the
Partition of 1947, the 2000 Camp David proposals) before
it grew worse after all the additional wars and bloodshed
which followed.

The Societal Issues

Most of the societal problems in Israel, save those emanating from the Arab-Palestinian minority which are getting
worse, are curable diseases, inasmuch as the integration of
new immigrants, the slow rapprochement between secular
and ultra-orthodox, the bridging of the gap between rich and
poor in times of economic crisis, and the rapid highways and
railways which link center to periphery and cities to townships and to rural areas, can through an improved educational system and generous social services, narrow the gulf
between the haves and have-nots, and upgrade the quality of
life in general in the country. The most obdurate to change
has been the secular- ultra orthodox divide, which in some
ways resembles the Jewish-Arab dichotomy. They are unlike
the national Orthodox Jews, who are modern and reasonable, involved in society and carry much of its idealism and
of the national missions, and constitute today the backbone
of the Israeli pioneering spirit of yesteryear. Previously, the
national tasks were assumed by the elite of 3% *kibbutzniks,*

who represented the cream of Israeli society and could be found in many positions of leadership, and in key intersections of volunteering jobs and military echelons, like senior officers and pilots. In those days of a guided economy and a socialist political system, their contribution in politics, the economy, the trade unions, social organization and the army, was way out of proportion to their size in the population. But with the dissolution of the cooperative ideal and the dismantlement of many kibbutz communities, by way of privatization, many of the ideals which had guided the state founders have also dissipated. The National-religious element, equivalent to the Kibbutz in size, and equally zealous in character, ideology and devotion, has emerged precisely at that moment of crisis and gradually replaced its predecessors. Today, they can be found at the forefront of settlement and of pioneering, at volunteering for security and social tasks, and at occupying higher and higher ranks in all walks of the military.

Israel is at a crucial juncture today, facing the asymmetrical wars which have been launched by Muslims of fundamentalist affiliation. Not only have the war tactics changed as a result, but also the extreme zeal with which their adherents are prepared to fight to death, or to explode in the process of eliminating their enemies, has totally altered the rules of the game. When the Muslim fighters are imbued within the religious belief that death is not only acceptable but even desirable, for the sake or entering the gates of Allah as *shahids,* then we are in the realm of the irrational, which is not the most effective way to wage war any longer. For those fighters have shown their mettle in the acts of al-Qa'ida terrorists who blew themselves up cold-bloodedly with civilian airplanes and against civilian targets, or of the Taliban in Pakistan and Afghanistan against American and NATO forces, or Hamas and Hizbullah who indiscriminately expose their own civilians by using them as shields, or bombard Israeli civilian settlements for the sake of mass killing. That kind of resolve and readiness for self sacrifice, cannot be countered by any rational war doctrine, and needs to be met with similar religious zeal. Among western and Israeli troops, where the value of life and love of life are cultivated, no force could remotely be mobilized to match this madness, which transcends heroic devotion in battle, usually the domain of the distinguished few, into a fanatically religious creed, which instigates masses to act in self-sacrifice. New tactics must be elaborated to fight this phenomenon, but in Israel it will be the national religious, generally speaking, who are likely to lead this new thinking, because they can combine the devotion stemming from their pioneering spirit and the steadfastness generated by their faith.

The ultra-Orthodox, themselves splintered into many groups and factions, some based on the "courts" of Hassidic dynasties of rabbis, others on their opponents, have nevertheless one thing in common: they are either a-Zionist or anti-Zionist, live in their own enclaves outside the mainstream of Israeli society and do not partake of its culture and pace of life. They are not productive in the sense that the ideal of their men is to devote their lives to study, hence their poverty, which is enhanced by their large families. They, together with the Israeli Arabs, constitute about one third of the population, but it is precisely that third which does not lift a finger for the welfare of the state, refuses to participate in its defense, and has no qualms about being, in the main, recipients of welfare handouts from the state rather than producers of its (their) prosperity. Worse, they regard themselves as laying outside the jurisdiction of the state, and do not adhere to the social contract which holds together any modern society, with a participatory democracy. Yes, they both appreciate democracy, not as a framework which allows them to flourish to the full extent of their capacity, and obligates them to ply to its rules and obligations, but only as a unilateral protection of their rights. But as soon as they are reminded of their duties, they are quick to remind the majority that they are "different" (Arabs or Ultra-Orthodox) and therefore the rules that govern the rest of the citizens do not apply to them. Both often rebel against the authority of the state and of its judiciary, and strive to as much autonomy as possible so as to avoid friction with the authorities. Both participate in the national elections, and even more intensely in the local ones, but they would not accept to be official members of the government for fear of shouldering responsibility for the Zionist state, or as they head anti-Zionist parties they would not be co-opted into any government to start with. Every disturbance of public order which they launch, is claimed as part of their "democratic right", but every prosecution to justice for a crime or a violation of the law they commit, is rejected as a "persecution", discrimination", a "conspiracy" against them; and the Israeli police who enforces it is blasted as "Nazi" or "Gestapo". Both totally negate the major ideals of the state : settlement, security, *Aliya* (Jewish immigration from abroad), and naturally would do everything they can to undo them or disturb their course.

So, like the Arab minority, they must have the choice between the two alternative courses: either to render services to the state and study in its educational system, with the prospects to become full-fledged, productive and creative citizens, entitled to higher learning and social benefits, or to remain plunged in their poverty and religious schools, at their expense, to lose government subsidies to their *yeshiva*, be deprived of their citizenship which grants them the leverage of their voting power, and be devoid of the government grants which permit them to linger in poverty instead of forcing them to a productive life to nurture their large families. The burden of security is so heavy for young Israelis who perform their duties, that recriminations are heard against those who do not shoulder their fair share and expect others to do the job while they pursue other careers without taking up any risks for their lives. Attempts were made to start a voluntary service in the army by ultra orthodox and to get them accustomed to its demands. But the small trickle of volunteers, and the mere idea that a part of the population may volunteer at will, while the other is obliged to serve, will explode one day in the face of the policy makers, as this discrimination becomes more and more untenable, and provides a pretext to the Arabs to bow out of service too. An overhaul of the system in this direction will have to be achieved if Israeli society wishes to continue its steadfast stand in the face of the new dangers it will be confronting in the coming years. To toughen its position outwardly, Israel must be certain, at first, to have solidified its inner front, with the reform in these two sectors taking precedence.

Another major reform is needed to preserve the scientific edge that Israel has had over its neighbors, and to cultivate an appealing living environment that would attract the best Jewish youth abroad to move to Israel. The key to both is education. It is not only unbearable that Israeli school children are no longer in the forefront of the best students in the various scientific disciplines, compared with other western countries, but they have surprisingly fallen far behind many Asian countries as well, in the key areas of physics and mathematics, which provide the scholarly infrastructure for a solid scientific base in the future. One of the major deficiencies of the system has been the catastrophic establishment of different independent "streams" in the educational process, which allowed the Arabs, the ultra religious, and even the moderate religious, leeway to advance their own educational curriculum, based on their convictions and worldview, rather than on a uniform program, common to all Israeli children in the public school system, and geared to promote knowledge and science. All these streams have been financed by the state, meaning that the tremendous financial effort exerted by the state to sustain the educational budget, the highest after security, has been expended to its own detriment. Furthermore, the two unproductive sectors of the population— the Arabs and the ultra Orthodox, who constitute about one third of the total due to their large families, not only lag behind in attaining the requisite high standards in science, but they instill in their curricula disrespect to the Zionist state, encourage its boycott and refusal to serve it or to obey its

laws, and idolize their own icons, like rabbis, Imams or political leaders, who incite against the state authority.

To start with, all streams must be annulled, and a uniform
curriculum in all schools must be pursued, with state encouragement, based on the regional schools that were mentioned
above, where all children, from all walks, groups, convictions and categories, share the same intensive program of
learning, at state expense. The recalcitrant would have to
budget their own schools, and it would not be long before
they will return to knock on the government doors, to ask
for financing in return for submitting to the state school program. Secondly, longer hours of study and more intensive
programs of schooling, should both inculcate in them more
knowledge and science, and more independent and daring
scientific thinking, backed by state of art laboratories for ex-
periments and innovation. The years of waste in pre-school,
where many children are taught by their ambitious parents
far ahead of their school age, demonstrate that children, at
least the gifted among them, are able to start learning much
earlier than the system expects them. For example, if we
could start school at 3 or 4 instead of six, we can complete
elementary grades by age 9 or 10, then six years of middle
school to be completed by age 16, and then college education for all to be completed by age 19. Certainly, the age
of military service would then be postponed by one year,
something that would raise the objections of the army, but in
return for another year of waiting for the new recruits, it will
get them much better educated. After military service, all
the young people, from all streams, convictions and groups,
will be able to decide whether they proceed to universities,
which will admit older and better trained students, and can
then attain higher achievements in science. There are two
prerequisites for this reform to work : that the hours of in-
struction should be prolonged from 4-6 to 6-8 daily, including a hot lunch at school and homework under guidance, in
place, by assistant teachers. Students would be so burdened
by study that they will not only learn and experience more

in a shorter time, but they will also have less time and less inclination for mischief, alcohol, drugs and violence in general. The second is a constant process of selection and encouragement of the outstanding and talented, so that in every school and at every grade, there should be a choice class for the best of the best, where great talent can be continuously absorbed and promoted. These would be the future scientists, and from among them would grow the Nobel Prizes. The entire educational system, which would thereby find itself more competitive and more focused, would also be uplifted if the best lift the rest upward.

The reform would not only rescue thousands from the primitive grip of sectoral education which perpetuates their backwardness, but would also facilitate the integration into the economy and society in general of these large parts thereof which are today left on the sidelines and feel a growing alienation. Even when Arabs and ultra-Orthodox Jews join politics, in order to gain their part of the pie, they remain in fact in the margins of the process, inasmuch as they either participate in coalition governments or support them in return for financial benefits for their sectors, or they engage in a political process which is alien to Israeli democracy and popular consensus. For example, the Ultra-religious do not undertake free democratic elections in their midst, and they derive the authority of their Knesset members from Rabbis who appointed them, not from free elections or from democratically-elected party institutions. Arab MK's may be elected to represent in the Knesset parties whose political platforms and ideologies are inherently inimical to the Zionist state of Israel. Both are nevertheless budgeted by the state, under political parties financing legislation, against its own principles. If those parties were financed only when they stood the test of democracy and loyalty to the state, just like the education of their membership only within the state system, then something would have been done to advance their integration into society and politics. Integration and dissent, inclusion and exclusion, bringing closer and alienating, cannot be pursued at the same time. You cannot use parties and then discard them, as is often the case today. If you signal to them that the policy is to assemble all elements of society around a set of ideals and principles, you also have to follow that up with legislation and applied policy.

One of the great blessings of Israeli society is its sense of solidarity and the great volunteering work which goes on as part of civil society to fill in the gaps left by the deficiencies of government. For example, in spite of the economic crisis which has hit Israel, like much of the world, no major dislocations in the food supply were noticed thanks to the multitude of volunteer welfare societies which took up to assure than no one was hungry. Food packages, which were donated by large companies, packed and dispatched by the volunteer organizations, and soup kitchens which processed donated food and provided hot meals daily for the deprived, made sure that the spirit of solidarity never failed, especially during the High Holidays, when the welfare of the poor is heeded by most average citizens. Based on this vast pool of good-will, any serious reform which can reinforce the strength of Israeli society to confront the tough days ahead, must be planned, executed and enforced. For example, the required changes in the environment to make Israel attractive to new immigrants. It is not enough to be economically prosperous to become attractive to the Jewish diasporas. Immigrants by choice to Israel in the 2000's, unlike the masses of immigrants from the Arab countries and the former Soviet Union, who were more rejected by their countries of origin than lured by Israel in the 1950s, 1960s and the 1990's, and arrived to their new land under duress, would expect a high quality of life in their new country. This consists of quality education for their children, an affable and hospitable society, a clean, aesthetic and healthy environment, respect for the law, safety in the streets, elimination of organized crime and reduction of petty crime. Many of those values can and must be instilled in the children through the school system, just like the preservation of the wild flora of this country in the 1950's, when the wide and omnipresent campaign, through posters, radio and press advertisements and class messages, bore stunning fruits and resulted in a high level effort of preservation.

This generation has become accustomed to that the spoken language has no rules. It is not only that slang words are introduced by youngsters, which are not always understood by the grown-ups, but basic errors in grammar are widespread, not only in market places, but in universities, by professors and students alike, in the Parliament, by ministers and Knesset members alike, and anyone who attempts to correct becomes a badger. In no parliament in the world would this distortion of the national language be tolerated, and become a model for emulation by the masses. Common people, especially children, tend to imitate what they hear, and they soon get entrenched in gross errors which they spread and perpetuate. Or, even when they learn at school the right rules, when they are fortunate enough to learn from knowledgeable teachers, they draw the conclusion that those rules do not matter, since they are not respected. From there, they quickly conclude that no rules matter in general, and each one can do what one wants. From the degenerate form of language one can rapidly apply that non-rule to the tone and content of speech, and engage in wild, uncivilized and violent conduct. Then, one tends to show contempt to other rules like driving, the public square, respect for cleanliness, for aesthetics, for courtesy, for loud behavior, and what have you. Accepting, sharing and respecting rules of common conduct are indivisible. When one respects rules, one respects any and all rules. And when one despises rules, then no rule will survive. To respect rules, children of all ages have to be involved in person. For example, if they are mobilized to correct the Hebrew of their parents, then maybe we will arrive to new standards of the language use. If children are encouraged to belong to youth movements, like boy scouts, and recruited for volunteer work as part of their curriculum, they will get used, through cleaning campaigns, to care about the environment, to plant flowers in public plazas and on window sills, to extend assistance to the elderly, the needy and the weak, and to regard those tasks as part of their upbringing.

The "liberalization" of the 1990s, when means of control were loosened, and wild parties were allowed for young groups, in the name of "freedom", created the sub-culture of drugs, of alcohol and of violence, once parents abdicated their role of parenthood and schools found themselves incapable and helpless in the face of mounting violence and of slackening supervision, where teachers were not allowed to discipline pupils for fear of being sued or attacked by parents. Basic values like respect for the teachers and for national symbols were neglected as "chauvinistic" and "nationalistic", and instead the "narratives" of the enemy were adopted and taught, under the titles of "liberalism" and "understanding the others". The result was that the Arabs in Israel saw their version of history adopted by the state and they increased their demands, not for reconciliation and understanding, but for alienation and secession. Rarely had the world seen such a self-destructive process of abdicating one's values and rules of self-preservation, in favor of embracing the enemy's theses of the conflict and its prescribed solutions. The educational system is the only avenue through which a national revival must be undertaken. But as it has been proven that schools can hardly determine the quality of pupils, and all they can do is to sort them out according to the basic cultural luggage they bring with them from home, parents must be made full partners to the educational process, and be encouraged to cooperate with the school system in the shaping of their children's make up and future. These are the main building blocks for a revival of the legendary Israeli pioneering spirit and collective effort to remake Israeli society and prepare it to encounter the challenges of the years to come.

Chapter 6

Israel's Geo-Strategic Upheaval

The new pattern of asymmetrical wars has shuffled the cards of Israel's strategic thinking. In the era of sanity and predictability, the strategic principles of self defense were clear and acted upon:

1. Due to Israel's narrow waist (8 miles in the coastal plain, which is also the most densely populated and the life artery of the country), any war had to be swiftly transferred to enemy territory. For not only had the IDF to seize, as quickly as possible, the dominating high ground for the successful conduct of the war, but most of the killing and destruction had to be made in enemy territory, as a deterrence from any attack.

2. Due to Israel's small population (during the 1967 War it was limited to 3 million people, compared to the Arabs' over 120 million), Israel could not maintain, unlike her Arab neighbors, a large standing army. Therefore, her defense was based on a small regular land force, to resist any surprise attack until reserve troops could be mobilized, equipped and sent to the fronts. A major role in this scheme was reserved to a large air-force which could interfere immediately to thwart enemy attacks until the main forces could be deployed.

3. To the extent possible, war on more than one front was to be avoided. Sometimes that strategy worked (as in the Sinai and Lebanese War, 1956 and 1982, respectively), but for the most part (in 1948, 1967, 1973), the involvement of many Arab states could not be avoided. In that case, they had to be tackled one by one, because tiny Israel could not

be expected to wield enough troops to decide the war on all fronts simultaneously.

4. For a time, Israel tried to build an "outer tier" in the outside circle beyond her immediate Arab neighbors, in order to help contain them, or at least pin down some of their forces in case of war. In the north, beyond Syria, it was Turkey which, though a Muslim country, was under the modernizing sweep of her civil parties, which shared the secular spirit of the Attaturk revolution. Turkey, which had captured a Syrian territory around Alexandretta, was in such hostile tension with its Syrian border, that it also found it expedient to connect with Israel, so as to threaten Damascus in a pincer move. To the east, it was Iran under the Shah, also an Islamic country, in historical enmity with the Arab world due to her Shi'ite Islam and her pro-Western stance, who also found it expedient to collaborate with Israel, and in so doing she was balancing the power of Iraq and Jordan, the two major constituents of Israel's "eastern front". To the south it was Imperial Ethiopia, which, due to its control of the sources of the Nile, on which Egypt depended, was thought to be able to keep Egypt, the largest and most powerful Arab country, in check. The concept of the "outer tier", which worked intermittently and partly, for a while, died out with the change of regime in all three countries that constituted it.

5. To the extent possible, to make sure that at least one world power supported the Israeli war endeavor, not only for the sake of diplomatic backing in international forums, but also for emergency economic and military supplies, should the war be prolonged and the war equipment undergo an unusual degree of attrition, like what happened in 1973. Apart from 1956 when the support came from France and Britain, in all wars thereafter the main backing came from the US.

6. The wars had to be swift and short, to allow the country to release its reserve recruits to their civilian jobs, so as to reactivate all aspects of the economy, which were half or fully paralyzed for the duration of the war. But in case of prolonged wars, like the 1948, 1973 and the Second Lebanese

Wars (2006), the country must be able to sustain the war efforts despite the civilian manpower difficulties.

7. The Rear had to remain outside the scope of the war, due to its vulnerability and the very high sensitivity to casualties in the small and solidarity-prone Israeli society.

While most of these principles were more or less abided by during the long years of conventional wars, the advent of the era of terrorism, which turned the situation upside down, compelled Israel to revise its strategy, to adopt new war doctrines or to perfect old ones, to buy or develop new weaponry, like drones and pilot-less aircraft, and to target individuals in the enemy camp, rather than confront armies, amidst a supreme effort to avoid the civilian casualties which would have served the enemy's strategy and aroused the fury of the world against Israel. Israel came to realize that unlike in previous wars, where military victories destroyed the enemy's forces for a while, until it could recover its strength and rehabilitate its forces, in the new asymmetrical wars, Israel was doomed to lose in any case, regardless of the results of the struggle in the battle field. With two major enemies-Egypt in the south and Jordan (and its potential partner in the Eastern Front- Iraq) in the East, out of the game due to their peace treaties with Israel, only Syria remains as an immediate conventional menace, while the others, though still powerful and potentially hostile in case of change of regime there, and though not exactly friendly to the neighbor they signed peace with, do not pose an immediate danger to Israel. In case the Muslim Brothers take over in Egypt, a possible reversal if the elections are honest and if Cairo desists from its monarchical designs in nominating Mubarak's son as successor, their first move, in sync with the Hamas, Syria and Iran, would be to abrogate the peace with Israel and revert to square one. In Jordan, the abnormal situation where an absolute king, who was elected by no one, rules his Palestinian-majority population by fiat, while maintaining a rubber-stamp "Parliament" which he can suspend or dissolve at any time, cannot endure for ever. A Palestinian take-over, to be added to the Palestinian state to be established in the West Bank (and probably Gaza), becomes a very likely possibility. In that eventuality, the rules of war will have to be reversed again.

Quite apart from all that, a new element has been weighing heavily against Israel in the military equation of the Middle-east. The military balance is no longer an Arab-Israeli affair, but since the Iranian Revolution in 1978, Iran has not only joined the Arabs against Israel, but has become the most vitriolic enemy of Israel, sworn and dedicated to its annihilation, on Islamic grounds that other Muslim states do not dare to invoke. So much so, and because it has been building a nuclear and missile arsenal to achieve its genocidal goal, that the Arabs have begun fearing its hegemony, which might turn against them. Strange bed-fellows are getting used to the idea of smooching together when Iran achieves its nuclear aims and the pro-Western Arabs are driven to some forms of collaboration with Israel, in order to escape Iran's domination and menace. The much talked about nuclearization of Iran can be analyzed *ad hominem,* focusing on the personality of Ahmadinajad, the President of Iran, who has often been compared to Hitler in both his dreams of *grandeur* and his visceral anti-Semitism; or *ad rem,* with a special emphasis on the technological achievements of Iran in its quest for regional power. But it can and should also be discussed in the context of the Islamic Revolution, which had been dubbed by Ayatullah Khomeini not merely as a domestic anti-Shah upheaval in Iran but as an international Islamic movement designed to extricate world Islam from its submissive torpor and launch it to prominence as a major player on the world arena. Moreover, though Iran had, by definition, never been part of the Arab-Israeli conflict, it has since the Revolution, launched itself in the forefront of the enemies of Israel, thus according to the Middle Eastern dispute a much more religious vein than it ever had and making it all that much more insoluble. For injecting massive doses of faith into an already difficult political situation certainly makes it more intractable due to the absolute demands made by Believers who feel they cannot negotiate away or compromise over what has been bequeathed to them by divinity.

This intricate and dangerous matter of Iran's nuclear weapons could also be tackled from its international aspects, namely not only the challenges put to it by the West and the UN which have nominally denied Iran's right to go nuclear, but mainly its open defiance of those challenges that stems from the personality of the leader, the religious nature of the regime and the general escalation in the Middle Eastern conflict. Particularly challenging are the concrete and repeated threats by Iran, a member of the UN, to "eliminate from the map" another member state -Israel, which have remained almost undisputed by other members of the world community beyond the inoffensive formula of "unacceptable" attached to them. In a normal world, any decent country or government should strive to oust Iran from the UN unless it reneged on its unheard of threats, but it seems that either Iran has so much clout, or that the rest of the world has been so apathetic to the fate of Israel and, once again, of the Jewish people, that Iran is having its way for now and its leader's promises of a new Holocaust (the first one has been categorically denied) are coming to be accepted as a matter of course.

Some Arab and Muslim media have criticized Iran's tactics of denial vis-a-vis Israel and the Jews, not so much due to its fallacy, immorality or genocidal import, but because they "inflict damage to the Muslim cause". One of them wrote:

> The extremist Iranian President may have gained some points in his vocal propaganda in the hate-mongering satellite channels, but diplomatically he only caused damage to his country which is going through a difficult period. He also caused severe damage to the Muslims by creating a political-cultural climate in which feelings of hate drown out the Muslims' noble and humane sentiments...

Ahmadinejad and his ideological followers are misleading themselves and the media when they say that the [Holocaust denial] conference was held for historical research, and that it put to the test the West's receptiveness of free speech and academic research... Those evil and despicable figures... who were invited to the conference, and who prevented Palestinian Attorney Mahamid[85] from participating in it, are they historians? And those six British Orthodox rabbis are neither historians nor do they deny the historicity of the Holocaust, they merely oppose the existence of the Jewish state before the coming of the Messiah. Ahmadinejad is using them as a fig leaf to cover up his moral shame, since he wants to wipe Israel off the map...

There are political activists who refuse to accept the Jewish Holocaust as justification for harming the Palestinians and denying their right to an independent state..., but they too express these views as political actors and not as researchers or historians...[86].

Ahmadinajad grew up in the *basiji,* the mass movement built by Khomeini at the onset of the Revolution, which turned into a militia where devotion and sacrifice were the key concepts in their human waves attacks against Iraq, regardless of the human losses involved. The principle cultivated by Khomeini taught that survival of the fighters was irrelevant, because it was participation in the battles of Allah, regardless of their result, which provided fulfillment and gratification[87]. So when this former son of the *basiji* went into politics, first as the Mayor of Teheran and then as President of his country, he was sure to implement politics of irrationality, whose consequences did not matter, even if that should involve huge loss of life for his own people. What counted was to carry out Iranian goals of *grandeur* via

---

[85]An Israeli-Arab attorney who attempted to attend the conference but was denied access to Iran.

[86]*Al-Sharq al-Awsat* (London) 16 Dec, 2006.

[87]Matthias Kuntzel, "Ahmadinejad's Demons", *The New Republic*, 24 April, 2007, pp 15-17.

nuclearization, and to fearlessly spread anti-Semitism and Holocaust denial as long as that was inspired by the Hidden Imam, the true master of the world, whose coming to install the rule of justice and plenty in the world was very much at hand.

Ahmadinejad's denials are many and stem from his absolute conviction that for the sake of the Hidden Imam, who has himself revealed his imminent coming to the deluding President of Iran, anything said or done is appropriate as long as it can serve the ultimate goal. So, if he is persuaded that the only legitimacy of the state of Israel in the eyes of the West is the Holocaust that it inflicted on the Jews, then denial of the Holocaust means also the delegitimation of the Jewish state as a step toward its elimination. On the one hand he boasts about his country's nuclear facilities and its inherent right to develop them, but at the same time he denies any intent to develop nuclear weapons. But he also refuses to allow open and complete international controls or to cease his nuclear effort or to relent on his plans to wipe Israel off the map, or to submit to world sanctions, all contradictory acts of denial, much in the style of his former *nemesis,* Saddam Hussein, who was swept out of the way, courtesy of the US. For if he does not entertain evil plans, then why does he repeat his declarations vis-à-vis Israel, and why does he not allow international supervision? His stubborn, purposeful, obsessive and one-track-mindedness leaves no doubt as to his determination to pursue his goals, and as to his deep religious convictions about their feasibility come what may. The consequences to his people, let alone to others, do not even seem to interest him. He has nothing of the pragmatism of his predecessors, Rafsanjani and Khatami, for he is bent on apocalyptic thinking. One cannot help think of Ahmadinejad's close parallels to Hitler, who ultimately brought disaster upon the world, his own people and himself, though having "revealed" that Hitler was Jewish, a close adviser of the Iranian President would have certainly rejected that comparison.[88]

---

[88]Muhsen Razay, the Secretary of the Council for the Protection of the State Interests, in an interview to Iranian Internet site Baztab, 28 Dec. 2006.

The man is a complicated one, and his blunt anti-Semitism and committed anti-Israel views have been sidelined
in the eyes of the world due to the prevalence of his nuclear
problem with the West, which senses that nuclear weapons
in the hands of this entirely irrational creature may generate a worldwide apocalypse. Think again of Hitler wielding
that kind of destructive power before he was destroyed. Like
Hitler, he has a plan that he pursues doggedly: to carry out
the legacy of Ayatullah Khomeini that his predecessors had
failed to do. That means, exporting the Islamic Revolution to
adjoining countries, strengthen Shi'ite Islam in its confrontation with the Sunnite majority in the Muslim world, become a regional power backed by nuclear weapons, use the
oil money to finance those plans even at the expense of the
welfare of his own people, build a web of support by major
world powers to counter any western attempts to reduce him
down to size, and eliminate the only adjoining power that
may stand in his way, namely Israel. We will examine those
goals one by one, in view of the fact that despite the many
opposition groups which watch with horror the road where
their leader is heading, notably the open criticism of revered
Ayatullah Muntazari[89], he seems to have gained the support
of Supreme Leader Ayatullah Khamena'i. For once, unlike
the first quarter century of the Revolution (1979-2005) when
the more or less pragmatic holders of power (Banu Sadr,
Rafsanjani and then Khatami) seemed to attenuate in deeds
the Islamic passion of the supreme leaders (Khomeini and
then Khamena'i), it is the holder of power who has now become the chief ideologue and engine of the Islamic Revolution, with no one in sight able or willing to contain or bridle
him.

Iran's dangerous unconventional threats on Israel, which
make up for the distance and lack of immediate boundaries with Israel, were supposed to create a new balance of
terror, like the one which maintained peace between East
and West during the cold war. But due to the irrationality of

---

[89]Roz (Iran), 16 April, 2007. See Memri Report, 24 May, 2006

Ahmadinejad and his present team, and his seeming indifference about the fate of his country and people in case of a nuclear conflict, in a culture which defies death and promotes sacrifice, it is to be feared that even in unconventional wars an asymmetry is created, where one side might not be deterred by the other, and might foolishly choose to take the risk, regardless of the resulting apocalypse. But even before we get there, Iran already controls two highly skilled, and supremely committed, ground forces—Hizbullah and Hamas, which can operate as *avant-gardes* geared to systematically erode the forces of the enemy by sustained shelling, by kindling border skirmishes, and causing enough civilian casualties on the Arab side to warrant UN condemnations, so as to discredit Israel and turn it into the aggressor, even if she is the victim of Iranian designs. The border wars of Lebanon in 2006 and in Gaza in 2008/9, have been the most dramatic illustration not only of this war doctrine but also of its stunning success. Both Iran and its two agents on Israel's borders, have practically undone the previous war strategies of Israel and forced it to alter them in some very unpredicted ways.

On the geo-political situation of Israel, not much will have changed if Israel withdraws from the high grounds of the West Bank which give it some strategic depth to defend the over-populated and over-industrialized coastal plain. Quite the contrary, due to the mounting military capacities of the Palestinians, particularly the Hamas in Gaza who have upgraded their arsenals of missiles, the main international airport of Israel can be paralyzed, and Israel isolated from the outside world, at the whim of any local Palestinian commander, who might not be content with the arrangements his political leaders may agree to. The security wall which Israel built along the West Bank to protect the towns and villages within Israel, is not only rejected as an "apartheid wall" by the Palestinians and the world community", but it will have no effect if either the Palestinians can access it from their side and sabotage its defensive efficacy, or train themselves to lob shells and missiles across it and disturb civilian life in Israel all the same. The 8-year lesson from Gaza, which was foolishly and unnecessarily evacuated in 2005, must serve as a guide to what is to come should Israel relinquish the high ground it is holding today. Besides, Israel's withdrawal from the West Bank will leave under Palestinian sovereign rule the main water aquifer of Israel, and will enable them, who have no concern for environment, to let their untreated sewer and industrial pollution to gravitate freely from the their high altitudes to Israel's low ground. What shall Israel do then? Fight a war to regain the territories? Who will accept a war for the sake of sewer and environment? The September 2009 Conference of the Fat'h in the West Bank, which was supposed to encourage the "moderate" elements among the Palestinians, ended up vowing the continuation of the "armed struggle" against Israel, in effect guaranteeing that the Palestinian forces being trained by the US and Europe today, will eventually turn their weapons against Israel. In case of a sudden Palestinian shelling of Israeli territory, the IDF can no longer transfer the battle to enemy territory, because there is none. In the south, Israel tried on Christmas 2008 to arrest the shelling from Gaza on Israeli villages, but since the Hamas was not recognized as a belligerent, it was Israel who was blamed and condemned. Does Israel wish to be in a similar situation along the much more complicated boundary of the West Bank?

Although Israel's population has remarkably increased since 1967, the parallel growth of the Arab population in the country, which is much more nationalistic than before, puts additional defense burdens on the home front. On the other hand, hardly does or will the small skirmishes and border operations require the massive mobilization of troops to deploy along Israel's endangered boundaries. The role of the air force did not diminish, although it is now done on the basis of accurate intelligence, with the purpose to hit terrorists before they launch their rockets, or to punish them after they did. Yes, fighter jets can still pass over Arab territories and sow awe among them, but short of an all-out war like that of Lebanon, or of Gaza, where massive bombardments were launched in an attempt to stop the missiles from raining over Israeli villages and towns, the air force will limit its main operational activity to drones and pilot-less aircraft to perform surgical attacks against known terrorists. In asymmetrical wars, new dilemmas emerge, as to who should be targeted, mainly because of the risk of collateral damage likely to harm non-combatants. Nevertheless, operations of this sort are constantly pursued, after the promises and the risks are evaluated on a case by case basis. For example, there was a case when Hamas leaders convened in their HQ in one of Gaza high-rises, which was otherwise inhabited by civilians. Similarly, there was solid intelligence about vast arsenals of weapons and explosives stored in the basements of such high rises. After many deliberations on the potential casualties that such gatherings and weapons could generate if left untreated, versus the tremendous civilian human loss on the enemy side, the decision was adopted of refraining from action. Conversely, in cases of targeted killing of specific terrorists in buildings and in cars, where it was judged that collateral damage would be minimal, the operation was launched, and Israel was condemned for "killing children", as if the other party was made of innocent saints. That dilemma is encountered by the Americans and NATO in Afghanistan and in Pakistan, and was equally tormenting the western forces which bombed Serbia and Kosovo, but it never stopped those who now clamor for "war crimes" against Palestinians, in spite of the fact that they too had engendered thousands of civilian casualties. A low intensity war of this sort does not require massive troops, only highly qualified few, except that when there is escalation and the need arises to move in order to mop up an area, then a large-scale operation would be needed.

Such a war is also asymmetrical inasmuch as it is waged by a regular Israeli army, not against the armed forces of Lebanon, which is a state but it does not control its territory, its troops and its policy, or against Palestinians who do not have a state as yet. Therefore, waging such a war, which has no designated enemy and cannot be directed against any belligerent government, renders victory impossible. Instead, those Muslim terrorist movements, which serve by proxy the interests of Syria and Iran, do not have any territory that they can lose, cannot be made to pay any price for their aggression, and are virtually immune to deterrence before the war, to punishment in its course, and to diplomatic chastisement in its aftermath. While they inflict heavy and concrete losses and damages on Israel, they become virtual when retribution is mounted against them. They can be found nowhere, they have no headquarters or bases and therefore their lifelines, support, financing and logistics cannot be found and destroyed. One can and does search for them, but since they are diffuse among existing civilians structures and hierarchies: family, clan, household, family property and businesses, they cannot be destroyed and annihilated like institutionalized military structures and formations, which are separate from civilian society. Here, the head of the clan, or the local cleric can also serve, *ex-officio,* as the head of the cell, and family storage cellars and barns can become the stockpiles of explosives and rockets, which evasive fighters would come to deploy and shoot, and then disappear into the fog of the night without leaving a trace. Whom can one hold responsible for the attack? The family who lives in place? If you bomb those positions in retaliation, you will be accused of "savagely" and "cruelly" attacking "peaceful civilians" and destroying their homes, and not long after the media would show the pictures of destruction and the UN would adopt resolutions condemning Israel. This is what happened in Lebanon and Gaza, proving that asymmetrical wars cannot be won. The defendant becomes so helpless, that his troops which had been built on rational principles of conventional warfare, are suddenly worthless and force a new thinking, a new strategy and new armaments. Not a better army is needed in this sort of struggle, but a better strategy, more cunning, wiser stratagems and more crafty wiles. And above all, when the course is chosen, to remain determined to carry it through whatever the resentment it causes among the hypocrite bleeding hearts of the world.

Since no purely conventional war will be possible in the future, unless a general breakdown pulls Egypt and Jordan back into the fold of warriors, there is no more sense to the idea that a multi front war has to be avoided. Because here, only a small fraction of the Israeli troops can be operated, at any front, against the evasive terrorist enemy, therefore small elite formations can be deployed simultaneously in various frontlines to tackle different threats at the same time. Under these circumstances, no decisive wars to end threats can take place, only intermittent battles of attrition which will erupt and vanish at the whim of the terrorists. In between these mini-wars, the terrorists would ask for a *hudna* to regroup and re-equip themselves, before they launch the next terrorist operation, or harassment by shelling against Israeli villages and towns. Strangely enough, Arab countries, both those who have made peace with Israel, and particularly those who have not, would feel obligated to put an end to the hostilities, because they cannot be seen as sitting-by, with arms folded, while their brethren are taking a beating from Israel. Muslim countries like Iran and Turkey, who are not direct parties to the conflict, and even farther ones like Pakistan and Afghanistan, will come to the rescue of the battered terrorists, but beyond diplomatic and moral support, they will not be able to do much. The lessons of Lebanon and Gaza have taught both the terrorists and their host countries, that the losses and damages inflicted on the economies and inhabitants of those lands, including the fighting groups therein, would warrant a more cautious strategy before they launch the next attack. The last thing they need would be the resentment of the populations among which they operate, if they do nothing to reconstruct the ruins, to pay indemnities for the damages, and to sooth the anger of the victims, lest they refuse to take the burden of the next war. And there are limits to how many times they can cause destruction and then make amends for it. This is the drawback of hiding behind a civil population which cannot be made to suffer endlessly in order to serve the purposes of the terrorists.

The most revolutionary change which shattered the Israeli strategic concept was the reliance on the outside tier of allies. To begin with Iran, a close alliance linked it to Israel, based on security considerations. The pro-western and modern Shah was inclined to reform an authoritarian rule, and silenced his opponents, the most prominent of whom was Ayatullah Khomeini, who left Iran for Iraq and lived there in exile for 15 years, until the Shah's agreement with Saddam over the Kurdish issue, forced the popular cleric into another exile in a suburb of Paris (Neaufle-le-chateau) in 1975. It is from there that Khomeini made a triumphant return to Tehran in February 1978, after the Shah had abdicated and the Islamic Revolution took over. Together with the fugitives of the previous regime, many Israeli and other diplomats escaped by the skin of their teeth and never saw Tehran again. In Turkey, the cold relations with Israel since it was established, because of the Arab objection to warm them, were replaced in the 1990s by an extraordinarily warm and close alliance, which was forged by successive civil governments in Ankara, and reached its peak in military and economic cooperation on a grand scale.[90] But things began to get sour during the prime-ministership of Necmettin Erbakan who was elected in 1996-8 on a Muslim ticket, which by definition did not stand for a close relationship with Israel, which was supported by the military who regarded themselves as the curators of Attaturk's legacy. In 1998 the Muslim Party was ousted by the army from government (they call that system a "democracy"), and prohibited from running again. But in the elections of December 2002, and again in 2006, the Muslim party under Erdogan and Gul, which replaced the

---

[90]See R. Israeli, "The Odd Couple: Turkey and Israel", *Orbis*, January, 2001, pp 165-179.

prohibited one, won the majority in Parliament and slowly began to take a distance from Israel and edge closer to Iran and Syria, thus jeopardizing those special relationships with Israel, and electing the Hamas and interests in the Arabs and Muslim worlds over them. In Ethiopia too, the alliance with Israel, which was based on the personal commitment of Haile Selassie its Emperor, vanished when the military under dictator Mengistu Mariam mounted a coup and scraped all the privileges which had accrued to Israel before. *Sic transit gloria mundi.*

Since the 1973 War, when the Cold War was still at its height, it was necessary for the US to align itself totally with Israel and secure an airlift to replace the rapidly wearing off hardware equipment, at the risk of a super-power confrontation. Thereafter, the US gradually enmeshed itself into the Middle East conflict and took over from the Soviet Union the political sponsorship of Egypt and then became also its chief military provider. That trend later facilitated the disengagement and then the peace treaties between Israel and Egypt (1979)and Israel and Jordan (1994). Throughout the past few decades the US became the sole power with which Israel took counsel for war and for peace, and the two countries, all proportions guarded between tiny Israel and superpower US, have even maintained a joint strategic team which convened twice annually to coordinate defense matters, including strategies, military appropriations, research and development, security threats and their thwarting, and even regional and global security concerns, like world terrorism, terrorist organizations, intelligence collaboration and the like. The degree of intimacy in those meetings has grown so close that even though Israel is not a formal ally of the US, it has come to be favored in many regards, like intelligence sharing, research and development of new sophisticated weaponry, especially in the high tech area, financial aid to facilitate the acquisition of new hardware, even "lending" to the IDF new equipment from the American stockpiles pending the delivery to Israel of its due equipment.

American support and constant cooperation are not invoked only in time of war or crisis, but has become a constant feature, either because crisis follows crisis in this era of continuous crisis, or due to the unpredictable evolution of world terrorism and the war against it. Asymmetrical wars, being limited, evasive, amorphic and without a stated exit, Israel (and the US) found themselves in permanent alert to thwart whatever new threat presents itself.

Asymmetrical wars are no longer swift and short, because they are low intensity and are made to be constant and continuous, with occasional peaks as they evolve. They are calculated by their initiators to harass, drive the enemy to attrition, drain its blood, its economy and its morale and bring it to realize that this is a war it cannot win, therefore better give it up. But unlike the US in Afghanistan, which may, after long years of struggle, as in Vietnam and Iraq, abandon the battlefront and go home, to wait to be attacked there, as on September 11, Israel has nowhere to go, therefore it better devise a plan of survival amidst constant war with no likelihood of deciding it one way or the other. Israel can never win that war, due to the interminable reserves or manpower, funds, hatred and commitment that the Arab and Muslim parties can wield. If it were possible, Israel could at least negotiate a long term cease-fire or, still better, a peace, imperfect as it may be. The problem is twofold: a cease fire (or its different varieties of *hudna,* truce or armistice, which were all tried but never held more than temporarily, in itself connotes that the conflict is not over, and the Muslim and Arab parties keep cultivating it and instilling in their masses the assurance of a future victory. Secondly when Israel made peace (with Egypt and Jordan thus far), it was concluded with the "moderate" pro-western rulers, who were themselves concerned about their position of power, which was threatened precisely by those who vowed continuous war against Israel, like the Muslim Brothers in both countries. After the peace was signed, its enemies in both countries continue to disgrace and disavow it, to ban and reject normalization with

Israel, and to threaten to abrogate the peace when they come
to power. It is not known how long might the present rulers
of Egypt and Jordan, or their successors, hold on to power,
but if democratization takes over, the position of peace re-
jectionism might well win and reverse the present state of
affairs. To predicate peace on authoritarianism, and to fear
that democracy might militate against it, is not a very hope-
ful idea to wake up every morning with.

And finally, the question of the home front has totally
been brought upside down, since it became literally what it
is—a home front, i.e. the frontline can no longer be kept
away from the non-combatant civilians, because in the era
of asymmetrical wars, the terrorists can both dispatch Islamikaze squads into the Israeli population centers and sow
destruction, death and fear, or from the perceived safety of
their shelters among their own civilian population, launch
both short range and long range missiles to cover practically
all Israeli towns and villages, including the Arab villages.
Unlike Israel and western countries, which at least make
an effort to minimize casualties among the civilian population of the enemy, in the case of Israel by spreading leaflets
warning of an incoming attack, calling home telephones to
warn against an impending bombing, or sending cellular
phone and Internet messages; and to lessen suffering among
civilians by distributing food and evacuating serious casualties to their own medical facilities, Muslim terrorists, in
Afghanistan, Iraq or the Middle East, seek, on the contrary,
to maximize civilian casualties among their enemies. Unlike the western attempts for discriminating surgical attacks
to differentiate between innocent civilians and the terrorists
who hide among them, the terrorists shell and bomb indiscriminately, and they care little where the bombs fall. In addition, they stock each bomb, rocket and shell with nails and
screws, to increase the numbers of the casualties beyond the
immediate hit, and to intensify the suffering of the casualties.
We know from their writings, posters and declarations, that
by maximizing the casualties on the one hand, something

which they cannot attain easily due to the good defenses Israel provides its citizens, and by exposing to the media their many civilian casualties to whom they provide no shelter or protection, they always achieve their goal of presenting their enemy as "cruel" and "ruthless", while they, as "evidenced" by the low numbers of the casualties they inflict, are the "humane" and "innocent victims". The media always fall in this trap, and so does world public opinion. Only when massive attacks like September 11, or Bali 2002, or the recurrent massacres in Iraq and Afghanistan yield a large number of western casualties, do the Muslim terrorists boast of their "great success", or "decisive victory", or "humiliation of the enemy's arrogance, and certain media fall again in that trap and aggrandize and spread the terrorist's "achievements".

Israel's war strategies have so much changed since the ushering in of the new era of terrorism and asymmetrical wars, that the old thinking and preparedness for war have to be totally revised. For one, not only does the new era proclaim continuous wars, but at low intensity, but they are also ideological wars, a true clash of civilizations. The gains and victories now sought by the terrorists are not assets, like territories and funds, namely quantitative issues which can be negotiated and agreed upon, but ideological ones, namely the Muslim ideology is set to take over all the rest. This is a cosmic qualitative struggle, which knows no compromises, understandings and negotiations, where those most obstructing the way to victory, i.e. the West and Israel, are targeted first. Hence the absolute necessity, and urgency, to devise new strategies.

Chapter 7

The Political Atomism in
Israel and its Price

Since Israel's inception, and even before, the major political body in that *ambiance* of pioneering and socialism,
when the *kibbutz* was the leading social ideal, and manual
work was promoted to the degree of religion, was a vari-
ety of labor parties, chief among them was *Mapai,* the acronym for the Party of Workers of the Land of Israel, which
was to hold the reins of power in the country for decades to
come. Though other splinter parties also existed, to the left
of *Mapai*, like *Mapam,* the acronym for the United Workers
Party, to differentiate from another group, *Ahdut Ha'avoda*
(United Labor or Labor Union), the predominance of *Mapai*
was unshakable. Just like the Soviet Block, where the appellation "Democratic" which preceded the official names
of East Germany, Romania etc, meant that there was no
democracy there, so the various "united" labor parties and
"united *kibbutz"* movements, meant that they were all splinter groups which could not dwell under the same roof. But
at least the differences were ideological, even if today they
seem to us ludicrous, and certainly not justifying dividing
kibbutzim and families in two, because they belonged to
two different "united" wings of the labor movement. Most
of the disagreements between parties were either personal,
between such towering ideologues as David Ben Gurion
and Berl Katznelson in *Mapai* and Meir Ya'ari and Jacob
Hazan in *Mapam.* They were all devoted Zionists, but they
viewed differently the idea of compromising with the Arabs

of Palestine, versus building up defenses against them as the establishment of the State of Israel loomed in the horizon. On the more international arena, the attitudes towards the Soviet Union and world communism deeply divided the various trends within Labor, from the pragmatic and realistic views of Ben Gurion who understood that Stalin was a tyrant who persecuted Jews and distorted the socialist message, to the romantic socialism of Ya'ari, who viewed Stalin as the Sun of nations, diminished his tyrannical image in order to aggrandize beyond measure the great promise of socialism, world peace, and of the fraternity between nations. So much so, that the communist block was dubbed in their parlance the peace camp, while the Americans, NATO and the West were the Imperialists.

As against these tendencies, which led the Zionist movement since its inception, though its most renown leader after Theodore Herzl was Chaim Weizmann, a man of more liberal convictions, stood in opposition the Revisionists, headed by Ze'ev Zhabotinsky, the father of the Beitar youth movement, which was often dubbed by the socialists as "fascists" and often likened to Mussolini's "brown shirts". In the battle for the souls of the very tiny Jewish constituencies in Palestine, the Revisionists took part and eventually engendered the Heruth Party, founded and led by Menachem Begin in 1948, who merged it with the Liberal Party in 1973, to form what we know today as the Likkud (Consolidation) Party, due to the many right-wing components that it brought together into that union. That was a major revolution in Israeli politics, since Begin who was considered until then outside the consensus, and was a severe critique of the government policies for his almost 30 years in opposition, when he headed a middle sized party, never strong enough to contend for the prime ministership, was suddenly catapulted to power by the elections of 1977. Begin, together with his Liberal partners, who had been co-opted into various coalition governments under *Mapai,* remained firm on his hawkish policies towards the Arabs, especially the Palestinians, whom he regarded as unworthy contenders for the Land of Israel that he refused to relinquish to them; and he also merged in his worldview the economic policies of his liberal partners, which would allow the country to break the shackles of socialist economics, and start a process of liberalization and privatization which would launch Israel into the modern era. That transition of power from one worldview to the other was the last time that a clear alternation was presented to the voters to decide about. Since then, the process of atomization in the political structure and culture of the country has become so fractious, and the choices so diversified and nuanced, and economic and social issues upgraded as the main concerns of the voters, that politics have been profoundly transformed.

The basic assumption in Israel had always been that Labor and its associates would ensure the welfare of Israeli society, though in the socialist style of a planned economy, a large public sector where trade unions are also large employers, but at the same time would stand fast on security affairs, due to the hawkish stands of David Ben-Gurion, who had never relented, at the same time, from seeking peaceful avenues to Israel's neighbors. In this mood of self-confidence in the government and in the future, the 1967 War broke out, after 11 years of almost complete quiet along the borders due to the post 1956 war's cease-fire arrangements, backed by UN troops in the Sinai. Those 11 years were also the best to date for Israel's development in terms of building an economic infrastructure and in absorbing the masses of new immigrants who flocked to the country. When the new war challenge came in May 1967, as President Nasser expelled the UN forces from the Sinai and closed the Tiran Straits to Israeli shipping, there was no doubt that when the ruling government of Levy Eshkol went to war, he was automatically assured of Begin's support. That assumption has greatly confirmed in the following years, that just as only the left can wage war without causing dissent or disagreement, so only the right could engage in peace, due to virtual assurance that the left would always support peace. The repeated tests of this thesis would constitute in the coming years the main basis for the frequent shifts in Israeli politics. During the 1967 pre-war crisis, as Israel was dipped in a profound anxiety due to the threats of the Arabs to annihilate her, weak and un-popular Eshkol brought into his government two representatives from the right wing opposition, including Begin. Little else in the history of Israeli politics had ever had such a tremendous impact on the legitimation of Begin's opposition, which had been under Ben Gurion literally ex-communicated beyond the pale. Begin, who had been dubbed by Ben Gurion a "clown" for his rhetorical fireworks, and whose party was systematically boycotted from joining any coalition government, was suddenly a legitimate minister in the Israeli cabinet, a fact that many Israelis had a hard time to digest. That would open the gate for him to rise to the prime ministership 10 years later, in May 1977.

The cooptation of Begin and his party into the Israeli government signaled the end of the bitter ideological debates within Israeli politics and the inauguration of the era of pragmatic policies based on two pillars: security for Israel and a sound economy to support the out of proportion military spending for such a small country, where almost one third of the population, the ultra-Orthodox and the Arabs, constituted a burden rather than an asset in the area of security and economic productivity. And so, over the years since, did the large two blocs, of the right and the left, have to collaborate within the same governments once they realized that they could not build their coalition on their own. The blunting of ideology, and the shaping of a national consensus, tended to increase the center of the political map and to blur even further the divide between left and right, and caused atomization of the political scene since no one political party was dominant any longer. Unlike the US, and the UK (the one a presidential and the other a parliamentary system), which maintained a two party alternation (Republicans and Democrats, and Tories and Labor, respectively) in spite of the blurring of ideology there too; but like Germany where the domination of the two parties (CDU and SPD) has also been waning, the two major parties in Israeli politics, (Labor and Likkud) which used to score 40% of the vote at their apex, and form governments at will, started to shrink to 30 and 20% and even below, enabling other variants to rise and making any coalition government utterly dependent on them. Again like in Germany, this situation at times forced the two major parties in Israel to form a "grand coalition" between the erstwhile rivals, not only because there was no other possibility to form a government, but also because the ideological gap had so much narrowed between them that a common platform could be worked out and agreed upon, to allow a government of "national unity" to step in, which as soon as the smell of approaching elections was in the air, reverted to their partisan and divisive onslaughts on each other, based on the former ideological rifts which often became irrelevant and obsolete.

Paradoxically, the more the ideological gap between the parties narrowed, which should have made for rapprochement between them, the more bitter their struggle to survive within their constituencies became, for it has been more and more difficult to point out to the real differences between them, and it was now necessary to counter the rise of new parties which competed for the same constituents. So, while the old-time Labor ended up as the third largest party, in the 2009 elections, and its partner to the left (Meretz, made out of vestiges of socialist *Mapam* and other "refugees" from Labor) was halved, many new left-leaning splinter groups emerged, like three green parties. In the previous elections of 2006, it was the other major group, the Likkud, which was smashed (shrinking from 40-odd Knesset members to barely 12), while most of that faction followed charismatic Ariel Sharon in splitting the Party and forming the Kadima center-right group, which together with Labor "refugees" like Shimon Peres, emerged as the largest, though considerably reduced, faction in the Knesset, which formed the government. But already in 2009 the Likkud more than doubled its constituency, while Kadima lost part of its, bringing about a change of government. But this time, it was the new right-wing parties, mainly constituted by former Russian immigrants, who have a penchant for right-wing politics, who emerged as the third largest party and became a crucial building bloc of the new government. In any case, one could see new Laborites in Israel presiding over the dismantling of their powerful trade unions and participating in governments which encouraged privatization, and right-wing economists widening social welfare and other unproductive outlays for the poor and unemployed. It turned out that the field of maneuver for politicians was quite narrow, and any elected government had to yield to social and political realities, beyond election promises and political platforms.

One of the most impressive shifts in the process of political atomization unfolded within the religious camp, while the Arab vote remained essentially stable, because being outside the pale of national consensus, they did not have new choices to make in order to placate their constituents. The only major adaptation occurred in the 1990s, when the Communist Party was dissolved as a result of the collapse of the Soviet Union, and its adepts either embraced new nationalistic or Muslim platforms, or joined the *Balad* Party, founded and led by Christian intellectual Azmi BIshara. But their anti-Israeli attitude did not change, their concern uniquely with the problems of their sector instead of being preoccupied by the affairs of the state on which parliament they sat, and their inadaptability to the Israeli system and alienation from it only deepened. Therefore, they entrenched themselves ever more deeply in the irrelevant margins of Israeli politics and will likely remain outside of it. But the religious parties were much more dynamic and adaptable. Differentiation has to be made nevertheless between the National Religious, who under various names have attained around 5-10 Knesset members, have participated in coalition governments and taken a central place in the political and cultural activity in the country; the Ultra religious of

Ashkenazi roots, who have constituted a stable group of 5-6 Knesset members, are not Zionists and vie for participation in government as a way to obtain their part in the national pie. But in order not to be compromised, they still refuse ministerial positions, so as not to share in the collective responsibility of the government, but in practice assume those duties from the formal position of vice-ministers.

The revelation of Israeli politics in the past few decades have been the Ultra-Orthodox Sephardic Shas Party, which has often filled the position of the third largest party when it attained around 15 Knesset members. They are more flexible and less doctrinaire than their Ashkenazi colleagues and mentors, and they willingly take up ministries in the government and are feverishly active in their constituencies. The problem is that they became marionettes of their Rabbi Ovadyah, whom they venerate for his Jewish learning, and follow his instructions to the letter. He is admittedly pragmatic and flexible, but when he does not accept the authority of the state and treats as "innocent" members of his party who were convicted and incarcerated for corruption, this does not encourage law abiding in his milieu. Furthermore, much of his constituency is encouraged to send their children to *yeshiva* schools, that guarantees their continued backwardness, unproductive life when they grow to adulthood; and dodge the military service which causes much resentment among Israelis their age who wish to share the heavy burden of security with others. They have been skillful in manipulating various governments whose majority depended on them, and they showed a proven capacity to adapt to any political platform which assured that their religious institutions obtained government funds. They have embarked on a social agenda of caring for the poor, for raising allocations to the deprived, the old and the handicapped, and have ensured a stable constituency to back them up, much thanks to the charismatic figure of their spiritual leader, who is much courted by senior Israeli politicians. However, in spite of the usually dovish conviction of the ultra-Orthodox, who elect people over land, and would rather compromise than risk lives, their constituency is rather hawkish, having originated from the Likkud rank and file, from the times of Begin, therefore the pragmatic leadership often leans rightward in order to placate them.

A brief historical survey of Israeli politics since the 1967 legitimation of Begin will illustrate the frequency and the extent of the shifts which have incessantly created new political formations, while nibbling at the preponderance of the two large blocs, and making the formation of Israeli governments ever more difficult, unstable and perilous. Moreover, to the old divisive issues of politics, foreign affairs, the economy and society, as outlined above, the emerging controversy about settlements throughout Judea and Samaria, especially in Jerusalem, has added a bone of contention to be debates during election campaigns, or when a clash between Israeli settlers and the Palestinians occupied the headlines in the Israeli press. Immediately after 1967, when the Arabs rejected any notion of peace or negotiations with Israel, only a small trickle of settlers infiltrated into those areas, often against the objection of the Labor authorities, which at the time informally cultivated the Allon Plan, which prescribed settlements only in the vacant territories in the Judean Desert and in the Jordan Valley, so as to safeguard strategically dominant territories for the defense of the West Bank, while refraining from increasing frictions within the densely populated areas of the Palestinians, when adding Israeli settlements in them. But after the Yom Kippur War of 1973, which evinced the vulnerability of Israel in case of surprise attacks, a large scale settlement movement, sponsored by the national religious and dubbed *Gush Emunim,* (the Bloc of the Faithful), undertook a vast program which within a few years settled on the land several urban centers like Qiryat Arba' and Ma'ale Adumim in Judea, Ariel and Qedumim in Samaria, Gush Katif in the Gaza Strip, and Katzerin in the Golan, which grew in leaps and bounds until they amounted to over 300,000 settlers in hundreds of new settlements. In addition,

Jerusalem, whose Jewish population was reinforced by some six new neighborhoods, perched on the heights surrounding the city, counts another quarter million souls.

Though, admittedly, many of the settlers were "environmental", i.e. non-religious Israelis who were either attached historically to those new areas, or were happy to procure for their families high-standard, spacious and detached homes at subsidized cost, the widespread religious ideology of the settlers, who made a virtue out of their strategic choice, brought the National Religious Party to its peak, and made it such a vital partner of various coalition governments, that the head of the party, ascended to the very pivotal post of Minister of Education and Culture in the Cabinet. Apart from the new sprawling urban neighborhood, which covered the empty hills of Judea and Samaria, and to some extent also of Gush Katif, which became essentially dormitory towns to which their dwellers returned at the end of their work in Israel, the settlers engaged in an amazingly advanced wave of development, which pulled those areas from their traditional slumber and pushed them some centuries forward. Flourishing farming communities with high productivity and super-modern agricultural technologies, based on hot-houses, began exporting flowers and off-season fruits and vegetables to Europe, wineries on the Golan, which had been covered with mines and military positions before, started to export top-grade and prize-winning wines to the entire world, and industrial zones, like Barqan in Samaria and Katzrin in the Golan, gave a developmental *élan* to those areas, the like of which they had never witnessed. In the process, tens of thousands of Arab workers found jobs and increased their own standards of living, by emulation of their Jewish neighbors, manifold. They got medical help in Israeli facilities and cultivated amicable relationships with their Jewish employers. This did not necessarily increase a loving relationship between Israelis and Palestinians, but it certainly became a showcase of co-existence between the two. True, some explosions of jealousy and narrow-mindedness occasionally marred the relationship, but in the whole a manageable neighborliness was maintained, stemming from the fact that most settled land was government owned, and in many of the cases where private land was seized for large development projects, the courts in Israel intervened and ensured fair compensation to the private owners.

Thus, slowly, the numbers of interested settlers and their supporters kept growing, and those who thought the National Religious Party as too lenient, shifted their support to the Ultra-religious Shas party which created and supported its own settlements, while the secular among them created other political splinter groups, such as Tehiya (Revival - later turned into the National Union), or went back to the Likkud, whose Head, Menachem Begin, upon being elected to power in 1977, vowed to increase manifold the settlement effort all over the place. The net result was that the National Religious Party, despite their pride over their settlements and their combination of *Yeshiva* colleges and military service, which catapulted its membership to high positions of leadership, has continued to dwindle to almost insignificance. But we have already mentioned that Shas discovered the social agenda, which they can brandish during the elections, and which enables them to drain the hawkish Sephardic vote from the national religious. Formerly some of the top leaders, like most of the rank and file of the National Religious, like Abu-Hatzeira and Yitzhak Levy, were Sephardic. Now, the National Religious, who are also serving the country, are middle class, and maintain their superb educational network, and are almost all purely Ashkenazi, while the Shas systematically drain to their much larger party the poor, the disaffected, the needy, who are less eager to put themselves to the service of their nation, and are almost exclusively Sephardic. Politics have become a matter of communal identity. Previously, after the 1973 war, when the Labor government was discredited and forced to resign in 1974, and its old guard with Golda Meir and Moshe Dayan, left in disgrace, the way was opened to the new generation of leaders.

The advent in 1974 of Yithak Rabin, the glorious Chief of Staff in the 1967 victory, who served as the Ambassador of Israel in Washington in 1973, and was not soiled by the 1973 fiasco, instilled a new hope into the political system. He tried to battle against the establishment of the Trade Union, the *Histadrut*, who, together with the dwindling *kibbutzim,* were the economic and political infrastructure of the Labor, which he was now called upon to restore. But he was naïve and inexperienced, and all he "succeeded" to achieve was to be ignored by the magnates of his party, and to negotiate "disengagement agreements" with the Egyptians, under American mediation. But his combat with the *histadrut* was too premature, and it would take another decade or two before that monster would lose its grip on Israel's economy. His rule was seen as elitistic, since he never went down the street to "dirty his hands" in popular politicking. All the while, Menachem Begin, who had brilliantly and relentlessly criticized the Labor government during and after the 1973 disarray of the country, in the face of the initial Israeli losses and failures in the war, continued to bombard the Rabin government after the Agranat Commission's findings were published. Many disaffected Sephardic Jews, who did not find a home in the prosperous, middle class, and Ashkenazi Labor, nor in Rabin a congenial and popular leader easy to access and to identify with, massively moved to Begin's new Likkud Party, concocted out of the Liberals and the Herut, since they viewed in its fiery and popular leader the man they sought. So much so that when Rabin tripped, and his National Religious partners, then at the height of their influence, abandoned him, his government fell apart and a tumultuous election campaign opened, where a new party, headed by former Chief of Staff and renowned archaeologist Yigael Yadin, *Dash* (the acronym for democracy and change), came to the fore, which would again shuffle all the political cards.

The founders of *Dash* were for the most part prominent members of the Labor Party who became disillusioned with their own leadership and decided to leave it and create a new structure from the outside. It was then clear that any achievement by the new comers would come by necessity at the expense of Labor, which had hitherto held the helm for almost 30 consecutive years, since the founding of the state. The elections results, in which Begin's Likkud and Dash middle class Ashkenazi produced the first collapse of Labor, which lost both some of its grassroots and some of its leadership. Dash, which rallied 15 Knesset members, a remarkable record for a new party, joined Begin to establish a government coalition, where the Likkud led politics and the economy, and Dash strove to control the social projects of urban renewal. But is was a one-election party, which was to shrink into a six-member faction in the next elections under the name of *Shinui* (change) which would later merge with other left-wing splinter groups and vanish with them. The dissolution of Dash and the disappointment that emerged from the much expected and hoped for change, returned Labor to its stature as the contender of the Likkud. The sensation Begin caused by pulling off the first Israeli peace treaty with Egypt in 1979, and forcing the main opposition of Labor to follow suit and help him overcome his own dissenters from within his party who opposed his policy, further blurred the lines between right and left. The next shuffling of the cards came in 1982, during the first Lebanese War, which the left claimed was a "war of choice", and Israel could have chosen to avoid it, while Begin, and his fiery Defense Minister Ariel Sharon, justified it as a war on terror which was designed to clean up the Lebanese border from the tyranny of the Palestinians, who had taken it over since they were expelled from Jordan in 1970. Once again, it was proven that while the support of the right could automatically be counted on when war was waged under Labor (like in 1967 and 1973), Labor would hammer at a Likkud government who initiated a war, and blast it to the point of breaking national consensus, as it did in 1981, when Begin decided to destroy the Osirak nuclear reactor near Baghdad. Conversely, while Labor lent support to the peace with Egypt signed by Begin, the Likkud was to seriously criticize the Oslo process initiated by the Rabin government.

The right-left controversy resulting from the Lebanon War, generated inter-party negotiations for sharing power, since no major bloc could govern on its own, and the blackmail that small factions could exercize produced a universal disgust from politics and politicians. Successive elections which resulted from unstable governments, that were given to the mercy of small parties or individual politicians who had their own private agendas to serve, generated a series of rotation governments, where the tied two major blocks agreed to share the prime-ministership by rotation, namely a two-year tenure for each, a devise which distorted democracy, since there was no longer coalition and opposition, once the two candidates for the top executive position divided the booty instead of competing for it. This deadlock was broken in the elections of 1992 when Rabin, returning from the political cold since his resignation of 1977, received a second chance from the Israeli electorate, not because of a majority he could rally, but because he was able to prevent his rival, Yitzhak Shamir of the Likkud, from forming a majority coalition. Even though in those elections the right got more votes than the left, many of them were lost because the many right wing factions, which run to the Knesset, were short of passing the threshold required by law. Rabin, with the help of the Arab votes in the Knesset, who could not care less about the issues at hand, as long as they obstructed the right wing, which they hated, from acceding to government, formed a government with the left-wing *Ratz-Meretz* party, which held until Rabin was assassinated in November 1995, causing again another turmoil in Israeli politics. The religious parties, who were used to obtain their booty in whatever government was in place, also joined, for a price. They received funds for their religious institutions, while the Arabs obtained a preferential treatment ("affirmative action"), to equalize their educational system with that of other

Israelis, and to push through curricula more nationalist and Palestinian-supportive, much to the exasperation of the rest of the Israeli population.

Disillusionment from the Oslo process, as terrorism escalated within Israel proper, brought many common Israelis to the conclusion that better less casualties without peace than more casualties with peace. Rabin's aura began to wane as he seemed unable to control terrorism, which on a certain month reached over 100 Israeli casualties, more than the annual toll prior to Oslo. Many Israelis were particularly grieved when that well-meaning Prime Minister did not have the public sensitivity to refrain from calling those dead the "casualties of peace", as if peace and war equally demanded victims. Then what is the difference between the two, inquired in disbelief the families of the killed? In the face of the more pressing demands of Arafat, under the threat of more terrorism, it stands to reason that he too began to lose faith in the process, but he could not bring himself to admit it in public, for he would have had to confess of the greatest error he did in his political career, and to resign in consequence. He was rescued from the horns of that terrible dilemma by his assassination, which turned him into an icon, especially in the left, all his faults were forgotten and he was hailed as the "visionary" of peace, as if falling dead by the hands of an abject assassin rendered him a saint. In fact, his glamour was fading before his terrible murder, and polls predicted a sweeping victory to his new young Likud leader, Benjamin Netanyahu. The latter had to wage an uphill campaign against Shimon Peres, who inherited Rabin's mantle and hoped to mobilize popular sympathy for the murdered Rabin to carry the vote. But it was not to be. The Rabin government emphasized education and upgrading the status of the Arabs in Israel, but his peace policies and politics ended up, in retrospect, as a major fiasco.

Two crucial repercussions of the public perception of the failure of the peace process, were the shift of the electorate slightly to the right, which enabled Netanyahu to form his

first government, and the beginning of the fading of the leftist Meretz, which was at its peak, with its successive leaders,
Shulamit Alloni, and then Yossi Sarid as a popular Minister of Education, who introduced the venomous Palestinian
poet, Mahmoud Darwish into the school curriculum, cared
for the poor and the disadvantaged, and instituted "peace
studies" in the school system as an intellectual and educational follow-up of Oslo. Since then that leftist party has
been steadily dwindling, from its peak of 12 MK's in 1998
to 3 in 2009. But the overall picture of the political arena did
not change: the Israeli electorate was split down the middle
between right and left, with the two major blocs alternat-
ing, and their satellite allies rising and fading according to
the fortunes of domestic and foreign policy. Netanyahu's
government predictably rested on a coalition with the religious parties, which permitted him a majority, but not a very
steady one. He was dragged to the Wye Plantation conference with Presidents Clinton and Arafat, as a follow up on
Oslo, but as soon as he emitted the slogan that Palestinians
would "receive only if they give", as a signal that the unilateral offerings of Rabin had come to an end, he was accused
by the left that he was sabotaging the "peace process" that
Rabin had inaugurated, unmindful that it had come unhinged
in Rabin's times precisely due to the his forgiving attitude
towards the repeated violations of the Palestinians.

Before Netanyahu's term was up, he had to call for new
elections, which allowed Ehud Barak, the new rising star of
the Labor Party, to win the prime-ministership, together with
his left-wing *Meretz* coalition. But Barak's term was short
lived, because his political promise, unlike his brilliant military career, proved empty, as he effected two major political
and military demarches which arguably ended in disaster:
He withdrew from southern Lebanon, as he promised in the
election campaign, something which would force Israel to
go to war there once again in 2006; and he pressed for Camp
David II in 2000, to finalize a deal with Yasser Arafat, only to
realize that he had no partner for a final deal. Instead, he got

the second *Intifada* during his term which he was unable to quell, thus losing his cabinet, Knesset and popular majority. He called for new elections in 2001, which the new leader of the Likkud, Ariel Sharon, the man who was credited as "Mister Security", won in a landslide, in the hope that he would put an end to the uncontrolled wave of terror which continued to spread in the country, in the face of an impotent and discredited government. Together with the vast losses of Labor and the parties to the left of it, and the marked rise of Sharon's right, a new element emerged in party politics, under the recycled name of *Shinui* (change), under the leadership of a tough-minded journalist, who rose dramatically, first with 6 MK's and then peaked with 15 MK's, who pretty much duplicated their 1977 predecessors, and reflected once again the elective potential of the floating vote, which occasionally steps in to decide the fate of elections. The head of that party, Joseph Lapid, became a very close associate of super-hawk Sharon, much the same way Yossi Sarid had become the ally of Rabin a decade earlier. Sharon immediately broke the taboo of not entering the territory of the Palestinian Authority, lest the "peace process be harmed", as the mantra of Rabin and Barak's times professed. In a tremendously popular quick sweep throughout the West Bank, terrorist niches and caches were discovered and blown up, with a minimum of civilian victims to the Palestinians, and of military casualties to the IDF.

As Sharon entrenched himself in power and achieved security along the borders, he also led negotiations with the Bush administration, who mediated the Road Map, and showed his support for the American President's "vision of two states" (it is hard to see any vision there, since that idea had been floating around for at least 4 decades earlier). But he retained his uncompromisingly hawkish attitude to the Palestinians, and repeatedly stated that the safety of Netzarim (a settlement in Gush Katif in Gaza) was as valuable as that of Tel-Aviv. But suddenly in 1994, as Sharon and his sons were edging towards indictment for mammoth acts of corruption in the business world, he performed an astonishing *volte-face,* which was massively supported by the liberal press of Israel, which viewed Israeli withdrawal as so much more important than an indictment for corruption that it decided to forsake one for the other. The new Attorney General, Menachem Mazuz, who had just been appointed by the Sharon government, with the support of Justice Minister Joseph Lapid, ordered the closure of the dossier for "lack of public interest", and the deal seems to have been completed. Sharon declared that Israel was now "reluctant to rule the Palestinians", something that had never bothered him before, and emitted the idea, which gathered steam with the vigorous support of Lapid and Deputy Prime Minister Ehud Olmert, who was primed to succeed him, that Israel would unilaterally evacuate the Gaza Strip within a year. Though much praise was heaped on Sharon by the Americans, the Europeans, some Arabs and the Israeli left, many remained skeptical, especially that at least half of the Israeli public, including half the Likkud Party, opposed the move very vehemently, mainly because it was to be carried out without agreement, and that unilateralism had never proved wise in Middle Eastern affairs.

Infighting within the Likkud became so intense, especially as the evacuation was implemented in 2005 and tormented the entire country during that traumatic process of uprooting by force 8,000 successful farmers and destroying their flourishing houses and settlements, that Sharon realized that he had lost his grip on his own party, and decided to secede and establish a new one - *Kadima (*Forward). Many "refugees" from the disintegrating Labor, notably Shimon Peres and more than half the Likkud ministers joined the new formation, and new elections were declared. During that campaign, Lapid's party was completely wiped out, some of its escapees joining Kadima, and the reduced Likkud once again elected Netanyahu as its leader. The elections brought about Kadima's victory, led by Olmert, who replaced Sharon who had sunk into a deep coma due to a massive cerebral stroke. Other repercussions flowed from those elections: Kadima emerged as the only party capable of forming a government, all the others having been severely crushed, Labor with 19 seats and Likkud with 12. Olmert, with great talent and skill formed a new center-left government with Labor and the religious, and launched an economic program, much along the blueprint of reform started by Netanyahu who had became Sharon's Finance Minister, and a plan to pursue the Sharon's policy of unilateral disengagement from Samaria too, under a new bombastic title of "consolidation". His term seemed stable and promising and his government steadfast, until the 2006 kidnapping of Gilad Shalit in Gaza, and the repetition of that scenario on the Lebanese border, drove the government into a hasty, ill-planned and ill-executed campaign against the Hizbullah. The war had hardly receded, and the Vinograd Commission had just been appointed to investigate its deficiencies, that Olmert's misdeeds began to emerge one after the other, and his accusations of multi-faceted corruption began to come to the fore. First as rumors, then as interminable police investigations, and then as indictments.

Besieged from all sides, Olmert attempted a repetition of the successful Sharon scenario, namely launch a daring and ambitious peace-plan with the Palestinians, based on large scale withdrawals from Samaria that would certainly be applauded by the Europeans and the Americans, in order to earn the attention of the same Attorney General, and the sympathy of the press and the public, away from his criminal woes. Partly because of his preoccupation with his approaching indictments, partly to compensate for the Vinograd Commission report which promised to be critical of his leadership, and partly to correct the bad image he and his Foreign Minister and rival, Tzipi Livni, had earned among the public as a result of their handling of the Lebanese war and its aftermath, he and his nemesis engaged in very intense negotiations with the Palestinian leadership for a permanent settlement, only to come to the conclusion that the maximum Israel could cede was still far beneath the minimum of what the Palestinians would accept. But he never disclosed the extent of the concessions he was ready to make. In the meantime, following the devastating Vinograd report, and the cumulative effect of the pending indictments, he was forced, by both his Labor partner and his competitor in the party, to resign before his term was up, and soon new elections were declared. This time, Kadima kept its strength, but the Likkud, in an impressive comeback, almost equaled it, while the Labor party was completely crushed (from 19 to 12 MKs), apparently putting an end to its long history as the, and then a, major government forming party.

However, together with the cutting of the two major parties to size (each represented by only less than 30 MKs), together comprising half the membership of the Knesset, another right-wing party, "Israel our Home", made out of mainly Russian-originating constituents, and headed by controversial Foreign Minister Avigdor Liberman, rose to the third place in the Knesset with its 15 MK's (out of 120 in total). This shows that not only the large political groupings which can form a coalition governments have been diminished, but that splinter groups who contend one or another aspect of their program, find it easy and expedient to run independently for their own list. This system of running, in a parliamentary regime, for lists rather than for regional or local constituencies, makes for fragmentation of the body politic on the one hand, and for dissolution of governments at the whim of one or two parties, who find themselves in disagreement with the prevalent coalition partner, or are dissatisfied with the fulfillment of the pledges which accompanied their alliance with the government. This has become so untenable, that governments can no longer survive their full term, and no long-term government program can be implemented. Governments then become like firemen who only extinguish fires, by satisfying everybody in preparation for the next elections. No long haul vision is encouraged, because no accountability is expected with governments that come and go. Other nations can afford that instability, not Israel.

Chapter 8

Threats to Israel's Survival

All in all, Israel has been, since its inception and against all odds, a very successful and promising enterprise. As such, it was conceived to last, except that the many errors it makes, domestically and externally, tend to erode its survivability and steadfastness, and therefore they need to be redressed of its own volition and design. Let us first identify the immediate menaces and then the possible ways to make amends to them, the most pressing and dangerous, to the level of rendering it existential, being the Iranian nuclear peril. The other serious threats are Jihadi terrorism and the attempt to rationalize it by demonizing Israel and de-legitimizing it. This in itself is an asymmetrical battle, in the sense that Israel is a tiny and embattled nation, whose legitimacy has been lately challenged on every step of the way, while the world looks on with indifference and shows no sign of moving to do anything, even in the face of President Sarkozi's appeal to the Security Council members in September, 2009 : "a member nation of the United nations is threatened with annihilation by another member. What do we do about it ?". The Secretary General of the UN, as well as the President of the United States who sat around that table, and should have been the first to raise that question, did not budge. Similarly, the pathetic castigation by Prime Minister Netanyahu at the General Assembly, one day earlier, to wit : "is there no decency? Is there no truth?", directed to the member states who stayed to listen to the speech of Sho'ah denial and hatred to the Jews by President Ahmadinejad, which should

have shamed the Secretary General and delegates of countries like Sweden, was totally ignored.

De-legitimation of Israel, or Anti-Semitrism as anti-Zionism

All this happened against the background of rising anti-Semitism in Europe, which a document of the Anti-Defamation
League has described as "greater acceptance of virulent anti-
Jewish attitudes", expressed in "viciously anti-Semitic cartoons in several major newspwers, alongside with editorials
comparing Israel to Nazi Germany", "various anti-Jewish
conspiracy theories" and the "all too common incidence of
Israeli flag burnings at protest", which rendered Jewish organizations "deeply concerned about the mainstreaming of anti-
Semitism, with more public expressions and greater public
acceptance of classic stereotypes"[91]. All this comes after the
Swedish *Aftenbladet* spread during the month of August 2009
abominable libels against Israel for "killing Palestinians in order to use their organs for transplant", and under the shadow
of the Goldstone Report, commissioned by the Commission
on Human Rights in Geneva, where such champions of democracy and human dignity as Sudan, Libya, Syria, Iran and
others, determine the rules of the game, to examine the "war
crimes " which Israel perpetrated in the Gaza war while attempting to defend itself against 8 years of bombardment and
shelling by the Hamas. That Commission had issued some 25
resolutions in the past few years, 20 of them against Israel, but
not the Darfur massacre, whose main perpetrator, President
Bashir, was indicted by the International Court in the Hague,
but never discussed or condemned by that Commission where
his representative sits.

It has become a recurrent truism that matters regarding
Jews, Israel, and Zionism acquire a worldwide resonance
that is out of proportion to their intrinsic news value. For
anything which relates to Israel, the sole Jewish state in existence, in contrast with the multitude of Christian, Muslim,

---

[91]ICEJ News, 22 September, 2009

Arab, and Buddhist entities, is placed under the magnifying glass and held to the highest standards of scrutiny. But why is it so? Is it because the "Jewish question," as Maxime Rodinson[92] has elected to call it, "persists", that the Jewish state attracts upon itself the old stereotypes, suspicions, and accusations that were always imputed to the Jews? In short, has Israel become the Jew of the Nations? The epithet "Jewish state" is in fact gratuitously appended to it by the Western media, while the Arab and Muslim countries prefer what is for them the derogatory attribute of "Zionist." While it is not fashionable and acceptable in liberal democracies to blame an ethnic or religious group or instigate against a minority, in a world that purports to be democratic and human-rights conscious, it is acceptable and fashionable to criticize, even calumniate, a state because that is always construed as a political debate, hence its legitimacy. So, essentially, while Arabs or Muslims or other adepts of dictatorial and totalitarian regimes have no compunctions of being openly anti-Semitic, and they use interchangeably Jews, Zionists, and Israelis, the hidden anti-Semites in the West adapt their language to the jargon which condemns Israel, drawing exactly on the same arguments as the avowed anti-Semites, but couching them in political terms. To do that, both groups need to link Jews with Israel, by either calling the latter the "Jewish state" (as in the West), implying that it carries with it the innate nature of the Jews, or by blaming directly the Jews, usually dubbing them "Zionists," or the "Zionist entity," not simply the Jews nor the "Jewish state," which would have compelled them to recognize that state.

We have already seen that by attacking the Jews and imputing the bad qualities inherent in the Jews to anything they produce, including their movement of national liberation—Zionism, and their state- Israel—anti- Semites thereby delegitimize Israel. But how do Westerners refer to that link, and

---

[92]Maxime Rodinson, Cult, Ghetto and State: The Persistence of the Jewish Question, al-Saqi Books, London

how do they use politics, not the ancient anti-Jewish religious and ethnic stereotypes to bash Israel? Moreover, if as some anti-Semites now claim, the ancient pernicious essence of the Jews, which used to be transmitted genetically, has now lost some of those characteristics due to their new existence in the state of Israel,[93] then how can a Westerner, unlike an Arab, continue to uphold anti-Semitic stereotypes with regard to Israel? Hatred to the Jews in the Christian world had been either based on religion or on social hostility towards those who were perceived as usurers, or on a quasi-ethnic suspicion towards those whose way of life set them apart from the majorities within which they lived. But in the contemporary world, where Jews have been officially absolved by recent popes from their religion's blame, and where their role in society and their life styles have become undistinguishable from those of the majority, what grounds can still exist to pursue anti-Semitism? Another question relates to the unbearable ease with which anyone, under one pretext or another, appoints oneself to pontificate and judge where the Jews allegedly went wrong, and suggest what they should do to amend for their faults, or what concessions they should do to redress the wrong; as if the Jews, and in consequence Israel, had become the yardstick to measure morality, and as if their conduct is anyone's business. Take the Kurds in comparison, who are also Muslims. They are a proud nation of 25 million, all living under oppression under the Turks, the Iraqis, the Iranians, and the Syrians, all battling and sacrificing for centuries, but they never got the attention that is given to Palestinians who are smaller in size, and of much more recent separate identity compared to the Kurds. Why? Because Israel is not directly involved with the Kurds, but holds the cards of the Palestinian fate. Therefore, the Palestinians are everyone's concern, everyone feels entitled to intervene on their behalf, bringing one of their leaders to admit that their cause won prominence only because their adversaries are Israelis and Jews.

---

[93]*Ibid*, p. 173.

At the same time, few have attempted to castigate the oppressors of the Kurds, still fewer have promoted their independence, and those who do, do so in a much more subdued and less judgmental fashion. Seldom has the question of the Kurds made such headlines or caused so many wars, or preoccupied the world powers or organizations the way Palestinians do. There are no Jews or Israelis to bash around there. Since every anti-Semite who harshly criticizes Israel to the point of turning the Jewish state into the Jew among states, claims his right to criticism, it is often difficult to draw the line between one and the other. The renowned Canadian Human Right Law Professor, Irwin Cotler, a former Minister of Justice in Ottawa and presently a member of Parliament there, has suggested guidelines, which mark the transition from criticism of Israel, which is legitimate, to plain and coarse anti-Semitism which is not. Critics become anti-Semites, he claims, when:

a. They publicly call for the destruction of Israel and the Jewish people. This is the case with the platforms of the PLO and the Hamas, some militant Islamic rulings as well as the Iranian threat to annihilate Israel, which we can call "genocidal anti-Semitism";

b. They deny the Jewish people's right to self-determination, delegitimize Israel as a state and attribute to Israel all the world's evil; we can call this "political anti-Semitism", inasmuch as other peoples' natural and historical rights are recognized, save the Jewish people;

c. They "Nazify "Israel ("ideological" anti-Semitism) and demonize it in a most insulting way by comparing it wrongly with its most horrifying butchers in history;

d. Israel is characterized, again wrongly, as the "perfidious enemy of Islam" ("theological" anti-Semitism);

e. Israel is attributed a mix of evil qualities by some intellectuals and elites ("cultural" anti-Semitism);

f. They call for boycotts or other economic restrictions on Israel ("economic" anti-Semitism);

g. They deny the Holocaust and re-write history as a way to deny Jews the sympathy they rightly received from the western world after, and as result of, the Holocaust;

h. They terrorize Israel by racist attacks and heaping false accusations against it (Like the Blood Libel, the *Protocols,* the Poison Affair[94] world conspiracy, poisoning of other people's soil and people, war crimes, massacres and the like), or casting it as "racist" itself, like in Durban, in Arab League conferences, the Human Rights Commission and the media);

i. They single out Israel for discriminatory treatment in the international arena through denial of equality before the law.[95]

Arab and Muslim propaganda, at large and in Europe, and anti-Semitic writers in the West, easily qualify for this questionable epithet since they handily pass these nine tests. This in itself creates in Israel the likeness of the eve of the Munich Surrender in 1938, of Czechoslovakia to Hitler. Then too, a tyrant vowed to eliminate Jews and just wanted a piece of his neighbor's territory to bring peace upon Europe, and he smiled under his moustache as the civilized nations of the West were capitulating to him. They were prepared to undergo humiliation in order to gain peace, but they ended up cashing in both humiliation and war. But this time the powers-that-be still have the opportunity in Geneva to avoid capitulation to Ahmadinejad's messengers, war in the Middle East and a nuclear holocaust; time will tell what they will elect to do, as the US has abdicated its leadership of the free world, and is committed to "engagement" instead. One of the most abject twists in the anti-Semites' attitude towards Israel as the Jewish state, and in the emotion-laden story of the relationship between Christians and Jews in history, has

---

[94]Raphael Israeli, *Poison: Manifestations of the Blood Libel*, Lexington, 2000.

[95]*www.jafi .org.il/agenda/2001/english/vk3-22/6asp.* Cited by Gerstenfeld, April 1, 2004.

been the surrogate use of the Arabs and Muslims by Western writers to castigate the Jews. There is something perverse in this twist inasmuch as both Christians and Jews had dwelt as tolerated *dhimmis* under Islam. But now those writers go to the defense of Arabs and Muslims as a means to whip Jews and Israel, and in so doing they find themselves in concert with their current Muslim compatriots in Europe whom they treat with much farther equality than Christians are treated in Muslim lands. Let us listen to what Maxime Rodinson says:

> Contrary to what has been said and written in Arab and Muslim circles, the condition of the Jews in the world of Islam was not idyllic. It is quite true that the negative aspects of the Jewish situation in Muslim countries has been exaggerated by Zionist propaganda.... It is quite true that the situation of Jews in Muslim countries over fifteen centuries has been better than in Christian countries....But this does not alter the fact that the status of *dhimmi* applied to Jews and Christians was inegalitarian and that if Judaism and Christianity were tolerated religions ...their believers were nonetheless considered enemies of the true faith. Appreciations of them were disparaging, suspicious and scornful. In the case of the Jews these attitudes found support in many passages from the Qur'an dating from the time when the Jewish tribes of Medina constituted Muhammed's main adversary, passages that can readily obliterate the favorable attitudes towards Jews and Christians reflected in other, earlier passages... Many instances of disparagement and suspicion of the Jews, and of slander against them therefore exist in the Muslim tradition. Especially at the popular level. Many proverbs testify to this.... The accusation of ritual murder, for instance, may be found in the *Thousand and One Nights...,* and the origin of Muslim sects which the Orthodox majorities consider as undermining Islam from within, is often ascribed to converted Jews. Extremist Shi'ism in the early years of Islam and and Fatimid Isma'ilism later, are two examples. In various Muslim countries public signs of contempt are attached to

Jews, and the most difficult and repugnant jobs are reserved for them...[96]

This sounds like a sober and balanced analysis of the situation until the instinct to attack Zionism and Israel suddenly draws from that historical survey some rather surprising and unrelated conclusions and interpretations:

There is no reason to portray [those attitudes towards the Jews] as crimes with which to stigmatize Islam, the Arabs or both—as the Zionists and their friends often do....But there is no reason to deny these facts either, as Arab and Muslim ideologues often do.... When they paint an unreasonably idealized portrait of Islamic society in the Middle Ages in which justice, benevolence and harmony alone prevailed—against the testimony of millions of Arab sources—they merely arouse the incredulity of non-Muslims and lead them to suspect that the reality was worse than it actually was...It was actually Zionism that stoked these smoldering embers. It could not have been otherwise when a group of Jews claiming to be the sole true representatives of the Jewish world laid claim to an indisputably Arab land, declaring that they intended to wrench it from the Arab world and turn it into a foreign state. It could only have been aggravated when this group of Jews realized its designs by force and with the aid of the powers of the Christian world.... The Arab anti-Zionist struggle, like all ideological struggles, uses all the weapons it can find. It is wonderful that this ideological struggle has so often forsaken the weapons of racial and religious hatred, and that its attacks have so often targeted only those directly responsible for the alienation of Arab Palestine, namely the followers of the Zionist movement.[97]

The total denial of the right of the Jewish people for statehood and the claim that it came to usurp a land that was "indisputably Arab", not only disparages the historical tie between the Jews and their country, but fails to explain how

---

[96]*Ibid*, pp. 184-6.
[97]*Ibid*. pp. 186-7.

dispute emerged from an "indisputable" situation. In order to make his thesis about the evil inherent in Israel and Zionism stick, he lends to them acts of injustice and arbitrariness ("they wrenched the land by force"), though he is conscious of the tremendous Zionist efforts to purchase the land from local Arabs and of the submission of the Zionists (and the local Arabs for that matter) to the rulers of the land, first the Ottomans and then the British Mandate, which far from being at the mercy of the Zionist predators, on the contrary acted, often ruthlessly, to oppress them. What is particularly stunning in this analysis is that after his long, well-documented litany of negative Arab/Muslim attitudes towards the Jews dating from the Middle Ages, the author concludes that it was modern Zionism, which lay at the basis of all those attitudes today, and that the Jews are to blame, due to their predatory practices, for the cumulative sentiment against them on the part of the Arabs. In fact, he justifies Arab anti-Semitism by legitimizing "all weapons" available in the anti-Zionist struggle in which he posits himself as an active participant. But disregarding the UN decision to partition Palestine, which Israel accepted and the Arabs rejected, and by claiming that the Arabs, who had never had a state in Palestine, were entitled to it and not the Jews who had been exiled from there, he is in fact singling out the Jewish people as the only one who has no right to statehood. That is bland anti-Semitism and that is the sort of argument that Muslims are seeking and using. But the peak of Rodinson's mischief against the Jews, under the guise of anti-Zionism, is when he lends advice to the Arabs how to disguise their anti-Semitism in order to make it more palatable to the world as anti-Zionism, and in his capacity as one of the most prominent European Orientalists of his generation, he knew he had not only the ear of Muslims in general, but that his popularity would skyrocket in the Arab and Muslim world whose propaganda work he was championing. He wrote:

> It was inevitable that in the ardor of the ideological struggle against Zionism, those Arabs most influenced by Muslim

religious orientation would seize upon the old religious and popular prejudices against the Jews in general. It was inevitable that certain fundamentalist Muslim organizations would link Zionism to the supposed general pernicious character of the Jews and Judaism. It was inevitable that the Muslim popular masses, once mobilized against Zionism, would call to mind popular traditions about the Jews and associate them with this combat. I recall all this as a warning. Zionist propaganda does its work by arguing that all anti-Zionist efforts of the Arabs and others are motivated by anti-Semitic propensities, by hatred of the Jews in general. The Zionist propagandists know very well that, for the time being at least, anti-Semitism arouses great revulsion among the majority of European and American public opinion. To denounce an action or assertion as anti- Semitic is thus to rally public opinion against it. The Arabs and some of their friends ought to understand that they are in effect aiding Zionist and Arabophobic propaganda whenever they denounce a Zionist act or thesis while explaining it, or appearing to explain it, by the eternal maleficence of the Jewish people, while accordingly seeking analogies to it in Jewish history, or while suggesting that the persecution of Jews was deserved, or did not actually take place, or was minimal. It does not help to conclude or preface such arguments with the proclamation: "we are not anti-Semites, the Arabs have never been anti-Semites" ... How many people have I seen who have made at first such proclamations, only later to hear critical, mocking, hostile, malevolent, disparaging ,or slanderous remarks against the Jews in general in Arab circles? They have concluded that they have been deceived by Arab propaganda and that the Zionists were right after all ... when they claimed that this propaganda was motivated at the bottom by anti-Semitism. They have then decided that the Zionist offices that organize bulk mailings or sales of translations of anti-Jewish pamphlets that circulate in the Arab countries were revealing the truth of the matter after all.

Every time an Arab government ... prints or distributes the *Protocols of the Elders of Zion*..., every time Arab publicists adopt such fabrications, they proffer effective aid to Zionist propaganda, which makes no mistake when it gives maximum publicity to all these acts. The question is whether the Arabs want to continue to accord Zionism such valuable assistance.[98]

The author, who is representative of the leftist anti-Semites in Europe, whose resonance in the Muslim world is considerable, is caught here in a pathetic attempt to hide his own virulent anti-Semitism by diverting it to anti-Zionist channels, but he himself implies that they amount to the same: if the Jews, of all peoples, are denied their right to statehood and therefore they are condemned to remain dispersed and persecuted among nations, what is that if not anti-Semitism? In no place does the author condemn the Arab anti-Semitic proclamations, because they are wrong morally and humanly or may cause incitement and social disruption, or close the doors to an Israel-Arab settlement politically. He just counsels the Arabs to desist from that anti-Semitic rhetoric because it is counterproductive and can hurt their cause. And despite the statements of some of them, openly and without compunctions, that they are anti-Jewish, that is anti-Semitic, the author tries to convince them (and himself) that they indeed are not. Because if they were, he cannot use them as his surrogate weapon to attack the Jews: you cannot use anti-Semites to lash out at Jews and then to claim that you meant Zionism. Equally pathetic is Rodinson's attempt to wean Arabs and Muslims from their crude anti-Semitism by telling them that the anti-Semitic material they are circulating (the *Protocols)* is fabricated. But what if they believe that it is not and that it is authentic, his insistence on the contrary notwithstanding? Why would they be different from the Europeans who fabricated it and continue to swear by it,

---

[98]*Ibid*, pp. 187-8

to propagate it and have even ended up believing in it themselves? And so, by concentrating on his Zionist subterfuge,
he simply belies his own argument about the deep-rooted
anti-Jewish sentiment in Arab and Muslim tradition, prior
to, and independently of Zionism, and exposes himself to
the counter argument that what is important to him is not the
anti-Semitic discourse, but the need to show, at any price,
that Zionism, that is the movement of national liberation of
the Jews, has no leg to stand on, should not and will not
succeed. Only thus, he believes, would the Jews be beaten
historically, by being denied a political rehabilitation in a
land that is not theirs, even if they should make some gains
temporarily by scoring sympathies when their Jewishness
comes under attack. For Rodinson and his likes, then, as for
Arabs and Muslims, the point is to raise doubts about the legitimacy of Israel by anti-Zionist allegations when possible,
and by straight anti-Semitic broadsides when necessary.

The persistence of anti-Jewish abominations in the Islamic world, which at times are backed by Western writers
like Rodinson, who target Israel and Zionism, has produced
a self-serving spiraling exaggeration of the anti-Jewish biases and stereotypes in both, thus attesting, Rodinson notwithstanding, to the common sources used by both, and to
the cross-nurturing of those two trends in the delegitimation
of Israel. For the more the Jews, and in consequence Zionism and Israel, are demonized beyond measure, the more
likely their image be tarnished, their reputation dimmed, and
their legitimacy questioned. So, while the old anti-Semitic
accusations had some kernel of reality to them (the rejection of Christ, living apart from others, sticking to their own
calendar, embracing and perpetuating different ways of language, dress and life, money-lending, and the like), these
things began to evolve after the troubled Christians, who saw
their stereotypes and beliefs threatened, escalated their anti-
Jewish biases into the domain of irrational fantasies. Indeed,
according to Gavin Langmuir, the accusations regarding the
ritual crucifixion of young Christian children, the attending

ritual cannibalism, and the attempts to destroy Christianity by poisoning wells and triggering the Black Death, were all later developments.[99] Says Langmuir:

> The falsity of those accusations seems glaringly obvious now, but that was not the case before Hitler. Of course, historians have long known that those accusations were made and that thousands of Jews were killed because of them. But not until the late 19th and the first half of the 20th century was there a serious attempt by some Jewish and non-Jewish historians to disprove them. They had a hard time convincing others, however, because of the way they went about it. Strangely enough, or perhaps all too understandably before Hitler and Freud, they did not focus on the accusations themselves; they focused on the Jews and tried to prove that Jews had never done such things. That defensive posture considered the Jews guilty until proven innocent, and it set the historians an almost impossible task, for it was and is impossible to prove conclusively that no Jews ever engaged in such physically possible conduct in secret. In a period of widespread hostility to Jews, however, the approach had the advantage for Jewish historians that they could try to exculpate Jews without criticizing Christianity directly—a feature that made the approach attractive to Christian historians as well. Its weakness was that it ignored the obvious. If the evidence to support the truth of the accusations was highly suspect, as it was, it was nonetheless certain that people had made those accusations and used them to justify the killing of thousands of Jews. The first question for objective historians should therefore have been, not whether Jews could have done something like that, but what had Christians in fact done? How did those accusations arise? Who made them and why? How did they "know" that Jews had done such things."[100]

---

[99]Gavin Langmuir, *Towards the Definition of anti-Semitism*, UC Press, Berkeley and Los Angeles, 1990, pp. 11-12.

[100]*Ibid*, p. 12.

These questions, which seem to have never bothered Muslim writers, are perhaps the crux of the matter, because this means tackling the issue of negative proof. The Jews had been accused in the Christian world since the 12th Century and then, by extension, in the Muslim world since the 19th Century, of blood libel and poisoning; those calumniations were taken as a matter of course, and the burden of providing the evidence of their innocence was squarely thrown on the Jews. How can one prove something that never existed? Positive evidence is part of the laws and ways of nations and civilizations, and it was always incumbent upon the accuser to substantiate his case. But to provide negative evidence, under the threat of otherwise being held as the culprit? Only Jews were submitted to that travesty. And as Langmuir has demonstrated, the Jews themselves, who were too meek to counter-accuse the Christians for those abominable and groundless calumniations, had elected instead to focus on their own innocence by trying to "prove" what cannot be proved. The Arabs and Muslims too have learned the same technique of accusation against the Jews, and it is no coincidence that the blood libel persists there. But the Arabs and Muslims in the 20th Century as well as post-Hitler Christians can persist in their blood libel accusations only because they can mobilize "positive evidence" on their side, if not direct then circumstantial, taken from the Qur'an and the *Hadith*, about the inherently evil nature of the Jews, and hence their liability to do anything, including blood ritual. Rodinson by himself has provided us with enough massive information on the disparaging nature of traditional Islamic literature, in addition to the evidence we have adduced, with regard to the Jews and the resulting inferior status of *dhimmitude* to which they were relegated, and that they had to share with Christians under Islam. But he said nothing of the submission of the Jews to that status and its acceptance as if it were an inexorable force. Much the same spirit had prompted the Jews under Christendom to apologize constantly and to prove their innocence when they were accused of blood libel, poisoning, and other unlikely abominations, rather than turn the tables on their calumniators and reproach them their unfounded libel. What we miss here is the toll that was levied on the Jewish psyche for generations, in both places, which made him feel and behave like the eternal culprit, thus encouraging the spiral of anti-Semitism. Admittedly, under the circumstances of discrimination, oppression, fear, and threat of extermination, exile and forced conversion, here was perhaps little the Jews could do to behave differently; and if they wanted to survive in the oppressive environment while carrying their freedom in their minds, they had no option but to stoop, resign, accept, adapt to the present, and dream of redemption in the future.[101]

The *dhimmi* condition was not only a legal, economic, religious, and politically subordinate status, but also, as Bat Ye'or has admirably shown,[102] a state of mind, which conditions the subject to submit to his fate, and continues to dominate his mind long after he has disengaged from that humiliating status. In a dramatic reversal of their erstwhile status of *dhimmis* under Islam, Christians have developed another aspect of *dhimmitude* (the term was coined by Bat Ye'or) and that is the tendency to exercise, as if it is right, a condescending and suspicious attitude towards the Jews. Nowadays, Jews can no longer be put in ghettoes or be made to wear the yellow patch, but they can be castigated, supervised, taken to task, and expected to behave by standards set by others. These are the common grounds on which Europeans and Muslims can collaborate. The Arabs and Muslims are still incredulous at the sudden upsurge of the Jews, who broke away from their allotted *dhimmi* status and spectacularly

---

[101]This aspect has been analyzed by Bat Ye'or in *Juifs et Chretiens sous l"islam: les Dhimmis face au Defi Integriste*, Paris, Berg International, 1994, pp. 107-113.

[102]For the study of the system of Dhimmitude, see Bat Yeo'rs *Les Chretientes d'Orient entre Jihad et Dhimmitude*, Paris, Cerf 1991, and its Hebrew and English versions, which have had wide resonance and contributed enormously to the understanding of the status of the Scriptuaries under Islam.

made it to the forefront of the modern world; some Westerners who still entertain their old anti-Semitic stereotypes
towards the Jews but cannot articulate them openly as of old,
turn against Zionism and Israel as an oblique way to compensate for the fashionable restraint from whipping the Jews
in the public square. Moreover, with a view of freeing themselves from the sense of guilt occasioned by the Holocaust,
many of those Christians, either following the Arabs or serving as models for them, have reversed the roles: the Jews
are now compared to the Nazis and the Palestinians to their
Jewish victims. Christians within the Arab world go even
further at the same time that they are still *dhimmis* under
Islam but also virulently anti-Jewish and anti-Israel in order
to endear themselves to their Arab society. They act thus because they must show to their seething Islamic environment
that they are no less anti-Zionist than the general populace,
in the process exposing their own sense of insecurity and
vulnerability in having to play the Islamic game, on Islamic
terms, in order to survive. So does the Vatican in licking the
boots of some of those worst regimes in an attempt to save
the dwindling Christian communities there from extinction.
It is evident at any rate that the continuous state of *dhimmitude* tends to corrupt the character and corrode the sense of
liberty of the shrinking and frightened Christian minorities
within the Muslim world, and these in turn feed their frustra-
tions and fears back to their coreligionists in the West who
seize upon them to reinforce and vindicate their own anti-
Semitism.[103]

As Langmuir points out, and as we know from many other
aspects of anti-Semitism in general, the blood accusation,
ritual cannibalism, well poisoning, ritual crucifixion, and
profanation hurled at the Jews have one thing in common:
irrationality,[104] though we are paradoxically attempting to
categorize them in rational fashion. The people who created

---

[103]Bat Ye'or, *Juifs et Chretiens etc.*, pp. 263-90.

[104]Op. cit., p. 13.

them and those who used them to incite massacres of Jews, never said that they themselves had actually observed Jews doing any of those things. The explanation of this irrational hatred of the Jews, according to Langmuir, was (and is):

> ... many Christians are plagued by a new kind of doubts, by conflicts between what they could and would know if they used their ability to think rationally and empirically, and what they wanted to believe.... Many people were able to face their religious doubts more or less directly or set them unthinkingly aside, and many were not fearful of the presence of the Jews [in their midst]. But many others could not or would not confront their doubts. Instead of examining what was really bothering them, they defended their beliefs by imagining that contemporary Jews were acting in ways that demonstrated empirically the truth of the Christian beliefs. To repress their doubts, they suppressed their capacity to think rationally and empirically, and instead imagined Jews according to their threatened beliefs. But doubts still plagued them, whether consciously or subconsciously. Their projections could not remove the real source of their anxiety, for it was buried deep within them, and their projections only drove the real problem farther underground. And since they could not recognize what was disturbing them, that only heightened their sense of a menace and their hatred of it and drove them to seek an outlet for their emotions. Revealingly, the surrogate on which they vented their hate was the Jews, the supreme symbol of disbelief.[105]

This same mechanism of irrationality may very well have applied to Muslim hatred towards Jews in the Middle East. In the Middle East, due to the ongoing intensity of the Arab-Israeli dispute, the same accusations have become part of the litany of complaints, for the most part having no leg to stand on, which have been poisoning systematically the minds of media readers, listeners and watchers, school textbooks, Friday prayer sermons, and political statements

---

[105]*Ibid*, pp. 13-14.

of Arab leaders and opinion makers. But unlike Langmuir's claim to the effect that the weight of irrationality has been decreasing after Hitler, who had brought it to its mad apex, there did not occur any corresponding decrease in the virulent anti-Semitism of Muslims in the world. So, while in Western democracies there are less manifest expressions of anti-Semitism, *inter alia* because they are punished by law, there remain grey areas of silence in the face of open Arab and Muslim anti-Semitism, which also serve the purpose of venting the persistent undercurrents of traditional European Jew-hatred. For when the Muslims deny the *Sho'ah* or the Palestinian delegate in the Commission of Human Rights in Geneva accuses the Israelis of injecting HIV positive to 300 Palestinian children in order to harm their reproductive organs, almost none of the Western delegates rose to protest, nor did the chanceries of Europe, who should have been horrified by this new manifestation of the blood libel[106]. Some Western media even actively aided the Palestinians in propagating the calumny in April 1983 blaming Israel for poisoning Palestinian school girls in the West Bank, and none of them showed the decency of apologizing for this horrible libel when the entire story proved a hoax.[107] This European assistance to Muslim libel against the Jews, whether intentional or through omission for the sake of protest, and probably geared to let Israel be unjustly bashed with impunity, has been taken in itself as an acquiescence in the Muslim accusations.

This in turn signifies: one, that passive anti-Semitism is permitted, or at least not harshly prosecuted, as long as the countries of Europe can wash their hands clean of any active Judeo-phobia within their boundaries; and two, this signals to the Muslims, in their lands and in Europe, that they can pursue their libel and their threats to destroy Israel

---

[106]See Raphael Israeli, *Poison: Manifestations of a Blood Libel*, Lexington Books, 2002, pp.14-15, 18-22, 45-6, 90-3, 214-17, 228-30, 231-33.

[107]*Ibid.*

and eliminate Israelis, because no one, least of all the UN and its "Human Rights Commission," would dare raise his voice against it. For no one is impressed by the UN Secretary General and Western leaders, who dub Iranian President genocidal threats against the Jews and politicidal menaces against Israel as "unacceptable," but do nothing to oust Iran from the UN until it repents. Worse, they continued their business deals with it as they were pursuing their preparations for another outburst of UN-sponsored anti-Semitism in Duban II. Many Europeans let the Muslims in Europe, the Middle East and the UN do the dirty job of anti-Semitism for them while they watch with delight their surrogates express similar sentiments to theirs. "Hatred of the Jews is found as a common denominator among people of otherwise irreconcilable beliefs and attitudes," lamented a student of Soviet anti-Semitism.[108]

There is perhaps no other explanation for the convergence of the tacit anti-Semitism of the West, especially France, and the explicit one, articulated by Arabs and Muslims. It was adopted and expressed by Muslim groups such as al-Qa'ida, *al-Muhajirun*, *Hizbu'l Tahrir*, and various brands of the Muslim Brotherhood, where it became an instrument of mobilization, incitement, propaganda and even policy. And the more it remains unchallenged by the rest of the world, the more it is likely to expand and deepen its roots, to assert itself, and to acquire permanence. On October 14, 1965, both the Soviet Union and Poland opposed the UN proposal that the Charter of Human Rights should contain a clause banning anti-Semitism. Instead, they pressed for an amendment—which others refused to adopt—advocating that Zionism, Nazism, and Neo-Nazism (in that order) be classified as "racial crimes."[109] Ten years later, the General Assembly did adopt the proposition that Zionism equaled racism, thus

---

[108]Emanuel Litvinoff (ed.). *Soviet anti-Semitism: the Paris Trial*, Widwood House, London, 1974, p. 1.

[109]*Ibid*, p. 4.

bringing to full circle the legitimation of anti-Semitism in the guise of anti-Zionism. If it was thought that no one could dare to attack the Jews openly, so their collective creations, like their movement of national liberation (Zionism) and their state (Israel) were put beyond the pale, signaling that from all the nations of the world, the Jews alone had no right to be liberated or to have a state of their own. That amounted to anti-Semitism pure and simple.

The transposition of the Jewish problem onto Israel and the resulting shift of anti-Semitism into anti-Zionism, seems to provide the key for the combined rage of the Arabs and Muslims and some Europeans in their common attitude towards contemporary Israel and Zionism. It was a great European, George Clemenceau, who while pointing to the great power and influence he was imputing to the Jews, also accused them of proving themselves "incapable of creating their own homeland."[110] This patronizing attitude has never extricated itself from the built-in contradiction among anti-Semites of recognizing Palestine, on the one hand, as the natural abode of the Jews, but on the other hand refusing to accept that the Zionist dream has precisely realized itself there. And after the establishment of the state of Israel, they will always hold it to a different standard of conduct than all countries, seeking as it were the seeds of its demise in its very existence, and perennially raising questions about its legitimacy. For this reason, Israel is not viewed like any other state. Fiji, Barbados, or Guinea, or any other God-forsaken place, which has not marked the world by any cultural, economic, scientific or religious traits, and which has emerged from nowhere into independence, are taken as a matter of course, their legitimacy is unshakable, and their statehood, self-determination, and territorial integrity are inviolable. Only Israel remains somehow different in spite of being one of the oldest and most persistent civilizations, and

---

[110]Cited in Walter Zenner, *Minorities in the Middle East: A Cross-Cultural Analysis*, SUNY, Albany, 1991, p. 65.

stands today at the forefront of the most advanced nations in the world.

Since the 1980s several high level European politicians have made radical anti Semitic declarations which accorded with Arab and Muslim positions and predisposed them to a total delegitimation of the Jewish state. In a public statement in 1982, Greek Socialist Prime Minister Andreas Papandreou compared Israelis to Nazis.[111] But no mainstream European leader went as far as Christian Democrat Giulio Andreotti, many times the Prime Minister and then the President of Italy, who declared in Geneva, during an inter-parliamentary conference in 1984, his endorsement for a Saddam Hussein's Iraqi motion, which equated Zionism with racism, supported the boycotting of Israel, and defended the right of the "armed struggle for the liberation of Palestine [that is terrorism to eliminate Israel]. Italy was then the only Western country to vote with the Soviet Bloc for this motion.[112] Later, such occurrences have become even more frequent. In April 2002, Franco Cavalli spoke at a demonstration of the Swiss-Palestinian Society in Bern. He was then the parliamentary leader of the Social Democratic Party (SP), which is part of the Swiss government coalition. He claimed that Israel, "very purposefully massacres an entire people" and undertakes the "systematic extermination of the Palestinians."[113] Was he ignorant of the comparatively higher number of Palestinians massacred by the Syrians, Lebanese, Jordanians, and their own infighting, or his anti-Semitism drove him to ignore the numbers? Or could he not explain why the Israelis were so inadequate and impotent at "annihilating" the Palestinians, if they are stronger and more numerous than

---

[111]Daniel Pedurant, "Anti-Semitism in Contemporary Greek Society," *Analysis of Current Trends in Anti-Semitism*, No 7, 1995, p. 10, Hebrew University, Jerusalem. Cited by Gerstenfeld, April 1, 2004.

[112]Maurizio Molinari, *La Sinistra E Gli Ebrei inn Italia*: 1967-1993, Milan, 1995, p. 115. Cited by Gerstenfeld, April 1, 2004, p. 16.

[113]"Israeli Kritik oder antisemitismus?," *Neue Zurcher Zeitung*, April 26, 2002.

ever before?. Senior members of the Greek Socialist Party routinely used Holocaust rhetoric to describe Israeli military actions against Arabs, even when they are defensive in nature. In March, Parliamentary Speaker in Athens, Apostolos Kaklamanis, referred to the "genocide" of the Palestinians, forgetting that no one people can undergo so many "genocides" and still survive. Jenny Tonge, a Liberal Democrat MP in the U.K. declared at a meeting of the Palestine Solidarity Campaign in 2004 that she might consider becoming a "suicide bomber" if she lived in the Palestinian territories. But in contrast to the other cases, her party distanced itself from her statement this time, explaining that it did not condone terrorism.[114]

Raising the very question of Israel's legitimacy, or even "recognizing its right to exist," in itself carries a connotation of suspicion, uncertainty, hesitation, temporariness, and remonstration, as if it were under probation, like a criminal on parole, who has to prove constantly that he deserves his freedom. If Israel concedes, withdraws, shrinks back to its "natural size" (as the Egyptians would have it), obeys, effaces itself, admits "guilt" or plies to demands from it, or submits to calumniations against it, in short behaves like a *dhimmi* of old, then it is considered by the nations of the world as peaceful, reasonable, moderate, and conciliatory. But when it stands up to its enemies, demands that its rights, territory, heritage, security, people, way of life, and sovereignty be safeguarded and respected, then the world is amazed at its "arrogance, self-assertion, aggression, selfishness, spirit of rebellion, fanaticism, extremism, and disregard of others". When diplomats and world leaders admit Israel's right to exist (thank you very much), this is often taken as a special favor done to it and some Jews are happy at the daily confirmation of that favor, which they were never accustomed to take as a matter of natural right. The *dhimmi* spirit that they perpetuate dictates to them a grateful mode of behavior

---

[114]See citations in Gerstenfeld, April 1, 2004, op. cit. p. 16.

towards anyone who condescends to affirm what otherwise would have been considered a matter of course. That is the reason why sixty years after independence Jews continue to express in their national anthem the "hope" of attaining freedom in their land. They cannot believe they did already. Consider this: a world leader of questionable reputation takes the liberty to pontificate and tell Israel that it has the "right to exist", but provided it evacuated territory, allowed Palestinian refugees to go back to their previous homes, gave up a certain amount of her defenses, and depended on international guarantees. This means that its right to exist was conditional on its meeting certain expectations, even if they run contrary to its interests or to its very chances of survival in its hostile environment.

Thus, not only is Israel, of all nations, is required to take steps towards its own demise, as a prerequisite to its conditional recognition by others, but this also implies that if it does not comply, its admission into the family of nations may be rescinded. Can anyone dare tell the British that they would be recognized only provided they return the Falklands to their owners; or the Americans, the Canadians, and the Australians that they can be recognized only if they restored rights to the dispossessed natives that they had conquered; or that the Japanese, Syrians, Iraqis, and Sudanese will be accepted only when they recognize their minorities and stop persecuting them; or Iran, China, and Egypt—only if they accepted democracy or stopped threatening their neighbors? Unthinkable? Not in the case of Israel, even though it cannot be reproached for any of those violations or improprieties. Take for example the question of Jerusalem, the capital of Israel and the Jewish people for the past 3,000 years. In December, 1995, the General Assembly of the UN adopted a resolution, with an overwhelming majority, as in previous years, denying the validity of the Israeli laws, which confirmed united Jerusalem as the capital of modern Israel once again. That resolution also condemned the "Judaization" of Jerusalem as if someone blamed the Chinese for the Sinifi cation of Beijing or the French for the Francisation of Paris, or Saudi Arabia for the Islamization of Mecca. When the Arabs dominated East Jerusalem, which they never made their capital, not only did they effect a full Arabization of the city, but they did that at the detriment of Jewish sites such as Temple Mount, the Mount of Olives, the Jewish Quarter, and no one complained (that is except for the Israelis, but those are not counted). But as soon as the Jews restored their sites to their sovereignty, without as much as touching the Aqsa compound, which the Muslims had knowingly constructed upon the holiest site of the Jews, then outcries about "Judaization" began, which was heralded as "threatening world peace." So, when the UN declared that the Israeli measures were "null and void," one wonders whether the restored Jewish Quarter, which had been destroyed by the Arabs, should have remained in ruins, or demolished again after it was repaired, or that the reparations of the cemetery of the Mount of Olives, which had been demolished by the Jordanians and its tombstones used to pave a road, should revert to its state of profanation in order to qualify for the ludicrous terms of that resolution.

In October 1996 the European community demanded that Israel should rescind all those measures of restoration and construction and return things to their "original state." Original since when? If the splendor of Jerusalem is returned to its Davidic and Solomonic original, then al-Aqsa Mosque should have been removed to allow for the original Temple to re-emerge. Or perhaps they meant that the latrines that the Jordanians had constructed on the sites of the synagogues that they destroyed in the Old Jewish Quarter of Jerusalem ,should be reinstituted on the ruins of those now reconstructed sites? The occasion for those European demands was the reopening of an ancient tunnel, dating back 2,400 years in history, to the times of the Jewish Hasmonean Dynasty, before there was any idea of Europe, of Christianity, Islam, Arabs, or Palestinians. And because the Muslim Palestinians who had usurped the holy Jewish Temple Mount, now claim that the tunnel endangered their holy sites, themselves built on the ruins of the ancient Jewish Temple, the Europeans moved to make Israel close it again. And all that, under the Palestinian threat of violence if Israel would not conform. Which one of those new European nations would have acquiesced in a situation where its right to relate to its past heritage was called into question? Jerusalem is but an example. At stake is the self-imputed right of Western countries to determine the standards of behavior to which Israel is held and their presumption to act as self-appointed supreme arbiters of that conduct. Exactly like the Jews in their midst, who were suspicious and accused until proven innocent, so is the Jewish state. It is in this sense that the Jewish state has become the Jew among states[115].

For decades, most nations took the right to call Israel "the Jewish State," or the "Tel Aviv Government," lending to it the same legitimacy as the "Vichy Government" had; they made their representations and sent their representatives to that non-existing address; the international media also dispatched their reports from Tel Aviv, while the pictures they showed often originated from Jerusalem, the seat of the government of Israel. All that in order to avoid recognition of Jerusalem, the ancient capital of Israel, which had predated their own respective capitals, as the reconstituted center of modern Israel. So widespread has that fiction been, that many people ended up believing that it was Tel Aviv, not Jerusalem, that was the capital of Israel. What other country in the world would have been submitted to such a treatment, or accepted the systematic negation of its legitimacy of which the choice of a capital city is part? This inordinately critical view of the Jews in history has somehow carried over and rubbed off to Israel as well, and directly aided the Arabs and Muslims in their rejection of Israel, lock, stock, and barrel. The intense scrutiny and obsessive coverage of Israel's every

---

[115]See Paul Giniewski, "Israel: Etat Juif ou Juif des Etats," *Politique Internationale*, No 74, Winter 1996-7, pp. 1-20.

fault and detail sends to Tel Aviv (but more to Jerusalem) regiments of reporters and correspondents, more than to any other world capital save Washington, DC. And all those journalists have to justify their presence in Jerusalem (under Tel Aviv disguise) and their hunger for news to feed their avid media. Thus, the most absurd of gossip can become reported news, and the most insignificant events can become "history." In reports about the *Intifadah,* for example, articles were written about the special wood used to manufacture police truncheons to maintain order, and the workshops where they were made. Similarly, we have seen that the tedious and repetitive detail that is of no interest elsewhere, finds its way to international media. The nature of the "Jewish" truncheon, which caused suffering to the Palestinians and also tarnished Jewish reputation, was only a symptom. No one has ever checked the truncheons used by the British police in Northern Ireland or by the French police in quelling street riots in the Parisian slums. But a Jewish truncheon deserves a special scrutiny. Palestinian children and adolescents can throw Molotov cocktails at Israeli police, occasionally killing, wounding, or maiming them, but those are "only kids" standing up courageously against their oppressors; to be repressed by police wielding those redoubtable Jewish truncheons, that is quite another matter, for Jews have to submit to special standards of conduct, unlike all others. A Palestinian spokesman made the remark: "We are so lucky that our enemies are the Israelis. If they were Singhalese, who would care to mention us?" Father Marcel Dubois, Head of the Dominican Order in Jerusalem, made a similar comment: "Had the occupied territories been under Margaret Thatcher's responsibility, the *Intifadah* would have lasted three days only, and no one would have talked about it any more."[116]

Both statements were corroborated by a member of the foreign press corps in Jerusalem—Thomas Friedman, of

---

[116]Marcel Dubois, "Judaisme, Christianisme et Philosophie," *Le Soir*, Paris, March 31, 1988.

the *New York Times,* who repeated the same observation in almost the same words: "the great luck of the Palestinians is that they are in a state of conflict with Israeli Jews."[117] This is the reason why the demonization of Israel in both Europe and the Muslim world is directly connected to the emergence of the Palestinian cause, which can be subsumed under the headline of "Palestinism". This trend has been particularly salient in France, not coincidentally also the home of the largest Muslim community on the continent (6 million out of a population of 60). During the election campaign of 2004 in France, the "Europalestine" list of candidates—founded and headed by a notorious Muslim anti-Semite actor, Dieudonne—made a relatively strong showing in some constituencies and totaled more than 50,000 votes, probably most of them Muslims, judging from their election stickers. Under huge advertisements in the streets of La Courneuve and other heavily Muslim populated areas of Paris, which announced the link between "peace in Europe and justice in the Middle East," more elaborated statements of faith, hatred, racism and bigotry could not be ignored: "The Martyrdom of the Palestinians people has lasted too long"; "The Palestinian issue has been shamefully marginalized in the corridors of power, in spite of its strong presence in the minds of thousands of citizens"; "Jerusalem to the Arabs"; "Death to the Jews"; "Allah Akbar!"; "Bush and Sharon got Saddam, but I pray that Bin Laden should escape them."[118]

As long as Muslim terrorism had been directed against Israel only, the European media usually put the blame on the Israelis; but only when it started to strike at western territory, did the Israeli position begin to encounter more understanding in Europe, where leader after leader showed sympathy for her. But for the diehard anti-Semites, as well as the Muslims of Europe, there has been no let up. Muslims continue

---

[117]Cited by David Makovsky in his "Media Report," The *Jerusalem Post*, August 25, 1989.

[118]Didier Hassoux, in *Liberation*, June 15, 2004.

their blunt anti-Semitic statements, while non-Muslims continue to deftly channel their hatred to anti-Zionism. It is no coincidence that the question of Israel's posture and reputation in the world is perceived by Muslims as pertinent to its legitimacy. They understand that a weak, disarmed, and bullied Israel can bring it more easily and more quickly to its demise, because no one wants to sustain a temporary or fleeting entity. A strong and internationally robust Israel, on the other hand, which can boast a sound economy, world acclaim for its military, scientific, and technological prowess and its dizzying pace of development, against all odds, would be that much more difficult to delegitimize, to eliminate, or to calumniate. Hence Arab economic boycotts against Israel to hurt its economy; the military and political siege around it to isolate it; terrorist attacks to discourage the flow of foreign tourists and investors, and new immigrants into it; its constant harassment with threats of war and violence to deflect its creative attention and sap its energies; and its libel, via demonization in an effort to undermine its standing and tarnish its soaring reputation as a strong high achiever and successful contributor to the world community. The Muslim dismal failure to attain any of those goals over the past half century has only galvanized their determination to redouble their efforts and try to achieve via "peace" what they could not accomplish by war. And when Israel refuses to surrender, Muslims and Europeans join the effort of vilification of the Zionist state. The pathetic British Teachers Union, who on occasions decided to boycott Israel academically; or the Norwegian consumers who tried a boycott of Israeli products, only showed them that the Zionist state can survive and flourish without them, their undeclared anti-Semitic sentiment notwithstanding.

The self-image of Israel as a Zionist state, namely one who claims a national home for the Jews in the land surrounding Zion (Jerusalem), has been the target of both Muslim propaganda and western anti-Semites to delegitimize the Jewish state. The concerted effort at the UN in 1975, by all

Muslims and anti-Semites to deprive Israel of its legitimacy, by ostracizing Zionism, was only the most spectacular manifestation of that trend. And although that abomination of outlawing one of the most successful movements of national liberation of the 20th century was redressed in 1991 when the General Assembly abolished its previous resolution equating Zionism with racism, Durban 2001, which was supposed to combat racism, ended up as an ugly demonstration of anti-Semites and Muslims against Jews, Zionism, and Israel which prompted Israel and the U.S.and other decent nations to leave the conference. The Muslim world celebrated, in spite of the fact that in the meantime both Egypt and Jordan signed peace treaties with the Zionist state. Less salient to public opinion is the persisting total and uncompromising negation of Zionism by Muslims, including those who made peace with Israel, and their ongoing commitment to eradicate it. This is evident in the daily and repetitive broadsides against Zionism in their media and other publications, and in their favorite reference to Israel as the "Zionist entity" and the substitution of the epithet "Zionist" for anything relating to Israel, like "Zionists" for Israelis, "Zionist policy" for Israeli policy, etc. Even the basic document of the Palestinians—their National Charter—vows to destroy all manifestations of "Zionism" in Palestine in its armed struggle against it. Eighteen years after Oslo, fifteen out of the thirty-three articles of that Charter, which was never amended, nor abrogated, continue to state that purpose. That goal seems to them to be more palatable to Westerners, who would oppose the explicit politicide of Israel, or the genocide of the Jews, as bluntly declared by Iran's President, but would accept the elimination of Zionism though they all would amount to the same.

The scandalous omissions and distortions and one-sided judgments, and no less the moral corruption of the Goldstone report's sponsor, the UN's Human Rights Commission, have further advanced the cause of those who wish to delegitimize Israel. For if a large part of the international

community endorses the report's conclusions and opts to put
Israel on trial—symbolically or literally—the clear message
to Israel will be the rescinding of its right to self-defense
against Hezbollah and Hamas, both of which are embedded
in civilian populations. That will require a basic rethinking
of Israel's current strategic policy of containing the terrorist enclaves on its northern and southern borders. In the
decades following the Six Day War, Israeli policy, upheld
by successive Labor and Likkud governments, was to deny
terrorists a foothold along any Israeli border. That was, in
part, the rationale behind Moshe Dayan's open bridges policy between Israel and Jordan in the 1970s, as well as Ariel
Sharon's West Bank settlement drive and the 1982 invasion
of Lebanon. When that war soured, so did the appeal of the
policy that inspired it. Israel's two unilateral withdrawals—
from Lebanon in 2000 and Gaza in 2005—both resulted in
the creation of terror enclaves on its borders, negating long-
standing strategy. The policy of prevention was replaced by
a policy of containment which was expressed in the 2006
operation against Hezbollah in Lebanon, and by the operation against Hamas in Gaza. In both those mini-wars, Israel
wrongly opted not to uproot the terrorist enclaves, believing
that the partial flexing of Israeli power would deter further
aggression. In this regard, The Goldstone report may well
mark the end of Israel's limited wars against terrorist groups.
Israel cannot afford to continue to be drawn into mini-wars
against terrorists hiding behind their own civilians to attack Israeli civilians, given that each such conflict inexo-
rably draws the Jewish state one step closer toward pariah
status. Limited victories on the battlefield are being turned
into major defeats in the arena of world opinion. That untenable situation may well leave Israel no choice but to return
to the post-1967 policy of preventing altogether the presence
of terror enclaves on its borders. Better, Israelis will argue,
to deal decisively with the terror threat and brace for temporary international outrage than subject our legitimacy to
constant attrition, even as the terrorist threat remains intact.

Israelis will be keenly watching the pace of Qassam rocket fire from Gaza for signs of an emboldened Hamas. If attacks do intensify, and the quiet achieved by the Gaza offensive is forfeited, the Israeli public will blame the Goldstone report. And Israelis' operative conclusions will likely lead to a less restrained response next time—the opposite result Judge Richard Goldstone sought to achieve in his attempt to deny Israel the right to self-defense. But in the process, the trend of Israeli delegitimation, whether intended or not by its author, may have gone beyond the point of no return [119].

Israeli concerns in this regard were voiced by its Prime Minister, Benjamin Netanyahu, in a warning he issued to the 47 countries of the UN Human Rights Council in Geneva on October first 2009, before it was due to vote on the report.

> It is expected that the Council will vote to accept the Goldstone findings, which conclude that both Israel and Hamas committed war crimes during Operation Cast Lead earlier this year. Israel launched the offensive after Gaza terrorists rained down thousands of rockets on Israeli towns and cities, killing over 20 people and making havoc of routine life in Israel's western Negev...This council has made, in recent years, more resolutions against Israel than any of the 180 countries around the world... If the committee decides to promote the Goldstone report, it would cause grave harm in three areas: It would grant legitimacy to the Hamas terrorist practice of attacking civilian targets while hiding behind other civilians. It would deal a blow to the UN status, reducing it to making "absurd" decisions. It would gravely harm the peace process, discouraging Israel from taking risks for peace for fear that it will not receive international backing. I hope a majority will come to their senses... We have no confidence in it; there is usually an automatic majority there against us. If a majority is found to negate this report, it will avoid this severe blow, but if not, the responsibility

---

[119]See Comment written by Yossi Klein Halevy, to the Goldstone Report for the Adelson Research Institute in Jerusalem, September, 2009,

will be on those countries who didn't pull themselves together in time. [120]

The Iranian Peril

The lethal danger that Iran poses to Israel has been outlined above, and its has not been alleviated by passing years. In sharp contrast with the growingly wimpish west, which beyond speeches dares not to impose really devastating sanctions, or to use force, Iran's President, his questionable standing at home notwithstanding, escalates annually his nuclear activity, his anti-semitic pronouncements, elevates Sho'ah denial to an article of faith, and is shamelessly applauded by many Islamic, third-world and other anti-semites. In September 2009, when the world realized that Iran not only did not reduce its uranium-enriching activity, in defiance of the world, but has built a second facility in Qom, to accelerate that process, there was an outrage for a while, but Obama's non-policy of "engagement", instead of severe American reaction, has not been affected. Moreover, it seems that the choice of Qom, the holy city of Shi'ism, may have been predicated on its "immunity" to retaliation, as if someone had built a nuclear enrichment in Mecca, Rome or Jerusalem. As we have seen so far, the Muslim world has expected the West to respect its calendar, principles, ambition etc, even when they may be lethal to others, while insisting that their right to terrorize, threaten and bash others, in "self-defense", remains indisputable. The UN looks on with total impotence, busy condemning Israel for defending itself and exonerating Iran for its deadly nuclear capacity-building, Sudan for its genocide of the Darfurians, and the rest of the Muslim world for its continuous orgies of daily killings in Iraq, Afghanistan, and its dismal record of human rights for their millions. So much so, that a writer mused that "searching for truth at the United Nations is like looking for kernels

---

[120]Prime Minister's Office Communique, 1st October, 2009

of wheat in a mountain of horse dung". His analysis is so perceptive that it is well worth citing:[121].

From the unscientific blather about global warming from our own Kevin Rudd and meaningless posturing by Barack Obama to Libya's President for Life and Eternity Muammar Gaddafi and his Iranian colleague-in-evil President Mahmoud Ahmadinejad, the nuggets are rare and, when they fall, they do so largely unheard. In the ridiculous non-judgmental process of giving all national leaders—dictators and democratically-elected figures alike—some freakish semblance of equal moral stature, the UN's unelected bureaucracy provides a ritual soap box for the grotesqueries of the world to parade their fantasies. But Rudd's boring lecture was not in the same league as the performances delivered by Gaddafi and Ahmadinejad, two monsters of truly global scale. Their ravings would constitute hate-speech in a number of Western nations but are sanctified within the confines of the UN as a demonstration of the organisation's commitment to freedom of expression. A freedom of expression which is not enjoyed by the populations of most of its member states from Africa, the Middle East and Asia.

The biggest lie is that promoted most vigorously by Ahmadinejad: That the Holocaust did not occur. Australia's delegation took the principled position and walked out but a number of other nations remained to hear this lunatic repeat his libel. To his enormous credit, Israeli Prime Minister Benjamin Netanyahu delivered a compelling rebuttal that demolished the Iranian's vile invective with clear logic backed by indisputable facts. He pointed out that Israel was founded by the UN nearly 62 years ago in recognition of the right of the Jews, an ancient people with a history stretching back some 3500 years, to a state of their own in their ancestral homeland. Directly addressing Ahmadinejad's lie, Netanyahu produced a copy of

---

[121]Piers Akerman," A playground for the vile and dangerous Australia's '*Daily Telegraph*', 30 September, 2009.

documents prepared by senior Nazi officials in 1942 which detailed plans to exterminate the Jewish people. There is no question about the authenticity of those documents. He then produced a copy of the construction plans for the Auschwitz-Birkenau concentration camp. One million Jews were murdered there. Again, there is no question about the authenticity of the documentation. And what of the Auschwitz survivors whose arms still bear the tattooed numbers branded on them by the Nazis, he asked? Are those tattoos a lie? Netanyahu noted that a third of all Jews perished at the hands of the Nazis and that, among many Jewish families, his own was affected. He praised the member nations who refused to listen to Ahmadine-jad's lies and commended them for standing up for moral clarity, saying they brought honour to their countries. But he was scathing about those who gave the Holocaust-denier a hearing, saying: "Have you no shame? Have you no decency? A mere six decades after the Holocaust, you give legitimacy to a man who denies that the murder of six million Jews took place and pledges to wipe out the Jewish state. What a disgrace! What a mockery of the charter of the United Nations!" he said. "Perhaps some of you think that this man and his odious regime threaten only the Jews. You're wrong. History has shown us time and again that what starts with attacks on the Jews eventually ends up engulfing many others." Netanyahu said the current Iranian regime was fueled by an extreme fundamentalism that had in the past 30 years swept the globe with a murderous violence and cold-blooded impartiality in its choice of victims. "It has callously slaughtered Muslims and Christians, Jews and Hindus and many others. Though it is comprised of different offshoots, the adherents of this unforgiving creed seek to return humanity to medieval times," he said. "Wherever they can, they impose a backward society where women, minorities, gays or anyone not deemed a true believer is brutally subjugated." The struggle against this fanaticism does not pit faith against faith nor civilization against civilization. It pits civilization against barbarism, the 21st century against the 9th century, those who sanctify life against those who glorify death. The primitivism of the 9th century ought to be no match for the progress and strengths of the 21st century. The allure of freedom, power of technology, reach of communications should surely win the day. But, he pointed out, the most urgent challenge facing the UN was to prevent the tyrants of Tehran from acquiring nuclear weapons. The big question is whether the member states of the UN are up to that challenge, is the international community prepared to confront a despotism that terrorises its own people as they bravely stand up for freedom? Unfortunately, there is no moral clarity at the UN, as Netanyahu says, the jury is still out and recent signs are not encouraging.

Matthias Kunzel, the German articulate Iran watcher, observes with disdain and sarcasm, that he international community has treated the recent disclosure of another secret uranium enrichment facility in Iran the way it has treated Tehran's previous violations of the Nuclear Non-Proliferation Treaty—with calls for yet more "dialogue", exactly as the UN Secretary General and leaders of the West have encountered the genocidal declarations of Ahmadinejad with the cynical and hypocritical exclamation: "unacceptable!", as if anyone were impressed. The world continued the pursuit of fruitless diplomacy at the talks between Iran and the five permanent members of the U.N. Security Council plus Germany, basing themselves on an incorrect understanding of international law, one that was spearheaded by the Europeans and is now "unfortunately shared by the U.S. president", says Kunzel, at the sight of the hapless western top diplomats, who wish to project a façade of a policy, while all they are doing is the non-policy of avoiding confrontation, like in 1938. "Any nation—including Iran—should have the right to access peaceful nuclear power," Barack Obama declared in his famous Cairo speech, "if it complies with its responsibilities under the Nuclear Non-Proliferation Treaty." The problem, says Kunzel, is that Iran is bound by its own constitution to violate the treaty, which is why insisting that the NPT still confers any rights on Iran is not only politically absurd but also wrong from a purely legal point of view. The treaty was signed by Iran in 1968 under the rule of Shah Mohammed Reza. It aims, as outlined in its preamble, at "further easing of international tension and the strengthening of trust between states." Its purpose is thus to stabilize the international system. The Islamic Republic, though, wants to abolish this "Satanic" secular world order and replace it with a *Sharia*-based system of Islamic rule. "The struggle will continue," promised Ayatollah Khomeini, "until the calls 'There Is No God but God' and 'Muhammad Is the Messenger of God' are echoed all over the world." The atom program is part of this revolutionary quest. "Iran's nuclearization," President Mahmoud Ahmadinejad told his supporters, "is the beginning of a very great change in the world." It would "be placed at the service of those who are determined to confront the bullying powers and aggressors." The opposition by Iran to the treaty's lofty intentions is not just politically affirmed but legally enshrined. Iran is probably the only country in the world that has declared comprehensive armament against "Allah's enemies" to be a constitutional requirement. In Article 151 of the Islamic Republic's constitution, Qu'ran verse 8/60 is cited as a binding precept for government policy: "Make ready for them all you can of armed forces and of horses tethered, that thereby you may dismay the enemy of Allah and your enemy, and others beside them whom you know not." To Western ears, this recourse to 7th-century scripture may seem quaint. But the mullahs are serious. Their idea of interpreting the Qur'an for the modern world is to replace "horses tethered" with "nuclear installations." An Islamic state like Iran can by definition not be considered a *bona fide* signatory to the NPT. The mullahs, although opposed to the treaty's overall purpose, never withdrew from the NPT in order to take advantage of the privileges the document grants its signatories.[122]

---

[122]Matthias Kunzel, "Iran has no Right for Nuclear Weapons", *Wall Street Journal*, 30 September, 2009

It is often assumed, writes Kunzel, that the NPT actually blocks access to the bomb. In reality, the opportunities afforded to aspiring nuclear-weapons makers are enormous. Article IV of the treaty enables signatories to produce all components necessary for a bomb under U.N supervision, as long as they do not combine these components into nuclear explosives. The significance of this loophole was explained in April 2007 by Hossein Shariatmadari, a confidante of Iran's "Supreme Leader" Ali Khamenei: "A country that has attained the knowledge and technology of uranium enrichment is only one step away from producing nuclear weapons. This [additional] step is not a scientific or a technical step, but a matter of political decision." Article X of the NPT further expands this loophole. A signatory state that, following President Obama's wishes, "complies with its responsibilities under the nuclear Non-Proliferation Treaty" could accumulate the most important components of a nuclear weapon under cover of the NPT, and then legally withdraw from the treaty by simply citing "extraordinary events." That's why President Bill Clinton in the 1990s, ignoring the faded Iranian signature on the NPT, denied the mullahs the right to any form of nuclear energy. On October 21, 2003, however, came a "very important turning point," as Hossein Mousavian, a high-ranking Iranian nuclear negotiator, described it. That was the day the foreign ministers of Great Britain, France and Germany—Jack Straw, Dominique de Villepin and Joschka Fischer—traveled to Tehran, despite major reservations on the part of the Bush Administration, to "recognize the right of Iran to enjoy peaceful use of nuclear energy in accordance with the nuclear Non-Proliferation Treaty," as the text of a declaration agreed by Iran and the three foreign ministers states. At that time, it was already known that Tehran had violated the NPT's monitoring regime for over 18 years by building secret nuclear facilities. Nevertheless, the paradoxical course of events continued: The more Tehran violated the NPT, the more generous the concessions by Europe, and later the U.S.—always using the treaty as justification. In his Cairo speech, Barack Obama also officially recognized Iran's alleged right to nuclear energy. Even after the existence of a second uranium enrichment facility was revealed, President Obama's tone remained conciliatory: "It is time for Iran to act immediately to restore the confidence of the international community by fulfilling its international obligations."

But Kunzel makes the point that as long as Iran is ruled by Khomenei's doctrine, this confidence can never exist. Tomorrow's talks will only encourage Tehran to continue feigning "trustworthiness." The refusal to acknowledge this reality could lead to a dangerous compromise—one that would allow Iranian uranium enrichment as long as Tehran permits U.N. monitoring. This would be a recipe for disaster. Allowing a theocratic regime dreaming of religious war to obtain nuclear weapons is a threat to humanity. It can neither be defused by the NPT provisions nor by continuing piecemeal sanctions. Short of a military strike, the only alternative is to make full use of Chapter VII of the U.N. Charter. In order to confront threats to peace, it suggests in article 41 the "complete or partial interruption of economic relations and of rail, sea, air, postal, telegraphic, radio, and other means of communication, and the severance of diplomatic relations." The time for "dialogue as usual" is over, forcefully asserts Kunzel[123].

In defiance of the world's outrage, Iran's top nuclear negotiator, Mr Jalili, announced that he and representatives of the Group 5+1 (the five permanent UN Security Council members plus Germany) had not discussed suspension of Iran's nuclear enrichment activities in their talks in Geneva, Switzerland at the end of September, 2009, as scheduled. "There was no discussion about the suspension of (Iran's) nuclear activities," the Secretary of Iran's Supreme National Security Council (SNSC) told reporters after he returned home from

---

[123]*Ibid.* Mr. Küntzel is author of "The Germans and Iran: The Past and Present of a Fateful Friendship," forthcoming in German in October 2009 with Wolf Jobst Siedler Jr. Belinda Cooper translated this article from the German.

Geneva talks, after the representatives of Iran and the six world nuclear powers ended their talks and agreed to meet again before the end of October, 2009. A meeting at the level of deputy heads of delegations was also planned before the heads of the two sides were to meet by the end of October.

"In Geneva talks, the central issues of Iran's package of proposals were explained. Readiness was announced for the establishment of joint cooperation on common concerns," Jalili said. "We concluded that the talks be continued and a framework be adopted for the continuation of the talks. It was agreed that the talks start at a lower level so that we could continue the talks in a bid to reach cooperation on common concerns envisioned in the Islamic Republic's package," Jalili noted. Namely, all elements are there for continuing to waste time until Iran's nuclearization is an irreversible *fait accompli*. He underlined that the talks were about maintaining and defending the Iranian nation's (nuclear) rights. Commenting upon Iran's newly announced enrichment plant in Fordo, south of the capital, Jalili said the new plant was constructed in line with Iran's measures to safeguard its enrichment program. "One of the measures was that we should have a center for enrichment with higher safety. Hence, we went after the new facilities which are under construction," the Iranian chief nuclear negotiator noted. Meantime, Jalili underlined that Tehran does not have a problem with inspection of the new plant by the International Atomic Energy Agency (IAEA) within the agency's regulations[124].

In fact, when Iran informed IAEA on 25 September, 2009 that it was building a second plant for the enrichment of uranium, there had already existed a widespread suspicion that Tehran had been secretly engaged in such a project. It is estimated that only when Iran thought that foreign intelligence agencies had discovered the plans over the new plant,

---

[124]"Jalili: Suspension of Iran's Enrichment Activities Excluded from Geneva Talks" News number: 880711135016:28|2009-10-03 Nuclear http://english.farsnews.com/newstext.php?nn=8807111350

did she resign to share the information with the West. But the main quandary remains the goal of such an additional project, which is due to house 3000 more gas-operated centrifuges, which carry out the enrichment task. Natanz, the main enrichment center, has the capacity of 54,000 centrifuges. At the current pace, it is estimated that Natanz can hardly produce enough low-quality uranium to fuel the reactor in Busher. In this case, if the additional plant can only produce 5% of the total, what is the big deal? Thus, the Iranian claim that the new plant is geared for peaceful purposes only, where a less than 5% concentration of uranium is needed, makes no sense at all. If it were no different from Natanz, it would have constituted only a fraction of that immense project. The other pretext provided by the Iranian president, to the effect that the new plant would only constitute a backup in the case the larger original is damaged, seems also to have no foot to stand on. Therefore, there are only two alternative explanations to the emergence of this new secret plan: either to enrich uranium to a higher grade for nuclear bombs, beyond the scrutiny of the IAEA, or to use it as a second stage enrichment to the first state in Natanz. The suspecting 5+1 nations have demanded that Iran arrest the entire process of enrichment by the end of December, 2009. But even that may be too late, if Iran, indeed, had received from Pakistan in the past the blueprint of the bomb. Even if Iran should officially relinquish her plans, it would be difficult to enforce and verify, or for Europe to insist on sanctions while she is benefiting hugely from its billions of commercial deals with Tehran.

World Jihadi Terrorism

Much more pernicious in its easier access and widespread diffusion, is the threat of world terrorism which is also intimately connected with Iran, where the annual convention of Terrorism International takes place. This is where the asymmetrical wars are elaborated to perfection and where they accumulate victory after victory, defy the great powers and find it easiest to confront Israel. For as America and NATO are coming to the conclusion that they cannot win the wars in Afghanistan and Iraq, and they decide, in consequence, to abandon the battlefield to the terrorists, and as the UN, via its Human Rights Commission, legitimizes terrorism and denies from its rivals the right to resist it, there is nothing that will deter terrorists to pursue their blueprint. As Pakistan and Afghanistan become more exposed to Western counter-attacks, new battlefields are developing in Somalia and the Yemen, where terrorists can find refuge and where Western-ers do not dare to venture. It is no coincidence that while the Hamas are pursuing their war of terror, at the same time that they cite the Goldstone recriminations against Israel and ig-nore those against themselves, the Palestinians threaten that they are preparing to turn their weapons and military skills, that the Americans are imparting to them, against Israel.

While the Palestinians are clamoring for renewal of ne-gotiations, provided Israel froze settlements, one of their leaders, Bassam Abu Sharif, a former senior advisor to late President Yasser Arafat, added his voice to a chorus of those raising the possibility of a third *Intifada*, or uprising against Israel. Namely, he, like other Palestinians, Arabs and Mus-lims, are determined to pursue that war of attrition against Israel, to which they can commit indefinitely, and which Is-rael cannot win, according to their estimate. In his words, "The Palestinians are preparing themselves to carry out an-other *Intifada* of independence and freedom in response to Israeli violations, massacres and policies against the Pales-tinians and their land, against Jerusalem, the confiscation of land and the geographic separation of the Palestinian terri-tories," said he. Several political figures from across the Pal-estinian spectrum have suggested lately that a new uprising is on its way in the wake of the violent clashes with Israeli police at the Al-Aqsa Mosque, just after the Muslim Rama-dan has ended in peace and security under Israeli protection, and the Jewish High Holidays began, namely time to cause disturbances as during the outbreak of the October 2000 *Intifada*. "The Palestinians are working to establish a fully sovereign state on the land, sea and airspace in accordance with UN Security Council Resolution 242, which has not been implemented since it was issued 42 years ago," he said. Abu Sharif said that indirect negotiations that will be held in New York will be the worst in the history of the Palestinian cause because they will be carried out while the Israeli government headed by Benjamin Netanyahu continues to seize land, alter the situation in Jerusalem, and expel Palestinians from the country. He concluded by urging Hamas and Fatah movements to sideline their partisan interests for the sake of the Palestinian cause. He also called for new elections and a resolution of internal disputes[125].

The resumption of shelling and bombing by the Hamas and its underlings along the Gaza border, the pledge of a new *Intifada* by the PLO, the threats against Israel by Iran in the UN, the renewed statements of al-Qai'ida about their long- term struggle with Israel, the capitulation of Israel when it surrendered 20 convicted murderers to the Hamas in return for a recording of Israeli prisoner Gilead Shalit, and the celebration in the Islamic world about the indictment of Israel by the Goldstone report, are all signaling the triumph of the asymmetrical wars, in contrast with the dismal failures of the Arab world which still pursues conventional strategies. The Hamas can register to its advantage not only the growing pace of delegitimizing Israel around the world, after Durban II and the Goldstone Report, but also the impunity with which their sponsor, Iran, has been succeeding in fooling the world and in having their way, in their nuclearization program. No wonder then, that they feel they have the upper hand, they can continue to kidnap Israeli soldiers to free their imprisoned terrorists, and that that they have no reason to alter their road.[126]

---

[125]Published on 30/09/2009 16:48 www.maannews.net/eng/ViewDetails.aspx?ID=228594

[126]Itamar Marcus and Nan Jacques Ziberdik, "PA an Hamas: Kidnapping Israeli Soldiers Key to Imprisoned Terrorists", *Palestinian Media Watch*, 29 September, 2009.

Chapter 9

The End to Appeasement

From Israel's sixty year experience, it is evident that what has aborted all its attempts to conclude peace, and has, on the contrary, escalated Arab and Muslim ambitions to annihilate it, was its pattern of capitulation to the temptation of appeasement. Each time its seemed that if Israel just made another step forward and conceded something more to the Arabs, it would have thereby advanced towards peace. However, when Israel has to face a culture which knows no compromise, and prizes victory over accommodation; when the enemy is a perpetually "humiliated" one, as much by its own failures as by what Israel is accused to have done; when education to hatred of the Jews has remained a constant in the Arab and Muslim systems; when the truth is not a concern and logical and factual proofs play no role in the worldview of the enemy; then appeasement is not likely to ever succeed in the long run, even if small gains are perceived to be made along the way. Peace, compromise and accommodation are the ways of democracies, which seek the common good and which produce settlements of problems by mutual negotiation and reciprocal agreement. Democracies know the price of non-agreement and of conflict, and try to avoid protracted wars which are very unpopular among their peoples. With tyrannical regimes, which incite to hatred and oppose peaceful settlements, and where there is no accountability of he rulers to their peoples, and they can perpetuate wars simply by their whims, for any diplomatic *demarche* on the part of democracies to succeed, it must avoid appeasement. For appeasement only strengthens the tyrant and aggrandizes his

ambitions, while a firm stand may awaken him into accepting the harsh reality and dealing with it.

Examples from the one century Arab-Jewish conflict in
Palestine, will illustrate the cultural, personal, political and
psychological *problematique* of appeasement, which has
been all too often resorted to by Israel, but has hitherto ham-
pered most attempts to reach a settlement between the parties. The most glaring examples are those addressing the cultural and religious convictions of our rivals, where for fear
of being or sounding "racist" or "uncivilized", we are ready
to countenance all the racist and uncivilized conduct towards
us, just in order to appear "good" in the eyes of the world.
Take the month of Ramadan, in September, 2009 with all
the extra-effort required by Israeli police to keep the order
on Temple Mount and around the Muslim mosque and the
esplanade therein. The police fulfilled its role admirably, not
one single incident occurred in that area during the whole
month, often at the expense of freedom of movement of
Jewish worshippers. But as soon as it was peacefully terminated, and the Jewish High Holidays began, throngs of
violent Muslim youth, incited by the Muslim Movement
in Israel, the Hamas and the Palestinian Authority, began
throwing rocks at Israeli worshippers, and any police intervention to impose peace and order, in defense of *bona fide*
worshippers, was lambasted by all Muslim and Arab countries, and the Muslims in Israel, as "Israeli attacks on Islam",
or "as "calculated disturbances by Israel of the Muslim Holy
places". "Moderate Jordan" even submitted an official letter of protest against "Israel's activities on the Mount". The
sensitivity of the place certainly dictates caution and delicate
handling. But knowing the roots of the problem and spreading it around the world, could certainly place it in the proper
context and prepare the Arabs to accept a firmer position
from Israel's side.

Muslim sources knew very well that the Aqsa Mosque
was constructed on the ruins of the Second Jewish Temple,
which was destroyed in AD 70 by the Romans. But since it

became the third holy place in Islam (after Mecca and Medina), Jewish rights, attachment to the place and historical claims, were obliterated. Since then, only Muslims exercized exclusive rights and let no one else advance his own. To that end, tons of Jewish archaeological findings were excavated by Muslims and dumped, in order to erase any traces of Jewish heritage, for fear that facts and science might refute their claims. When Israel seized Temple Mount after 2000 years of exile, the Muslims expected that Jews would now enforce the same principle of exclusivity and apply rights of access and of restoration to Jews only. But the Israelis, in order to appease Muslims, left them in exclusive control of the Mount, thus confirming their hold on the entire "holy basin", and reinforcing their belief that no one else shared that privilege. Their reasoning was that if Jews truly believed in their attachment to the place, they would have certainly behaved as they were expected. Conversely, in the Patriarchs' Tomb in Hebron, which Muslims had turned into a mosque, and excluded Jews from there over many centuries, the Israelis who took over in 1967, partitioned the rights of prayer between Jews and Muslims, and that arrangement, which is much resented by Muslims, has been in operation ever since. Had the Israelis enforced the same arrangements on Temple Mount since 1967, namely to let the mosques operate, but side by side to also allow Jewish activity, the Muslims would have learned, like other civilized people, to share with others the sanctity of the place. But they did not learn, they continue to attack Jewish worshippers, but are themselves immune to any claim or attack by others.

This is only the tip of the iceberg. For, appeasement of this sort has, all along, ravaged the relationship between Israel and Muslim countries, when at every turn, Israel sought to please the Muslims (something it never achieved) or at least to reconcile them, but it always earned scorn, contempt and hatred, never respect for its gesture, because behind every seemingly positive move there must always hide some dark conspiracy. And so, four decades after Israel took over the Holy Basin, those who exclude others and obliterate any traces of other cultures, are still holding the place exclusively, while the civilized people who were generous enough to wish to share, are kept out. And whenever there is talk of negotiation for a final settlement, the Muslims reiterate their total rejection and exclusion of Jews and Israel, and expect their claims alone to be recognized and accepted by the world. That is the classic case of appeasement and its price. Other cases unfold almost daily in Israel's dealings with the Palestinians and other Muslims. During Ramadan, Arabs in Israel and in the territories expect their prisoners to be released, their festival to be respected, but during the Jewish High Holidays those are the days they chose for their *Intifada* in 2000 and for ite commemoration the years after. The Jewish synagogues which were turned over under Oslo, provided the Palestinians guarded them and preserved their sanctity, were burned down into ashes by Palestinians at the outbreak of the *Intifada* (in Jericho, Joseph Tomb in Nablus and the Rachel Tomb near Bethlehem). Because Israelis were foolish to accept Palestinian assurances without ironclad guarantees that they would comply.

Appeasement and its cost are at the base of many agreements signed by Israel with the Palestinians and other Arabs and Muslims, and their aftermath. For example the Oslo series of "agreements", which would not have been needed if were what they were supposed to be—agreements. So many of them were there that none of them stuck. Because, instead of making every accord performance-bound, namely that nothing would proceed if the Palestinians did not fulfill their duties (Like collecting illegal weapons, put an end to violence, extradite terrorists or punish them, and the like) they simply reneged, and the Israelis, instead to halting the entire procedure, ignored the Palestinian violations "lest the entire peace process came to an end"—an act of appeasement *par excellence,* which cost the invalidity of the entire agreement and its slow death by strangulation. It seems that every time this happened, the Arabs justified that as the "public good", or "Muslim good", or "Arab good", which means that a contract, especially an international one, is not a document which obliges both parties to fulfill it in detail, a concept that was anchored in Roman law, but an instrument to force the non-Muslim signatory to stand by its commitment, but the Muslims are exempt from implementation if the Muslim common good is not served. That is based on the Hudaibiya precedent which was violated by Muhammed, but justified thereafter as the "Muslim common good". And for the sake of appeasement, no one attempts to shake the belief in this common good, something which tends to confirm it and ensure its repetition.

Religion pushes the conflict one notch up, because it renders it un-negotiable and insoluble. So, like in the case of the peace between Egypt and Israel, where it was all founded on rational notions of law, sovereignty and international commitments, (though it was post factum rationalized as a follow-up to the Hudaibiya model), so could an agreement with the Palestinians, (not Hamas) be worked out. Israel has already experienced both a rational accord with the PLO in Oslo (which has not worked) and the repeated *hudna* agreements with Hamas, which are inspired from the Hudaibiya precedent. When Muslims promise to achieve something by force, including genocide if necessary, like in the case of Ahmadinejad, against which no one in the Islamic world protests, it has to be taken seriously, not simply as a form of rhetorical exaggeration. Therefore, Israel must preempt, otherwise it will become the victim, while decent people of the world will just sit and watch. Failing to act would accustom the world to view Muslims and Arabs being permanently at Israel's throats, and Israel as permanently threatened. To avoid that from happening, the world would engage in diplomacy and "engagement", which means appeasement.

When acts of aggression and other hostilities break out, and out of a seeming concern for human lives, a salami tactic of slow death and low-intensity punishment of the aggressor is pursued in order to minimize the numbers of "innocent" casualties, assuming that all non-combatants are innocent. That allows the aggressor to continue its attacks indefinitely, being virtually immune from a total and decisive counter-attack of extermination which would also, in the long run, cause the many casualties on both sides one wished to avoid in the first place. For example, if Germany were spared the blanket bombings of its cities, then its capacity to go on fighting and exploiting its huge pool of manpower and solid industrial base would have prolonged the war indefinitely, resulting in many more casualties to both the aggressor and its victims. Similarly, there is no telling how many more casualties would the Pacific War have cost, on both sides, had the atomic bomb not put an abrupt end to it. Many more cities in Japan would have had to be annihilated by conventional bombings, like Dresden, and many more American marines slaughtered on the beaches of the country, before Japan would have surrendered. In both modes of destruction, the results in terms of ruins and victims, were horrific. But, it would have been much more economic and life sparing, had the bombs been dropped earlier, and in a more lethal pace and intensity, and put the end to the war more rapidly. The people of Germany and of Japan supported their governments and hailed them as long as they were victorious and conquering other countries and enslaving their inhabitants. If there was a widespread support for the governments in place, can any body claim that the people who lent support were "innocent"? Similarly, when a mass gathering of Hizbullah or Hamas convenes in the open in Beirut or in Gaza, with all their leaders present and inciting that supportive crowd, would it not be sparing many human lives, in the final analysis, if that assembly were bombed and strafed, rather than see its members launch deadly terrorist attacks on civilians in multiple assaults? If the US knew on September 10 that a group of 19 murderers were gathering somewhere in preparation for their attack the next day, wouldn't it have made sense to eliminate them preemptively, possibly with some collateral innocent people, rather than "spare" the innocent and abort the preemption, just to watch the much more horrific massacre of the Twin Towers innocents the next day?

And yet, because of "restraining moral considerations", which in fact are manifestations of appeasement, most civilized nations would refrain from preemptive action in those cases. The rationale is simple: in preemption one can only be sure of its casualties and damage, never can one persuade others of the greater damage that was spared because of the preemption, and therefore, at the price of disparaging the preemptive strike even when it seems inevitable, the appeasement of the victim would take precedence and the condemnation of the defender would follow. Even when the defensive strike comes in reprisal for what was done, the defender would be reproached for not preserving "proportionality" or for targeting people instead of "bringing them to justice", or "executing them without trial". What is proportionality? Logically, it would mean that the reaction should never exceed the action which triggered the reprisal. Namely, if Hamas blew up a bus and killed 20 odd passengers in Israel, or a Hamas terrorist exploded a bomb in a restaurant and killed another 20 civilians, wiping out entire families, Israel should act likewise, and start blowing up Palestinian restaurants and buses, which is a much easier, if harrowing, task to perform than a complicated military operation where casualties can fall. Israel, like other civilized countries, would never do that. How does one keep proportionality? Instead of killing one for one, which is perfectly proportional, or 10 for one in order to deter by the high price, should Israel kill only one for every massacre of twenty? That is less than proportional, and Israel would not do it either.

While asymmetrical wars seek to cause maximum casualties to the enemy-uniformed and civilians, innocent and culprits, children and women, in order to demoralize and sow fear in the enemy, civilized nation wish to catch the criminals, or pinpoint them for elimination (like Churchill against Hitler, Bush against Saddam and Bin-Laden). When Israel does that, it is also condemned for "assassination", which is a criminal term, thus *a priori* making a mockery of proportionality in reprisal, and paralyzing the defensive capacity of Israel. Israel, like the US, would be happy to capture the culprits and bring them to justice. But they permanently hide among civilians, innocent or not, no one would extradite them, even not the Palestinians under their Oslo commitment, therefore there is no alternative to their elimination individually, when there is an opportunity, even if occasionally there is collateral damage. There is even an advantage to their elimination over their incarceration, because sooner of later the most notorious murderers among them would be demanded for release by their organizations in exchange for other hostages that they will have taken, in other acts of terrorism. If Israel has to release bigger criminals in order to obtain the freedom of one of her servicemen, then better to eliminate than to incarcerate terrorists.

The consequence of this reasoning is that if there is a way, by using more targeted violence, even at the price of more immediate casualties, to bring about the end of a conflict, instead of letting it fester for years, and lowering its flames for the sake of appeasing the enemies or their supporters, then one should resort to it. In the final analysis, less casualties and less damage would be caused if the conflict is shortened and its intensity enhanced. If in Vietnam, a shorter and more massive American intervention was adopted at once, instead of the incremental escalation which dragged the US into the quagmire and ended in loss and defeat, then many less Vietnamese and Americans would have died and much less destruction and demoralization would have been caused. Similarly, if in Lebanon and Gaza (2006 and 2009) a massive Israeli and crushing victory could have wiped the Hizbullah and Hamas out, then less casualties, less destruction and less damage to the Palestinian cause would have been caused. A low intensity without decisive results, is the game of the asymmetrical wars; a crushing and massive victory over the terrorists and the change of reality, is the game of the powers which seek to defeat terrorists and prevent them from rising again. Many Iraqs, Afghanistans, Guantanamos, Gazas and their likes, are needed to deal terrorism a lethal blow. Desisting from these steps in the middle and not bringing them to completion, will admittedly appease some moods, if temporarily, but the war on terror will drag on and cause more damage, more casualties and more destruction.

These same principles apply to the Muslim ownership of nuclear weapons. Through appeasement, Ahmadinejad's Iran has been fooling the world and gaining precious time to attain the bomb. When he does, this will be irreversible. Other nations have also stockpiled arsenals of nuclear weapons. But they are neither threatening others with extermination, nor embracing totally irrational policies, like expecting the impending "return of the Imam", or adopting practical measures to welcome him in the streets of Tehran. Holding a millenarian religious belief is one thing, but taking operational steps towards the implementation of messianism is quite another. For such a fanatic to possess nuclear arms spells out apocalypse, which he does not fear but welcomes. If Iran under this regime does obtain nuclear weapons, it would take much more appeasement than hitherto to talk its ruler into refraining from using it, but the fear would always remain that he might. If one follows the niceties of international law, of diplomacy and engagement, instead of brutal confrontation with this type of fanatic tyrant, the world would become a worse and less safe place, not a better one. Diplomacy is the domain of the civilized, the rational and the pragmatic, for whom politics are the art of the possible, not the domain of the fanatic, the romantic and the irrational, for whom politics are the realization of the seemingly impossible dreams and ideals.

For the sake of appeasement, the West, and many of its underlings in the Islamic world, have come to differentiate between the minority "extremist Islam", that of the fanatic al-Qa'ida or the Taliban, which has to be battled ; and the majority of "moderate" and "peaceful Islam", which seeks accommodation with the West, loathes terrorism and can be dealt with amiably. Had the West blamed Islam as a whole, it would have been accused of "Islamophobia" or of racism, hardly the recipe to endear it to the Muslim masses in the world. However, not only are there no two "Islams", differentiated in doctrine and principles, but Muslims themselves reject such distinction. Sheikh Yussuf al-Qaradawi, the paramount Muslim judicial figure, who was made universally popular via *al-Jazeera* network, is not only the idol of the so-called "fundamentalists", but also of all pious Muslims throughout the world. The masses who demonstrate, often violently, for Muslim causes in Cairo, Islamabad, Jakarta or Casablanca, are plain common Muslims, just as are the jubilant crowds who celebrated after September 11 or after innocent Israelis are blown up. Could anyone tell who pursues moderate Islam and who holds fanatic beliefs there? The notions of Jihad, submission to Allah, the Holy Book, *Shari'a* Law, the Five *Arkan* of Islam and the other Islamic principles, are neither extremist nor moderate, they are Islamic. There are Muslims, who may be more observing than others, but those who observe, observe Islam, neither an extreme nor a moderate form thereof. Just to dub that faith "moderate" and "peace loving", serves no other purpose than appeasement, and drives some Believers to pursue their atrocities and outrages once they got the seal of approval as "peaceful".

Though the active *Jihadis* (not their Islamic faith) are a minority, that some evaluate at 15% of the 1.3 billion Muslims, namely in the order of about 200 million, that is enough to make the phenomenon frightening. But more scary is the widespread support that the *Jihadis* have among various strata of Islamic society: journalists, professionals, politicians, scholars, clerics and common people. Even more alarming are the very few voices, mostly in the West, of moderate Muslims who dare to stand up to the terrorists, to suggest reforms in Islam and to disavow the faith which drives people to such atrocities. Most startling are the numbers of scholars, journalists and other knowledgeable Muslims, who take advantage of the freedom of expression in the West to diffuse there their intolerance of other faiths or to promote the principles of Jihad or the aggression of Islam. Such figures are Sheikh Qaradawi, already mentioned above, who serves as the Head of the Supreme *Fatwa* Council in Europe, who circulates freely between European capitals and has befriended some leaders there, or abd al Bari Atwan, an editor of the London-based *al-Quds al-Arabi*, which endorses al-Qai'ida and Bin-Laden without reserve, and supports acts of Jihad, including Islamikaze acts of terror against Israel.

Islam was born and grew in a *Jihadi* ambiance of world dominion, which no Islamic authority has ever desisted from embracing. Whether Jihad is pursued openly by war, like al-Qa'ida and the Taliban's confrontation with the West, or by immigration into the West and the spread of the Islamic faith through gradual, continuous and unrelenting *da'wa,* most *Jihadi* spokesmen avow their ultimate aim of controlling the world and altering its inhabitants' believes. They often cite the Qur'an[127], the Word of Allah, with which no one can argue and no one can deny or refute, to wit: "They desire that you should disbelieve as they have disbelieved, so that you might be alike; therefore, take not among them friends until they fly [their homes] in Allah's way. But if they turn back, then seize them and kill them wherever you find them, and take not among them a friend or a helper". Baydawi, the authoritative commentator (d. 1315), interprets this to mean that whosoever turns back from belief *(irtadd),* openly or secretly, take him and kill him wheresoever you find him, like any other Infidel. Separate yourself from him altogether. Do not accept intercession in his regard. Much of the education to hatred of others in the Islamic world is based on these verses. So is demonization of the West and Israel, which ultimately signifies total rejection of the other and its annihilation. Trying to accommodate Muslims in general by

---

[127]Sura 4, verse 89

claiming that their "peaceful" religion is "moderate", only facilitates the appeasement of the aggressor and puts a stamp of approval to this clear murderous doctrine which Muslim official commentary is not trying to hide.

Disregard for these basics, and wishful thinking that their venom had subsided over the years, has led to tragic errors in western and Israeli policies. America has attempted, after September 11, to prevail on Saudi authorities to alter their educational programs, but the pace and substance of those "reforms" have left much to be desired. All that was "altered" have been the declarations of some clerics that "terrorism is anti-Islamic", statements that have been hailed as "progress", "steps in the right direction", but were all attempts at appeasement, while in fact the Saudi (and the rest of Muslims') definition of terrorism implies that against unbelievers like Israel, or for the sake of "resistance" like in Palestine, Iraq, Afghanistan and Kashmir, those acts of *istishhad* (self-sacrifice for the sake of Allah) are totally permissible. Attention should be paid, therefore, not to the formulae that are emitted to cheat the West or to placate it, but to the inner interpretations which are diffused among the Muslim publics, because they are the only ones valid.

Even before the establishment of Israel, the Jewish *Yishuv* in Palestine sought accommodation with the local Arabs, under the false belief that if soothed and appeased they would be amenable. The Jews erroneously thought that by being fair and generous to the Arabs, and making proof of the common good that would accrue to both by Jewish settlement and Jewish development, the Arabs would come to recognize the benefits of a Jewish homeland in their midst. But culturally, they were unable to accept that where they had dismally failed for generations, when under Muslim-Ottoman rule the country was desolated, both economically and demographically, and its cities, including Jerusalem, were neglected backwaters which did not even deserve to be district capitals, should flourish under the Jews. The Jews indeed dried the swamps, which had been allowed to devastate the country for centuries, planted trees where the Arabs had permitted their goats to decimate the entire flora, settled deserts and rocky hills into splendid oases, and built plants to provide manufactured goods locally and jobs to the influx of incoming Arabs form the adjoining countries. Nevertheless, the attempts made by the leaders of the *yishuv* to strike a bargain with the Arabs came to nil, once the indigenous Bedouins and the incoming Arab immigrants realized that accepting the growth of a successful Jewish entity would only bring out their own failure to do the same. Since then, they always elected to bring Israel down rather than to raise themselves to its level, and the more Israel tried to meet them half way, the more negative they became.

The Arabs who became Israelis exemplify the complexity of those feelings. They have advanced economically, culturally and in other ways, but one can only hear complaints from them, in spite of the fact that their life expectancy has grown by two decades (from 50 to 70), that they get the best socialized health care available anywhere, enjoy advanced and technological education, their agriculture jumped one millennium forward (from medieval donkey-drawn wooden plows to hot houses and high productivity), their standard of living and per capital income are manifold higher than that of the adjoining Arab world, they are exempt from military services, are entitled to all social services without lifting a finger for the state defense, pay less taxes, national and local than other Israelis, constitute a security burden on Israel, and constantly complain that they are discriminated against, and wish the Jewish state which has raised their stature and pulled them out of poverty and deprivation, to become Arab state, so that they revert to their pre-state of Israel level, something like Gaza or worse. Israel continues to placate and sooth their hurt egos and to provide them more and more lucrative benefits, in a vain hope to appease them and avoid their uprising. But the uprising is here already, and all the Arabs need is to be shaken up and to face a sharp choice between the bounties the state has to offer, like freedom, democracy, prosperity and high standard of living, and their continued alienation which engenders bitterness, a sense of victimhood and disloyalty, which often transgresses into treason.

Similarly, with the Arabs surrounding Israel in hostility, all the exercises at appeasement, compromise and accommodation have been interpreted as weakness and rejected, because if suggested by Israel they must be at the detriment of the Arabs. Already during the 1930's, based upon the precedent of the Faisal—Weizmann Accord at the end of the Ottoman rule, David Ben—Gurion, the leader of the Jewish *Yishuv,* led negotiation with Arab leaders with a view of coming to some agreement and avoiding war, but they all came to nil, as the Arabs refused to share Palestine with the Jews, and all they "agreed" to, which would have certainly been violated immediately if accepted, was some kind of Jewish autonomy under Arab rules, which would have left the country poor and festering, and their regime tyrannical and underdeveloping. That scenario was repeated by King Abdallah of Transjordan, who entered the war of 1948 uninvited, just to satisfy his ambitions of gaining some recognition if he ruled Western Palestine, including Jerusalem, which was not his domain, in order to enhance his Allah-forsaken backwater desert kingdom based in Amman. After the war, he and the rest of the Arabs refused to recognized the armistice lines as permanent ones, for fear or turning Israel into a permanent feature of the Middle East. Since then, they have tried, on many occasions to destroy Israel, but every time they are defeated, they go back to the previous arrangements that they had rejected, in the hope of improving their positions pending the day when they can prevail.

Under the Armistice Agreement with Jordan the famous Article 8 was formulated which obliged Jordan to recognize the free access to the humanitarian and holy sites left under the Armistice, on the Jordanian side of the border. But Jordan, had no intention of respecting that crucial article from the outset, since it would have permitted Jews to operate the Hebrew University and the Hadassah hospital on Mount Scopus, reactivate the Mount of Olives cemetery, and accede to the Wailing Wall and other Jewish holy sites. As soon as that became known, instead of threatening to blow up the whole agreement and resume hostilities, which could have resulted in the expulsion of the Jordanians from Jerusalem and the West Bank, Israel acquiesced in the situation, which only encouraged the Arabs to more contraventions, until the 1967 War blew in their face. In an effort to preserve the armistice, even at the price of violation of one of its main clauses, for the sake of preserving the peace, Israel ended up invalidating the entire concept of armistice from its main content and intention, and as a transition towards a permanent peace, and perpetuated the state of war with the Arab peoples, that has not receded ever since, the signed accords with Arab regimes notwithstanding.

When in 1956, the *Fidayeen* terrorist activities from Gaza and the West Bank against Israel made life in the country untenable, Israel joined Britain and France in the Suez War, which was calculated to diminish Nasser's stature in the world, remove the siege in the Tiran Straits, which permitted the operation of the Eilat port, and put an end to the terrorist activity, Israel gained real quiet for 11 years, because it insisted on a UN peace policing force. That was the quietest decade in Israel's history, which permitted it a rapid development and a rebuilding of its armed forces, based on the strategy of deterrence gained during the *blitz* armored warfare of 1956, which defeated the Egyptian armies in a few days. When Nasser felt strong enough, and reintroduced his troops into Sinai in 1967, thus re-imposing the siege on the Gulf of Eilat/Aqaba, and expelling the UN forces, to which the meek Secretary General U Thant acceded without a fight, Israel learned that no international guarantees were to be trusted, because when the chips were down, the guarantors tended to ignore their commitments and to appease the aggressors. Only the firm stand of Israel at that time, even though it felt isolated in the face of the threats of its annihilation by Egypt and its "peaceful" partners like King Hussein of Jordan, broke the siege and assigned to Israel new boundaries which allowed a deep hinterland of a few hundred miles, instead on the very few miles which had never been able to safeguard Israel from a surprise attack.

The idea started to crystallize in Israel, after the two lessons of 1949 and 1956, when Israel seized vast swaths of territory in Sinai, but then gave them up without any *quid-pro-quo* that would guarantee its security and scuttle the need for future wars, when the 1967 War found the Israelis not only battle hardened and more self-confident by their immense victory, but also rich in past experience. This time, they refused to settle for anything less than a peace accord, and a total demilitarization of Sinai, if Israel were to withdraw. The problem was that the Arabs were still accustomed to the idea that all they had to pay for aggression was to make the horrific concession of agreeing to peace. Namely, anytime they agreed to peace, however nominal and empty of content it might be, the retrieval of their territories was guaranteed. What incentive would they then have for refraining from aggression altogether, if they stood to regain their losses by simply uttering the word "peace"? Only if they knew they would lose territory by waging war and massacring other people, (like Japan and Germany in WWII) was there a chance that they might strive to avert war next time around. After that settlement with the Egyptians was concluded in the 1979 peace accord, it quickly became a precedent for all other Arab countries, who wish to recuperate "their" territories to the last inch, without feeling any obligation to pay anything for their aggression. That was the recipe for the never ending cycle of hostility between Israel and the Arabs.

Many Israelis fear that unless they make concessions and accept all of the Arabs' demands, in territories and otherwise, there is no chance that peace could be reached. But experience shows that it is exactly the reverse: the more any party is allowed to get away with his aggression, the more aggressive it is bound to become in the future. Conversely, the more heavily it will be fined for its aggression, the less likely would it be to repeat the aggression. Therefore those who hurry to make concession are not necessarily those who would bring peace, though they pose as "peaceniks", while those who insist on making the enemy pay the price of its aggression, might end up as the true pursuers of peace. To yield territories to the Palestinians or Syrians today, while they are still advertising their hatred to Israel and their commitment to obliterate it, can only indicate that Israel has accepted those terms and encouraged the Arabs to pursue them. The Oslo process may be the best illustration of this hypothesis. The Syrians and Jordanians opened fire along their armistice lines with Israel in June 1967, when they thought that they could join Nasser's bandwagon and take their part of the spoils of Nasser's anticipated victory. They failed, and their failure cannot be rewarded by an unconditional Israeli withdrawal from territories whose seizure was crucial in defeating their attacks. IF Israel should withdraw, as the Syrians demand even before any negotiations start, that would not only reverse normal international processes where only at the end of negotiations are there agreed results thereto, but that would signal to them that no risk is attached to any future attack on their part, since no losses will be incurred even in case of defeat. The reverse can be fatal for Israel, because its defeat in war can mean the end of its existence. Nonetheless, not a few Israelis advocate Israel's withdrawals, hoping that pleasing the tyrants of Damascus may produce peace.

Similarly, the faulty Oslo Accords, which generated the establishment of the Palestinian Authority and a peace with Jordan, constituted tragic errors on the part of Israel, whose price Israel continues to disburse without getting any *quid pro quo* nor a world recognition of her sacrifices. Israel had seized the West Bank following a Jordanian aggression along the entire armistice line, and it forfeited those territories when its armies were defeated. In recognition of that state of affairs, Jordan renounced the West Bank in August, 1988, leaving Israel and the Palestinians, who had not been a party in the conflict, to contend for it. Instead of proposing a solution to the indigenous Palestinians, Israel committed the folly to invite the head of the PLO and his armies from exile in Tunisia, to head the Palestinian Authority (PA), naively believing that Arafat, who had devoted a lifetime to hate the Jews and vowing their demise, would suddenly wish peace with them. In that foolish, careless and mindless belief which had no leg to stand on, the Rabin government also blindly equipped those enemy troops with weapons in order to "maintain peace and order" according to the terms of Oslo, which banned totally violence and terrorism. Instead, those forces, which continued to grow from 10,000 to 40,000, were held by Arafat under a dozen of different security organizations, playing one against the other, and making sure that no particular one prevailed. All of them turned their Israeli-supplied guns against Israeli troops, the numbers of armies and militias were inflated incessantly, and new weapons, banned under Oslo, were smuggled in, while Arafat was clamoring for a Jihad to liberate Jerusalem.

Had Rabin and his wishful-thinking Cabinet reacted in time, seized the illegal weapons and ceased the entire process until rectified, the situation would have been different. But the Israeli governments continued to appease Arafat, the rest of the Arabs and the Americans, by looking the other way while Arafat violated the agreements, smuggled in weapons, vowing Jihad and refusing to collect illegal weapons, streamlining his security apparatus into one rational organization, battling against terrorism which continued unabated, or at least extraditing or imprisoning the terrorists who sought shelter in the Palestinian cities which were surrendered by Israel to Palestinian rule, and became instead nests of terror under Palestinian supervision. So much so that appeasement became the official policy of the government, and somewhat also of the one which followed, until the crisis broke to the open and it grew evident that peace would not emanate from

Oslo. Even its own initiators and authors, were so much disgusted from it that they held parallel negotiations with inconsequential Palestinians in order to draw an alternative "agreement" to replace the one that failed. It is unclear what made them believe that what had been dismally aborted by one Palestinian leadership, would fare better under another, less empowered than the other. It seems that their reputation had been so deeply staked on Oslo, and they themselves realized that they were so duped by their "partners in peace" whom they came to trust religiously, that they were prepared to try another course that could salvage the entire process and their own careers.

Since then, "occupation" became the key word for the Palestinian struggle. They claimed that any land occupied in 1967 was "occupied land" by an act of aggression and demanded that it be evacuated and handed to them, as if Israel had initiated the seizing of the land and as if they had been the original owners from whom the land was seized in self-defense. Israel failed to explain to the world, that the West Bank was not "occupied" as an act of expansionism, to match the Soviet occupation of the Baltic states or of Eastern Europe, or the German search of a *lebensraum* to settle its expanding population. Quite the contrary, Israel's population of three million then, was supplicating all Arabs to recognize its armistice borders as the permanent ones, but they refused. But once attacked and poised to eliminate its attackers, it had to move inside the territories and to hold them until a permanent settlement is found. That was the reason why Israel did not annex the West Bank, except for Jerusalem its capital, where the anomaly of partition could not obtain any longer, and it had been violated by the Arabs in any case. But to hold those territories, the tiny population of Israel could not maintain a large army, therefore it had to resort to its old system of settling soldiers-farmers on the borders, who performed the double task of populating those areas and guarding them at the same time. That was the genesis of the Israeli settlements. Had the Arabs hastened to negotiate and settle, they could have caught the situation in its preliminary stage. But as they waited, the temporary settlements became permanent, families raised children and left the military framework, and over the years they grew into full-fledged Israeli towns and villages that no peace process can shake from their base.

That is the price the Arabs had to pay for their 1967 aggression and for their refusal thereafter to discuss some compromise. Any conflict that is left festering for so long, acquires a dynamic of its own, and finds new avenues, by trial and error, to adapt to the realities of life. Hills that were rocky and deserted in the West Bank, or impoverished Arab neighborhoods in East Jerusalem where unemployment, with their lack of social services, and the tyrants which enslaved and exploited them, find themselves after 40 years, drawn into the 21st Century, much more developed and advanced, with social services and employment that they had never encountered before. Certainly, all Arabs in the West Bank would have elected to have those benefits under Arab rule, and they very much resent the defense wall which has split villages and is termed the "apartheid wall". But under Arab rule, which most Jerusalemite Arabs would hate to experience again, all those goodies would not have accrued to them, and if they had to choose, they would prefer remaining under Israel. They know that Israeli "apartheid" is just an exaggerated propaganda slogan, because under it they enjoy much more freedom than under any Arab or Muslim government that they are aware of. In an apartheid state, they would not be able to travel in the same buses or to enter in the same malls or to eat in the same restaurants and lodging in the same hotels. They know these are words, and little by little they come to realize that their aggression in 1967 had a price tag, which is much less terrible than the Arab propaganda describes it.

During all these conflicts and processes, Arab and Muslim cultures, which are not open to rational criticism or to a grilling self-reckoning, submit totally to their own propaganda and are closed to other arguments. Unlike the state of Israel or the IDF, which have over the years submitted themselves to commissions of inquiry, and have, as a result, dismissed or sued in justice hundreds of senior officials and officers, such a procedure is unknown in those cultures. Never would a ruler there establish such a commission to inquire into his deeds, nor would he admit any fault, and certainly would not let any factor outside his apparatus of power to accuse anyone or take any step against anyone. Similarly, all the school text-books submit to the same propaganda, which is hammered into the heads of pupils and public with a uniformity that does not allow any different voice to be voiced. For example, in a border incident between Israel and any Arab troops, never would it occur to them to interview an Israeli or to cite an Israeli version of the story. Thus, in any incident, the Israelis are cruel, killing children, demolishing houses, persecuting the poor Palestinians, who of course did no fault. In Israel, all the major Arabic networks are represented and they usu-ally enjoy the same freedom as the others, so that nothing can happen in Israel without all the opinions being heard. So, the plain propaganda inculcated into their heads, which knows no boundary between truth and lie, reality and fantasy, ends up making up exclusively their worldview. It is very difficult to combat these horrific stereotypes which only increase hatred and demonize the enemy to the extreme, never recognizing any error or misdeed of theirs. We are not talking here about slogans to raise the morale or to diminish the enemy, which are common in all wars within all cultures, but about crude lies which invent "citations" that never were, acts that never happened or intentions which could only be guessed or im-puted by evil minds to others. There is no other way to pen-etrate this thick curtain but to talk directly to the people on the other side, by leaflets or extended services, to imprint in their minds that the stereotypes they were made to cultivate had no relation to reality.

There were occasions where the Israeli government was so piqued by anti-Semitic surges in various countries, that it either cut relations with them or lowered its diplomatic representation in them in protest. For example, when Jorg Haider, the notorious Austrian anti-Semite's nationalist party entered the governmental coalition in Vienna in the 1990's, the Israeli government was quick to cut off relations, despite the fact that Haider personally never acted against Jews, and he apologized for the anti-Jewish remarks he made. On the other hand, when Arafat's wife made venomous anti-Semitic remarks in the presence of Hillary Clinton, then the First Lady, or Bashar al-Asad when welcoming the Pope in Damascus, or the Egyptians and Jordanians, on a daily basis, in their government-supervised press, Israel seeks to talk to them, at times courts them even as they pursue their blood libels and other anti-Semitic lambasting in their public squares. Maybe if Israel boycotted all the anti-Semites it would end up isolated and forlorn in the world, but it is very confusing to public opinion, when it chooses to hold different people by different standards in different times and places. If anti-Semitism is to be resisted, then always and everywhere on every circumstance. Also diminishing to Israel's image, is its pursuit of tyrants like Mubarak of Egypt and King Abdallah of Jordan, who have a problem of legitimacy, but it holds them as "partners" in the "peace process", not realizing that they are in there to advance their own interests and that they would never take a pro-Israeli stand in any confrontation between Israel and other Arabs. If at least those leaders visited Israel regularly, as decent and honest partners, something could be said in favor of those frequent "consultations". But it is the Israeli leaders who travel so often to seek their "advice", something which is perceived in the Arab world as a humiliating move. In all problems brought before them, those leaders have followed the Arab line, urged Israel to accept the Arab Peace Plan, which seeks to demote Israel, pressed it to release thousands of convicted criminals, instead of prevailing upon the Palestinians to free a an Israeli soldier who had been kidnapped and incarcerated for life, and dragged their feet for years, from putting an end to Hamas smuggling of weapons through tunnels to Gaza from Egyptian territory.

Compromising with Arabs on any topic has proved unproductive, because their policy of demonization, delegitimation and genocide of Israel and Zionism is based on a blind hatred of Jews. Therefore, any gesture of goodwill on its part is perceived as a dark conspiracy, any compromise as a weakness. They have no use for compromises or negotiations, they want a total capitulation of Israel to their wishes and a smashing victory over it. Therefore, like the Allies' attitude towards Germany and Japan, in W W II, where unconditional capitulation of the Axis was demanded, only sound defeats of the Arabs, once and again, can shake them up into reality. They have much to lose from wars and defeats, mostly in terms of humiliation. So, only decisive strikes against them, where they hurt, but in a measured and rational way, can show them that aggression would not work and would only cost them more humiliation in their shame-prone culture. The key for Israel is to prepare the grounds in the world for diversified alliances in the Third World, instead of counting exclusively on the Americans and being given to their mercy, once and again. To the campaign of conquest of Europe that Islam has launched in recent decades, and their parallel campaign of intimidating poor countries in the Third World to support them, a counter attack must be mounted by all those that feel threatened by Islam, lest Western values are eroded once Western countries are made to succumb, one by one, to Islamic *sahri's* laws.

In the Muslim world, the pains and aches of all the wrongs of the world are squarely put on America and Israel's shoulders. The victim mentality has become part of their make-up. Violence against the West exploded in 2006, in connection with the Cartoon affair, and many dozens of people perished and western embassies were set aflame. When the Pope dared say anything about Muslims, the violence against the Church has become so intolerable that he was made to repent in public, something which only increased Muslim demands.

To Muslim terrorism, which provokes an endless string of thousands of victims, mainly among Muslims themselves, this does not appear to be too heavy a price to pay, if the end result got the powerful Soviets out of Afghanistan; Spain, Britain and Japan, and the mighty US, out of Iraq; and ultimately NATO out of Afghanistan, Israel out of Palestine, Spain out of Andalusia, China out of Uyghur Xinjiang, and India out of Kashmir. Every non-Muslim step backward is viewed in the Muslim world as a great victory, which only increases their appetite for more, and stokes the fire of Jihad more intensely. The "moderate" and "pro-western" regimes in the Islamic world, which seem to still support the West are doing so only because the Jihadist movements are set to remove them from their positions of power, therefore they must count on American power to survive. Take American support away from Afghanistan, Iraq, Pakistan, Mubarak, the Palestinian Authority, the fake Lebanese non-government, and you will see them succumb in no time to *Jihadists* like the Taliban and the Qa'ida, in South and Central Asia, or the Hizbullah and Hamas in the Middle East.

Very often we are tempted by the proposition that if we only could be rational, fair, decent, honest and well-meaning, the others will too. But when we remember tyrants in history, who in retribution for loyalty of minorities or conquered peoples, or for a civilized behavior on their part, an eagerness to acculturate, and their contribution to local cultures, were demonized and exterminated, we realize that, unfortunately, we are not always rewarded in accordance with our deeds and conduct. What is meant here are not only the murderous regimes of the Nazis and Communism, which have eliminated many of their own peoples and brought misery upon much of the world, but the historical conquests and expansion of Islam, where entire cultures have been wiped out without a trace, in their zealous haste to convert the world into their *dar-al-Islam*. Twice, in the 8th Century, and then in the 15th Century, they tried to subjugate the Christian world, the first time in the Iberian Peninsula from the south, and the second time in the Balkans from the east, and in both instances that rule of oppression and annihilation lasted several centuries until overturned. The undercurrents of humiliation, jealousy, bitterness and sense of vengeance in that culture of *lex talionis* are brewing under the surface, and when they explode into the open, they will be as cruel, demonic and unforgiving as the Mongol sweep into the civilized world in medieval times.

In the past, many "agreements" were concluded between Israel and the Arab world. The American Super-power has been trying for decades to promote such an agreement between the parties, as a "confidence building", in order to jumpstart negotiations between the parties, as if negotiations in themselves can remedy the situation. In fact, hundreds of sessions have been held between the parties, on the highest level as well as on the technical level of experts, but the suspicions and mistrust between the parties have never been deeper, and the gap between them so unbridgeable. This emanates from the basic attitude of the parties and their expectations from a possible settlement. The Israelis, and westerners in general when they consider negotiations, view negotiations as quantitative issues, which undergo a give-and-take process, at the end of which there is a meeting of minds which translates into an agreement or a treaty. The Arabs, and particularly Muslims who inject into the dispute also religious absolutes, are not prepared to negotiate because they want everything and now. For example, Temple Mount being so sensitive to the parties, logic and civility would dictate a formula of compromise whereby both sides would live and let live, and reach a compromise in terms of time or space. But Muslims, who demand exclusivity, cannot even negotiate a compromise, let alone accept it. Therefore, only if such a middle of the way arrangement is imposed on them, like in Hebron, is there likely to be a de-facto *modus vivendi,* short of an official "agreement" which can never be reached.

The situation in Gaza escalated into war because of the steps of appeasement adopted by Israel. At first, Israel controlled the Philadephi border area between Gaza and Egypt, making sure that nothing could be smuggled into the Strip. But the Americans pressed Israel into abandoning that strip under the "guarantee" that EU observers would man the border crossings and ensure that no illegal smuggling went through. Israel foolishly agreed, but as soon as the Hamas launched violence, the EU observers withdrew and the American intervention evaporated, and Israel was left alone to battle the lethal consequences. It was as if a fire brigade had been put in place to watch the fires, but it withdrew as soon as the fires broke out. Great foresight and political savvy indeed, when Condoleezza Rice did not have to bear the consequences of her pressures and threats. The end result was that smuggling of arms got out of hand, the Hamas rearmed and began its bombings and shelling of Israel, and Israel had to retaliate with the results we know. The Goldstone Report should have placed the blame on the American Secretary of State, who for the sake of appeasing the Europeans and the Arabs, forced the Israelis, who foolishly succumbed to her pressures for the sake of appeasing her, to remove the necessary precautionary measures which alone could have prevented the war and its aftermath.

Stability has become an icon in the West, for the sake of which they are prepared to appease, to plead and to ignore their own principles and ideals. But there are bad stabilities (like the Soviet Union in its time, Saddam's Iraq or Iran today, which must be cleared and removed in order to put good stabilities instead. America has to decide, does is want a stable Saudi Arabia where democracy, human rights are only a dream, or instability there until the regime is taken over by popular democracy, which might eventually fall into the hands of *Jihadist*s who will create a new instability? In the Palestinian camp, the Hamas came on top in elections that were encouraged by the US. America is hated in the Arab world because it says one thing and does another: it cannot predicate its choice of free elections on certain results (as it had hoped), so it has to accept their outcome. After all, there is no much difference in ideology between Abu Mazen and Isma'il Haniye. Both are opposed to a settlement with Israel which would leave the refugees outside the framework of any agreement, both want to re-divide Jerusalem, and both refuse to accept Israel as a Jewish state; both are anti-Semitic, both have threatened "armed struggle", i.e. terrorism against Israel, and both have not hidden their ambition to see the state of Palestine engulfing ultimately all historical Palestine. The only difference is that Hamas does not wish to talk with Israel, while Abu Mazen is willing under certain conditions. From Israel's viewpoint, maybe the former is preferable, because then it will not be hard pressed to appease it, while the latter, who enjoys western support due to his supposed "moderation", would require more appeasement, at Israel's expense and possible demise.

Summary

The Imperative of Revival

In view of the overwhelming difficulties which Israel has been facing in the past decade, with the change of strategy by the Muslim world, from conventional to asymmetrical wars, where their risks of defeat as smaller but their propaganda gains are remarkably higher, Israel must devise a new strategy for her survival in the bad neighborhood where she happens to be located, in the face of the recalcitrant Arab and Muslim worlds to accept her as a legitimate Jewish entity in the area. The Americans can give an advice or force Israel to act on their misjudgments, but they do not bear the consequences or pay the price. Therefore, Israel must re-organize domestically, and adopt novel policies outwardly, so as to make it clear to the world that it would extract a price from anyone who tries to hurt her or her interests or Jewish communities around the world, and that she would stand by western values and defend them, even as the West shows signs of fatigue in defending its own geographic and spiritual turf. That would require far-reaching reforms at home, social, educational and political; and in the relations with the world. Instead of merely draining Israel's resources for the sake of its survival, it ought to reset them in the service of its revival. In other words, it is time to move from defense to offense.

Home Reform

Domestically, Israel is in much need to strengthen itself, to unify its society, to reform its political regime, to reinforce its economy in directions which lend precedence to brain resources and human development, to place quality of life at the top of its priorities, so as to make it attractive to returning Israelis and to new Jewish immigrants, and to mobilize the country to withstand outside pressures by galvanizing its resolve and strengthening its capacity to resist outside pressures. Time is pressing, therefore all those flags have to be raised simultaneously, so that the reforms that were outlined above be undertaken forthwith. In order for Israel to keep its edge on the hostile environment which surrounds it, it must focus on excellence in all its doings, starting with education for its children, from age 3 through college, with a curriculum that is value-bound with Judaism and Zionism at its core, keeping the pupils busy many more hours than hitherto, so that they can absorb not only humanistic and social studies but also high levels of science, including the rudiments of laboratory research, free and creative thinking and encouragement and rewarding of distinction. Studies should start daily with the raising of the national flag and end with extra-curricular activity for the benefit of society: extra-classes for the weak, assistance to the elderly and the handicapped, volunteer work in the community to clean up the public square, to improve the environment, to pick fruits and vegetables for farmers at the peak seasons, and use the proceeds for school and student enhancement.

To provide incentives to the young, school must not only be free throughout (from 3 to 19, namely kindergarten to college) as outlined above, but Israeli citizenship must be made conditional on a basket of services rendered to the sate by those who wish to join the ranks of its citizenry. First, one has to enroll in the regional schools, founded and funded by the state, where a similar core program is studied, which includes Judaism, Zionism, Bible, History of the Jews and of their neighbors through the ages, philosophy, politics and a strong emphasis on science, with the best encouraged to develop to the full their capacities in special classes in each school. Special talents have to be selected early on and introduced to special areas of research by personal mentors selected from the academic faculty of the universities, who will regard that as part of their duties. Their salaries will be decided, among others, by the numbers of school students which they sponsor and see through their successful studies. School will also raise children to care for the community, the environment, the state, their physical and mental health. When they attain age 19, after college, they will be ready to enroll in national service, be it military or otherwise, which will also entitle them to citizenship, including the right to vote and be elected. Those who elect to stay outside the circle, will be enabled to study their own curriculum at their own expense in their private schools. Nevertheless, the option to join the citizenry will always remain open to them when they accomplish their national duties, otherwise, they will only remain as residents in the country, without citizens rights, including social welfare, free education, vote and citizenship.

The imparting of the same values to all its children would ensure the tightening of Israeli society and the cultivation of its solidarity and high quality, and would contribute immensely also to the reduction of the social and political gaps. That would be the opportunity to also launch the reform in the Arab sector of society, to uniformize it and integrate it into the whole, and to overhaul the political system. A strong, stable and independent executive is direly needed in Israel, which could be immune to the whims of the political parties. An urgent election reform ought to be adopted forthwith, which would raise the threshold of the elected parties to at least 10%, so as to oblige all the splinter groups to cluster around larger bodies, so as to cut down the number of parties and facilitate the formation of government; and a Chief Executive must be elected directly by the people, either along the American presidential model, with the proper checks and balances instituted, or along the French Parliamentarian model, where the Prime Minister is responsible to Parliament, for legitimacy and majority rule, while the directly elected President maintains supreme power, the direction of foreign and security affairs, and discretion of deciding the crucial issues of the state. Such a structure is vital to insure rapid response by the executive in times of crisis, without incurring the perennial danger of a vanishing government coalition when any political party is not satisfied that its interests were fulfilled.

The question of the Arabs is as serious and as urgent. The era of the blurred identities and indecision of the government must end, and clear choices must be faced. Arabs in Israel must be confronted with the choices that every individual can decide for oneself, free of the shackles of community pressures and indoctrination. They can no longer clamor for citizens rights and at the same time take hostile positions, in speech and in deed, against the state of which they wish to be the happy and privileged recipients of its bounty. No one can impose on them an identity and no one can deprive them of their natural and chosen course when they have elected one. Those who will have elected to join the state school system, and will when reaching adulthood to enlist in national service and fulfill their duties, will also become a complete part of Israeli society with all the rights that accrue to any citizen. Those who do not, will retain their right to continue to reside in Israel with rights to work and elect their local authorities, but if they choose to identify as Palestinians, they will also be the citizens of the Palestinian state when there is one. And so, Israel would no longer feel threatened demographically by its Arab citizens, and would conceivably become less sensitive to the issue of being recognized as a Jewish state, which presently has been marring the peace process, when there is one.

The urgency of these reforms stems from the probability that the two sectors of the population most likely to be affected by the reform of tying citizenship to fulfilling duties to the state, would be the Arabs (20%) and the Ultra-religious (some 15%), namely more than a third of the total population in the aggregate, and rapidly increasing due to their faster natural growth. This means that will come a

time in the coming decades, where the solid majority existing today, which would potentially support these reforms in
the Knesset, could vanish, and the present structure of Israeli politics, together with the deep suspicion between the
parties that each one of them might conclude, in secret, a
deal with the Arabs and the Ultra-religious against all others,
could deal a deadly blow to any hope of democratic reform.

Re-orienting Foreign Relations

It sounds almost absurd to speak of "foreign policy" of such
a tiny nation as Israel, at a time when even America and
other powers, far from possessing a foreign policy blueprint
which is deliberated and adopted in the shadows of secretive
chanceries, are content enough to respond adequately to the
triggers from the outside. The world wars, like the wars in
Vietnam, Iraq or Afghanistan, which have absorbed the energies and resources of America in the past century, were not
planned "policies", but improvised responses to initiatives
forced from the outside. Of course, one can claim that those
responses are the policy of the US, but they still connote the
sense that even great powers are devoid of choices in foreign
affairs, so much more so a small and modest country like Israel. Therefore, it would be much more relevant and wiser to
speak about "foreign affairs", or "foreign relations", rather
than "foreign policy", which is virtually non-existent.

Within these parameters, Israel does not have many
choices: either to be a client of a great power, as it has
been under American tutelage almost since its inception,
with the attending dependence on others, or to distribute
the risks in more directions, by diversifying its alliances
or creating its own, with countries who embrace similar
principles or have similar needs. The strategy of the Outer
Tier having failed, two of its building bricks (Turkey and
Iran) having embraced Islamic revival, new ideas have
to be sought to construct new approaches. For Israel, the
greatest immediate concerns are three circles of conflict :
with the Palestinians over the same land, with the attending

issue of Israeli Arabs, who are also Palestinian for all intents and purposes; with the Arab world, which consists of 22 nations who provide the support and the hinterland of the Palestinian issue; and with the Islamic world, which consists of 57 nations, including Iran and Turkey, who constitute the backbone of the Muslim-Western confrontation. But Israel belongs economically, culturally and emotionally to the western world, which today consist mainly of North America and Western Europe, and has to think out new ways to relate to that world or to its forlorn extensions in Latin America, or to other western nations, like Canada and Australia, who under the threat of Islam may come to find common denominators with Israel.

While for now Israel remains solidly in the American orbit, and its choices for diversification are quite limited, some new alliances can be envisioned and launched, built on economic and security interests, like the ones recently constructed in Central Asia with the former Soviet nations, in spite of their essentially Muslim populations. Israel has the great advantage of emerging as a small new but successful nation, which made it from deprived and underdeveloped into a developed country, at the level of Western Europe, with a strong edge in certain areas of high-tech, agriculture, water management, the military, medicine and science. IN order to strengthen that reputation, Israel must prioritize its scientific research by encouraging excellence in all levels of education. Nobel prizes, whatever they are worth, being the present-day gauge of scientific achievement, and the small nation of Israel having won 10 of them in the past few years (more than any nation, save the US) in spite of its small size and its status as a new country without a long tradition of scientific research, permanence in that line of development might be the key for future expansion of foreign relations. The continuous growth of Israel in the economic and scientific and technological spheres, lend her an appeal among developing nations that other powers do not have. Israel is also too small and too insignificant to either threaten the countries which seek its help, or to come under pressure from it for *quid pro quo's* in return for its assistance.

A growing threat is looming in the West from the mounting Jihadi movement in the world, with the struggles in Iraq, Afghanistan and Pakistan still undecided, and a Muslim country like Iran developing its nuclear arsenal. The latter is in a position to wait for American withdrawal in the Middle East in order to take its place. In this situation, many frightened and threatened nations, would find partial comfort in a closer alliance with Israel, or would even, like the rich but week Gulf countries, find shelter under its nuclear umbrella. Powers like China, Brazil, Russia and India, which have economically and politically emerged as the next tier of great powers in the 21st Century, or western nations like Canada and Australia, where the residue of goodwill towards Israel and the Jewish people on the one hand, and their traditional sharing of values with Israel on the other, may warrant new emphases on Israel's foreign relations in the future. The UN and other international bodies count their weight and influence in terms of votes, not values and not principles of right and justice. If Israel could begin to accumulate new pools of supports in Asia, Africa and Latin America, as it did in the 1960's, it could wield during crucial votes in those organizations enough support to at least avoid being repeatedly sanctioned, if not openly gaining a solid advocacy.

A new concept must be adopted in international relations, namely that there are insoluble problems. The Western "accountant mentality", which near every column of problems had to seek a parallel column of solutions, invented for this purpose an entire discipline of "conflict resolution", which for decades theorized and researched and granted fellowships for the study of that new invention, before they admitted that such a creature did not exist and that what one could do, at most, was "conflict management". Indeed, there are many political and societal problems in every country and society which are not soluble, like drugs, traffic accidents, teen-age pregnancy, children delinquency and others, which cannot be resolved. All we can do is reduce their effect and render life possible side-by-side with them. So are conflicts and have always been, especially when they depend on the whims of tyrants who are not accountable to their peoples and can trigger an armed conflict by an edict. Democracies, which are headed by legitimate leaders who are accountable, do not trigger conflicts, they only respond to them. This is the situation of the asymmetrical conflict between Israel and its neighbors. The latter have tried to attack repeatedly, and she must respond to survive. As long as they keep the desire and ambition to attack, she will keep the instinct to survive and defend herself. But the problem will remain insoluble, until they become accountable democracies themselves.

Much in international relations does not depend on Israel, which is, most of the time, unable to intervene one way or the other. But at least in the Middle East, where it maintains a stature of a major actor, it can leave an impact in the relations with its neighbors, without losing sight of the dangers surrounding her. Moreover, after the Goldstone Report, which virtually deprives her of her right to self-defense, she would be hard pressed in the future to take any excessive risks to her security for the sake of attaining peace, a prerequisite that has been urged on her in recent decades, without assurance that she will be backed in the future if the "guaranteed" arrangements fail, as they have in Oslo. Therefore, Israel's calculations must be built on the assumption that when the chips are down, she would have to operate on her own. For example, if there is to be a settlement with Syria on the Golan, Israel cannot, at the outset of the process, undertake to withdraw from the Golan, for fear that the Syrians might change their mind in accordance with the whims of the dictator who would rule in his time. First of all, it must be impressed on Syria that the situation cannot revert, under any circumstances, to June 5, 1967. Not only because the Syrians have to pay for their aggression, which had cost many lives and much anxiety, but because the Golan is one of the main water sources of Israel, which cannot be left to depend on the next aggression of Damascus, if it should retreat totally. Therefore, any solution must be left to the test of time in the long haul. Only if successive Syrian governments prove friendly, open and peaceful over a long period of several decades, and Israel regains confidence that their aggression is no longer promoted in the public, could Israel consider a gradual retreat over a long period of time.

The Palestinians are quite another affair. We have already noticed that a prerequisite for negotiation with them is that both sides recognize mutually the right of self-determination of both the Jewish and the Palestinians peoples, and the recognition of the PLO versus Zionism as the movements of national liberation of both parties. When that is established and recognized, then the entire territory of historical Palestine, i.e. Israel, the West Bank and Jordan, should come to the table of negotiations, with the purpose of partitioning that entire land between its two owners: the Israeli Jews, and Palestinian Arabs. The Hashemites of Jordan, who are only a regime, not a land or a people, have to be subsumed under the large Palestino-Jordanian state, whose Palestinian majority can decide for itself what sort of regime it wishes to have. That large unification is imperative, because a state in the West Bank (and Gaza) contains only a third of the Palestinian people (3.5 out of 10 million), and if allowed to rise it would continue to knock on Israeli doors for the settlement of the rest (as Arafat had demanded in 2000, and now Abu Mazen is subsuming under the Right of Return for Palestinian refugees, which Israel cannot accept, and no peace will prevail. After such an agreement is worked out for the partition, an equal and reciprocal formula will be worked out which will allow the populations of both side who will have remained in the land that is not theirs, three options: either to sell their properties and move to their home countries (Israel for the Jews and Palestino-Jordan for the Palestinians, including the Arabs of Israel); or to swear allegiance to their country of residence and become its full-fledge citizens; or remain where they are as permanent residents, owing their political loyalty to their home country.

This solution is not ideal, but it could provide much to fill the ambitions of both parties without completely satisfying either. Great statesmanship consists of seizing the bad before it becomes worse. We are still in a situation where we can settle the majority of the Palestinian people on its land without compromising the security of Israel, and while neutralizing the lethal threat of Israeli Arabs on their (Israeli) state while they support their (Palestinian) people. If we wait much longer, even this solution will be no longer feasible, as the two populations continue to inextricably enmesh themselves into each other and render their condition much akin to Bosnia. Is a bloody Bosnian war what is needed? But even if the PLO should accept this avenue, the other half of the Palestinian people, represented by the Hamas, which refuses to recognize Israel and negotiate with it on any level, will continue to wage a war of terror and claim that its members are civilian non-combatants who are immune to reprisals, similar to the claims made today by the Taliban and al-Qa'ida in Afghanistan. On the issue of combating terrorists who hide within a civil population, there exists a vast array of opinions, which push a general public acceptance of such a war, and the casualties involved, beyond consensus. And in democratic societies, which are accountable to their constituencies, no war can be waged and won without such a consensus. Terrorists precisely capitalize on these assumptions, and they seem to win the debate, as evidenced by the dwindling support in the US for the escalating war in Afghanistan.

A lively debate took place in Amitai Etzioni's blog at the end of September, 2009, among prominent sociologists and political scientists on this issue, on which much of the security of the West will hinge in the coming months and years. But there seems to be a vast array of differences among them. Some, like Michael Gross, Professor of Political Science at the University of Haifa, Israel, finds a wide gap between Al Qa'ida terrorists, other nationalist terrorists and guerrillas (e.g. Hamas),and other proxy guerrillas (Hezbollah) and regular soldiers supporting a terrorist regime (e.g. in Sudan or Myanmar). Most of these are akin to guerrillas (that is combatants) rather than terrorists (who may be criminals or war criminals). In these settings, civilians may perform all sorts of jobs making some civilian combatants vulnerable to certain kinds of harm (sometimes lethal, sometimes non-lethal) depending upon their level of participation. The traditional combatant-noncombatant dichotomy of the Geneva Conventions is replaced with a continuous participation scale with a great many actors stuck in the middle. There are in fact different kinds of civilian combatants and each is subject to different forms of harm. But the erroneous differentiation that Gross makes between the military and political wings of those terrorist movements, which was invented by their leaderships precisely in order to escape punishment, should not give shelter to either, because no major action is undertaken by those organizations without the explicit order of the political leadership.

Another valid point that Gross makes is that it is misleading to suggest that "terrorists should not be killed when they can be safely detained." This requires a great deal of explanation (what is "safely detained?"). Except that he imputes equal rights to terrorists and criminals, a mistake done by Tony Blair after the London 2005 underground explosions. A criminal seeks personal gain by his crime, therefore he is punished by both incarceration and deprivation from the gain he sought. Terrorists take lethal risks to their lives for no gain, due to their ideological/religious convictions. They are punished for their ideologies which they sought to implement in the public square. He stipulates that law enforcement demands the attempt to arrest and detain, while the law of war does not (although there are limits on disabling force). He determines that terrorists are combatants first and criminals second. On the field, the law of armed conflict applies.

Once captured, those guerrillas who are terrorists enjoy due process, while with ordinary soldiers, there is no call to try and arrest them during the time they pose an armed threat. He further asserts, in response to Etzioni's invoking the efficacy of warnings, suggesting that anyone who ignores a warning may be presumed hostile, that the Second Lebanon War (2006) and Gaza War of early 2009, decisively refuted this assumption. Often, hostile forces leave under the cover of warning. Often, those who stay cannot leave (the sick, elderly or children, for example) or find the roads clogged and many of these victims had no nearby place to find a respite from the fighting.[128]

Richard Moodey, a Professor of Sociology at Gannon University, while finding Etzioni's arguments" to be reasonable and persuasive, thinks they might be more persuasive if he were to distinguish more consistently between "terrorists" and "suspected terrorists." He argues that the legislative establishment of a different kind of tribunal with rules different from those of both civilian and military courts, makes sense, but that suspects should not be labeled "terrorists" until they have been found guilty. The emphasis put on prevention entails the surveillance, interrogation, and possible detention of categories of people who are not, as individuals, under suspicion. This makes it especially important that the damning label of "terrorist" not be applied indiscriminately. He asserts that while not admitting as much, Etzioni in fact embraced Peter Ustinov's maxim, "terrorism is the war of the poor, and war is the terrorism of the rich". He invokes the deliberate bombing of civilians in WWII in London, Dresden, Tokyo, Hiroshima, and Nagasaki seem to him to illustrate Ustinov's notion of the "terrorism of the rich", and he suggests to modify the "Ustinov principle" by asserting: terrorism is the war of the poor, the weak, and the anonymous;

---

[128]I was suggested in the blog that many of these points are addressed in Michael Gross' upcoming book, *Moral Dilemmas of Modern War: Torture, Assassination and Blackmail in an Age of Asymmetric Conflict.*

war is the terrorism of the rich, the strong, and the famous. Clausewitz, he emphasizes, is celebrated for having said that war is diplomacy carried out by other means. Only the wealthy, the powerful, and the famous have the resources to either to continue diplomacy instead of going to war, or to go to war as another means of gaining their objectives, whether those objectives are noble or foul. The poor, the weak, and the anonymous do not have the resources to engage either in war or diplomacy.

Max Singer, a Senior Fellow at the Hudson Institute, commented that the best way to reduce the harm of war is to win it as quickly as possible. He invoked the example of the long El Salvador war, which lasted, after the guerrillas had been decisively rejected by the population, only because the guerrillas could reasonably hope that their allies in Washington would convince the US to pull out. If US participation had been whole-hearted and apparently unshakeable the guerrillas would have had to stop a lot sooner than they did. The problem is that in order to win a war quickly, one has to wage massive armies and overwhelming fire power, which cause more casualties than a democratic society can stomach. One can find oneself in praise of the German *blitzkrieg* for being rapid and short, but knowing what happened after the Germans won so rapidly, one would certainly abstain from doing so. Here too, ambivalence reigns supreme and justifications can be procured both ways to support a quick and massive war, for its economy of civilian lives, and its minimalization of civilian hardships, or condemn it for its violence and heart-tearing scenes of extensive destruction and casualties among non-combatants, however we define them. Professor Mario Bunge, of the Chair of Logic and Metaphysics at McGill University, was right assuming that all wars are all dirty, for after all, violence in warfare is a virtue, not a shortcoming. In modern wars, more civilians are affected than combatants, and the only way to keep one's hands clean is to prevent war by all means-except for defense against military aggression. Well, most wars begin by military aggression by one of the parties. We return to square one: what is aggression? How do we define the aggressor? In the Muslim culture, where the very existence of a perceived enemy of Islam is aggression, as is the presence of the enemy in a territory perceived as Islamic (Palestine, Andalusia, Kashmir), we again revert to the quandary of the identity of the aggressor.

For Jan Narveson, a Professor of Philosophy at the University of Waterloo it is clear that the people that we are dealing with "just love enemies who are willing to go the extra mile". It is all but impossible, he says, to avoid civilian casualties, especially when the enemy has not only no interest whatever in avoiding them, but positively makes its living by not avoiding them. Khwaja Iftikhar Ahmed, Founder and President of the Inter Faith Harmony Foundation of Muslims of India and Chairman of the National Consultative Body of Indian Muslims, contends that life is dear to Muslims, but life in the hereafter remains the real motivation to practically all the followers of Islam. They very strongly believe in the will of God and destiny. In their psyche there is no fear of death. Muslims as a community are never able to reconcile with acceptance of supremacy and hegemony. If they cannot fight with technology, a section of misguided elements can take to suicidal techniques, but they find it impossible to surrender to such forces. Therefore he suggests to the west not to impose itself; instead, to facilitate the change. Things will happen much faster and to the mutual good of one and all. Afghanistan is no different, he argues. .Pushing the moderate, secular and progressive elements in Muslim societies and countries can serve much better than coercion, war or aggression. "Our civilized modern western world allowed Sadat, Zulfiqar Ali Bhutto, the Shah of Iran, Benazir Bhutto, and many like them in the Muslim world, to die in mysterious circumstances, and then we talk of change".

Beyond what Israel could and should do, in terms of domestic policy and foreign relations, there is a constant erosion in the positions taken by the Powers-that-be and the international organizations, with regard to the Middle East and the struggle against world terrorism. Hypocrisy reigns supreme when the Nobel Prize for peace is awarded to Barack Obama the same days he was contemplating dispatching more troops to Afghanistan; when the liberal British *The Guardian* omits from the list of all Nobel Peace Prize winners, which he compiled to celebrate Obama's win, the three Israelis who won it[129]; when American and Nato forces have been massacring thousands of civilians in Iraq, Afghanistan and until recently in the Balkans, but lecturing Israel about disproportional or excessive power; or when Javier Solana sermonizes Israel about its "occupation" of its own country, while his Spain is still colonizing Ceuta and Melilla in North Africa, with much less legitimacy than Israel's presence in the West Bank and Jerusalem; or when the Secretary General of the UN attends sessions bashing one of the members of his organization, and shaking hands with the man who promised to wipe Israel off the map. Now a new calamity has descended on Israel, as the members of the international Quartet, which was conceived as the supreme international body to supervise the Road Map, has reneged on its major principle of reciprocity and turned it to another empty document.

The unfortunate Oslo Accord, which stipulated what each party was committed to implement, failed because there was no test of conditionality between steps to be adopted. Therefore, the Palestinians continued to clamor for more Israeli withdrawals even as they violated all the other clauses, chief among which was cessation of violence. The Wye Plantation Agreement was signed by Netanyahu under the slogan: "they will receive only if they give" attempted to redress this situation, but to no much avail. The Road Map done under Sharon, sought to correct this situation and established the principle of testing under each stage the reciprocity of implementation, before the parties proceeded to the next. Now

---

[129]Tom Gross, *National Review Online Saturday*, October 10, 2009

comes the policy statement of the Quartet in New York, on September 24, 2009, which discards the principle of reciprocity, which is a fundamental axiom in international law and in legal contracts in general, and empties that document from its validity, if only one party is held responsible for its fulfillment. It would be like obligating a house owner to vacate his property and turn it over to the buyer even if the latter did not make the payments agreed upon in the contract. In fact, the statement of the Quartet astoundingly urges the parties to "act on their previous agreements and obligations—in particular adherence to the road map, irrespective of reciprocity". Thus, the "performance-based"—movement from one stage to the next, was contingent upon the fulfillment by both Israelis and Palestinians of their respective responsibilities. Now this critical element appeared to have been removed. True, the erosion of the road map was helped by past Israeli governments that plunged into permanent-status negotiations before the Palestinians fulfilled their obligations. But it is the new formal position of the Quartet that provides the final blow to the road map's carefully structured conditionality.[130]

Contrary to the new haste embraced by Obama to see Israel withdraw beyond the 1967 lines, without making the Arabs pay for their aggression which generatd the seizure of their territory, President George W. Bush had sent a letter to prime minister Ariel Sharon in April 2004, stating that it was unrealistic to expect that Israel would withdraw from its large "population centers" in the West Bank. This acknowledgement of the settlement blocs granted a portion of the settlements a degree of legitimacy that Obama's new direction denied. Bush had also accepted the fact that Israel was not going to withdraw to the 1967 lines and was entitled to "defensible borders." The Bush letter, moreover, received massive support from both houses of the US Congress in

---

[130]Dore Gold, "The Quartet's disturbing shift and America's new direction", *The Jerusalem Post*, Oct. 2, 2009

June 2004, providing it with bipartisan backing (including Rep. Rahm Emanuel and Sen. Hillary Clinton). Given the language Obama used at the UN - and the Quartet now backed—it is not surprising that his administration has not openly committed itself to the 2004 letter. The Quartet statement also goes out of its way to back the Palestinian Authority's new plan for building the institutions of a over the next 24 months— which was drafted by Palestinian Prime Minister Salaam Fayad. On the one hand, the Fayad Plan appears to address Israel's call for bottom-up peacemaking by tackling head-on the lack of sufficient self-governing bodies on the Palestinian side. On the other hand, it is a program that leads the Palestinian Authority seven-eighths of the way to an independent Palestinian state, leaving ambiguous how the Palestinians get to the finish line. What it leaves open is the possibility of a unilateral declaration of statehood by the Palestinians or by someone else.[131]

For a unilateral action by the Palestinians to declare their own state, just like in Kosovo, it seems that the Quartet, with the strong support of the EU, and the latent encouragement of the US, will be pushing the Palestinians to make that unilateral declaration even when they are not yet ready for self-government, not least of all, due to their internal split with the Hamas. When they all recognize that state, they will be turning that arrangement into an imposed solution. If this is the situation, then Israel ought to think up its own unilateral solutions, like beginning to implement unilaterally the Palestinian blueprint suggested above, verify with the two houses of Congress if they too have reneged on their support to the Road Map, and whether they too reject Bush's assurances to Israel, short of which Israel would not have taken the risks it took. A whole new ball game will then open in the Middle East, if the Hamas and Iran are allowed to make gains and the deterrent power of Israel to recede and sink. Many things may happen, not peace.

---

[131]Ibid.

Bibliography

Documents

1. The Holy Qur'an
2. The Goldstone Report. The Goldstone Commission published its over 500 pp. report on 15 September, 2009.
3. *Qira'a fi Fiqh al-Shahada*, (Readings in Islamic Martyrology) was published in 1988 as a special addendum to *al-Islam wa-Filastin* (Islam and Palestine) that appeared in Nocosia, Cyprus, and has been the ideological supporter of the Palestinian Islamikaze operations against Israel
4. Press Communiques, the Israeli Prime Minister's Office.

World Press

Al Ahram (cairo)

Al-Akhbar (Egypt)

Daily Telegraph

Egyptian Gazette

Al-Gumhuriyya, (Cairo)

Baztab Iranian Internet site,

Haaretz (Tel Aviv)

ICEJ News

Al-'Ilm (Science) Egypt,

Iqra' Television (Saudi Arabia and Egypt)

Iran News

al-Islam wa-Filastin (Cyprus)

Al-Istiqlal (the Weekly of Islamic Jihad in Gaza)

al-Jazeera (Qatar)

Jerusalem Post, (Jerusalem)

Journal of Terrorism and Political Violence,

Kayhan, (Tehran)

Le Point, (Paris)
Le Soir,(Paris)
Liberation, (Paris)
Al Manar Television, (Lebanon-Hizbullah)
Memri (Jerusalem and Washington DC)
al-Mujahidin
Al-Mustaqbal (Lebanon)
National Post
National Review Online
Neue Zurcher Zeitung (Zurich)
The New Republic
Nativ (Israel)
October, (Cairo)
Orbis
Palestinian Media Watch
Politique Internationale
Al Quds al-Arabi (London),
Al-Risalah, (Gaza)
Al-Riyadh (Saudi Arabia)
Roz (Iran),
al-Sha'b (Egypt)
Al-Sharq al-Awsat (London)
The Times (London)
Al-'Ukadh (Saudi Arabia)
Al-Usbu' (Egypt)
Valeurs Actuelles, (Paris)
Al-Wafd ((Egypt)
Wall Street Journal
al Wifaq
www.jafi.org.il/agenda/2001/english/vk3-22/6as

Books

Abbas, *The Secret Ties between the Nazis and the Zionist Movement Leadership* (Arabic), Dar Ibn Rushd, Amman, 1984.

Bat Ye'or, *Juifs et Chretiens sous l'islam: les Dhimmis face au Defi Integriste*, Paris, Berg International, 1994.

Bat Yeo'r *Les Chretientes d'Orient entre Jihad et Dhimmitude*, Paris, Cerf 1991.

Gerstenfeld, Manfred, "Antisemitism: Integral to European Culture", in *Post Holocaust and Antisemitism*, No 19, 1 April, 2004, p. 4, published by the Jerusalem Center of Public Affairs.

Giniewski, Paul, "Israel: Etat Juif ou Juif des Etats," *Politique Internationale*, No 74, Winter 1996-7, pp. 1-20.

"Israeli Kritik oder antisemitismus?," *Neue Zurcher Zeitung*, April 26, 2002.

Israeli Raphael, *Man of Defiance: a Political Biography of Anwar Sadat*, Weindenfeld and Nicolson, London, 1985.

Israeli, Raphael, *Peace is in the Eye of the Beholder*, Mouton, Berlin and NY, 1985.

Israeli, Raphael, *Palestinians Between Israel and Jordan: Squaring the Triangle*, Praeger, NY, 1991.

Israeli, Raphael, *Poison: Modern Manifestations of Blood Libel*, Lexington Books, 2002.

Israeli, Raphael, *Islamikaze: Manifestations of Islamic Martyrology*, Frank Cass, London, 2003.

Israeli, Raphael, *Jerusalem Divided: the Israeli-Jordan Armistice Regime 1947-1967*, Frank Cass, London, 2003.

Israeli, Raphael, *Fundamentalist Islam and Israel*, University Press of America, Lanham, 1993.

Israeli, Raphael, *The Iraq War: Hidden Agendas and Babylonian Intrigues*, Sussex Academic Press, Brighton, 2004.

Israeli, Raphael, "State and Religion in the Emerging Palestinian Entity", in *Palestinians Between Nationalism and Islam*, Vallentine Mitchell, London, 2008, pp.147-170.

Israeli, Raphael, *The Islamic Challenge in Europe*, Transaction, N. J. 2008, p. 39.

Israeli, Raphael, *Muslim Minorities, in the Modern States*, Transaction , N.J., 2009.

Israeli, Raphael, Muslim anti-Semitism in Christian Europe: Elemental and Residual anti-Semitism, Transaction, New Jersey, 2009.

Khadduri, Majid, War and Peace in Islam, Johns Hopkins, 1969.

Langmuir, Gavin, *Towards the Definition of anti-Semitism*, UC Press, Berkeley and Los Angeles, 1990.

Litvinoff, Emanuel (ed.). *Soviet anti-Semitism: the Paris Trial*, Widwood House, London, 1974.

Molinari, Maurizio , *La Sinistra E Gli Ebrei inn Italia: 1967-1993*, Milan, 1995.

Rodinson, Maxime, *Cult, Ghetto and State: The Persistence of the Jewish Question*, al-Saqi Books, London.

Zenner, Walter, *Minorities in the Middle East: A Cross-Cultural Analysis*, SUNY, Albany, 1991.

Articles

Abu Gheith, Suleiman (Al-Qa'ida Spokesman) in an article titled "In the Shadow of the Lances", see *Memri*, June 12, 2002.

Akerman, Piers, "A playground for the vile and dangerous Australia's *'Daily Telegraph'*., 30 September, 2009.

Ayman al-Zawahiri's article in *al-Mujahidin*, see *Memri*, June 12, 2002.

Dubois, Marcel "Judaisme, Christianisme et Philosophie," *Le Soir*, Paris, March 31, 1988.

Durie, Mark, "On Islamic Antisemitism," *ICJS Research*, Melbourne, June 23, 2008.

Ginat, Gitit, "Freedom fighter", *www. haaretz.com*, 18 May, 2006.

Gold, Dore, "The Quartet's disturbing shift and America's new direction", *The Jerusalem Post*, Oct. 2, 2009.

Gross, Tom, *National Review Online*, Saturday, October 10, 2009.

Hassoux, Didier, in *Liberation*, June 15, 2004.

Israeli, Raphael, "The Role of Islam in President Sadat's Thought", *Jerusalem Journal of International Relations*, Vol 4, No 4, 1980.

Israeli, Raphael, "The Charter of Allah", *In Islam and Israel*, University Press of America, ch 7, pp. 123-170.

Israeli, Raphael, "The Odd Couple: Turkey and Israel", *Orbis*, January, 2001, pp 165-179.

Israeli, Raphael, "Identity and State-building: Educating Palestinian Children after Oslo," *Journal of Terrorism and Political Violence*, Spring 2002.

Klein Halevy, Yossi, "Comment on the Goldstone Report", the Adelson Research Institute in Jerusalem, September, 2009.

Kuntzel, Matthias, "Ahmadinajad's Demons", *The New Republic*, 24 April, 2007, pp 15-17.

Kunzel, Matthias , "Iran has no Right for Nuclear Weapons", *Wall Street Journal*, 30 September, 2009.

Lewis, Bernard, "How did the Infidels Win", *National Post*, 1 June, 2002.

Makovsky, David, in his "Media Report," *The Jerusalem Post*, August 25, 1989.

Marcus, Itamar and Nan Jacques Ziberdik, "PA and Hamas: Kidnapping Israeli Soldiers Key to Imprisoned Terrorists", *Palestinian Media Watch*, 29 September, 2009.

Meyer, Claude, "Interview with Jean-Claude Milner", *Actualites Juives Hebdo*, No 823, No 823, 11 December, 2003.

Muhsen Razay, the Secretary of the Council for the Protection of the State Interests, in an interview to Iranian Internet site Baztab, 28 Dec. 2006.

Norfolk, Andrew, "Our Followers must live in Peace until Strong enough to wage Jihad", *The Times*, 8 September, 2007.

Pedurant, Daniel "Anti-Semitism in Contemporary Greek Society," *Analysis of Current Trends in Anti-Semitism*, No 7, 1995, Hebrew University, Jerusalem.

Qaradawi, Sheikh, "Homosexuals Should be Punished like Fornicators, but their Harm is less when not done in Public", *Al-Jazeera*, 5 June, 2005.

Sharon, Moshe,"Hudna and Sulhin Islam" (Hebrew), *Nativ*, Summer 2002.

Index

Analytical Index of Names, Places, Terms and Events